ASIAN RELIGIONS IN PRACTICE

PRINCETON READINGS IN RELIGIONS

Donald S. Lopez, Jr., Editor

TITLES IN THE SERIES

Religions of India in Practice edited by Donald S. Lopez, Jr.

Buddhism in Practice edited by Donald S. Lopez, Jr.

Religions of China in Practice edited by Donald S. Lopez, Jr.

Religions of Tibet in Practice edited by Donald S. Lopez, Jr.

Religions of Japan in Practice edited by George J. Tanabe, Jr.

Asian Religions in Practice: An Introduction
edited by Donald S. Lopez, Jr.

ASIAN RELIGIONS

IN PRACTICE

AN INTRODUCTION

Donald S. Lopez, Jr., Editor

PRINCETON READINGS IN RELIGIONS

PRINCETON UNIVERSITY PRESS

PRINCETON, NEW JERSEY

Published by Princeton University Press, 41 William Street,
Princeton, New Jersey 08540
In the United Kingdom: Princeton University Press, Chichester, West Sussex

Library of Congress Cataloging-in-Publication Data
Asian religions in practice : an introduction / Donald S. Lopez, Jr., editor.
p. cm. — (Princeton readings in religions)
Includes bibliographical references.
ISBN 0-691-00513-3 (pbk. : alk. paper)
1. Asia—Religion. 2. Asia—Religious life and customs.
I. Lopez, Donald S., 1952– . II. Series.
BL1032.A85 1999
200′.95—dc21 98-47112

This book has been composed in Berkeley

The paper used in this publication meets the minimum requirements of
ANSI/NISO Z39.48-1992 (R1997) (*Permanence of Paper*)

http://pup.princeton.edu

Printed in the United States of America

1 3 5 7 9 10 8 6 4 2

CONTENTS

ASIAN RELIGIONS IN PRACTICE

INTRODUCTION

Donald S. Lopez, Jr.

Princeton Readings in Religions is a new series of anthologies on the religions of the world, representing the significant advances that have been made in the study of religions in the last thirty years. The sourcebooks used by previous generations of students, whether for Judaism and Christianity or for the religions of Asia and the Middle East, placed a heavy emphasis on "canonical works." Princeton Readings in Religions provides a different configuration of texts in an attempt to better represent the range of religious practices, placing particular emphasis on the ways in which texts have been used in diverse contexts. The series seeks to provide new ways to read and understand the religions of the world, breaking down the sometimes misleading stereotypes inherited from the past in an effort to provide both more expansive and more focused perspectives on the richness and diversity of religious expressions.

Five volumes in the series have been published to date: *Religions of India in Practice* (1995), *Buddhism in Practice* (1995), *Religions of China in Practice* (1996), *Religions of Tibet in Practice* (1997), and *Religions of Japan in Practice* (1999). Each of these large volumes contains a wealth of material, focusing not so much on the classical texts of the traditions, but bringing together works (the majority never previously translated into a western language) that are central to religious practice in Asia. The volumes present types of discourse (rituals, folktales, biographies, apocrypha, prayers, and oral narratives) and voices (vernacular, esoteric, domestic, and female) that have not been sufficiently represented in earlier anthologies and accounts of the religions of Asia.

The utility of an anthology is not, however, simply to be measured by its contents; every collection also faces the problem of context, a problem caused by the fact that any anthology necessarily requires that texts be moved from a variety of locations and gathered together to form a new book. If a selection is a portion of a larger work, it is also removed from its place as part of a larger whole. When an anthology is composed of translations, as in the case of the Princeton series, there is the inevitable decontextualization entailed by the act of translation, with its unavoidable sacrifice of much of the aesthetics of expression. In the case of religious works, the text is often removed from the place of its production, from the ritual of which it is often a part, and from the diction of its recitation. The text is also displaced through juxtaposition, as one text is set next to another. To anthologize, therefore, is to isolate the text from the social histories of its author and its audience.

Thus, beyond the task of translating the original texts and then organizing the texts thematically into an anthology, there is the task of narration. In the Princeton Readings in Religions, this crucial function is performed in each volume by a substantial introduction by an expert scholar. These introductions have been praised for the various ways in which they have brought together the best and most current research into a clear and informative overview of the histories, doctrines, and practices of the religions of Asia. The present volume assembles those five introductions for readers interested in studying the vast scope and historical sweep of Asian religions. Each introduction faces the difficult challenge of providing a full sense of the complexity and richness of these traditions without becoming lost in detail, of calling into question long unquestioned stereotypes without adopting yet another Olympian perspective, and of offering a clear and compelling narrative, while resisting the urge to essentialize.

In his essay on the religions of India, Richard Davis presents a historical survey of the challenges and transformations that have occurred there, from the Aryan migrations of 2000 B.C.E. to the present. In the process, he introduces the famous Indian religions: Hinduism, Buddhism, Islam, Jainism, and Sikhism, as well as the nameless tradition, the religion of the home and village. At the same time, he notes the many continuities that exist among these traditions, making it sometimes problematic to identify them as distinct and self-conscious "isms." Hinduism presents an interesting example. The term can be traced back to the Indo-Aryan word for sea, *sindhu*, which was used also for the Indus River; Persians who lived to the west of the Indus modified it to *hind* and used it to refer also to the land of the Indus valley; in Greek and Latin, *hind* became *india* and was used to designate the uncharted world beyond the Indus; eventually, Muslims used *hindu* to refer to the native peoples of South Asia. The word was used more specifically to refer to those residents of India who did not convert to Islam, thus gaining its first "religious" connotation. It was not a term, however, used by "Hindus" to refer to themselves.

In the nineteenth century, officers of the British Raj began to use the word Hinduism, especially for purposes of the census, to refer to a putative system of religious beliefs and practices of those who were not adherents of Islam, Christianity, Sikhism, or Jainism (Buddhism had disappeared from India centuries before). The term was finally taken up as a self-referential appellation by non-Muslim, non-Jain, non-Sikh, non-Christian, non-Parsi, non-Jewish Indians in an effort to construct a religious identity that could challenge and surpass in age and authority that of the Christian colonizers and their missionaries. Since then, scholars, both European and Indian, have projected the term retrospectively to name a great historical range of indigenous Indian religious formations. Prior to the nineteenth century, these groups did not have a name for, nor did they consider themselves members of, a single religious community. In this way, an indigenous term for a geographical feature, the Indus River, evolved, through a series of formations, into an abstract noun used to name one of the "world religions." One of the ironies is that since the partition of British India into India and Pakistan in 1947, the inhabitants of the Indus River Valley (now in Pakistan) are not Hindus but Muslims.

In my essay on Buddhism, I offer a survey of Buddhist doctrine and practice under the rubric of the most famous of traditional Buddhist categories: the three jewels of the Buddha, the dharma, and the sangha. The Buddha is the enlightened one, a name used first as an epithet for an Indian prince who in the sixth century is said to have awakened from the sleep of ignorance to a new state of awareness. Precisely what the nature of that awareness was would become a source of controversy among Buddhist schools throughout the centuries, but all agreed that the Buddha had discovered a path out of the sufferings of birth, aging, sickness, and death. What the Buddha taught was called the dharma. These teachings would come to encompass a vast literature, much of it composed long after the Buddha's death, but often represented as having been spoken by him, beginning with the words, "Thus did I hear." The Buddha quickly gathered a group of disciples around him, a group that was called the sangha or "community." The term referred sometimes to those who had followed the Buddha's path to enlightenment, sometimes to a local group of monks and nuns, and sometimes to the collective institution of Buddhism. The Buddha, dharma, and sangha are called the three jewels because they are rarely encountered in the cycle of rebirth, and when they are encountered, they are of great value. A Buddhist is traditionally defined as someone who seeks refuge from the travails of life in these three jewels, repeating three times, "I go for refuge to the Buddha, I go for refuge to the dharma, I go for refuge to the sangha." With the development of Buddhist traditions across millennia and across continents, Buddha, dharma, and sangha took on new and different meanings, each claiming the authority of the Buddha himself. My essay asks the reader to consider, then, "Who is the Buddha?" "What is the dharma?" and "Who belongs to the sangha?"

Stephen Teiser begins his essay on the religions of China by noting some of the problems entailed by organizing our understanding of Chinese religions under the traditional headings of Confucianism, Daoism, and Buddhism. He nonetheless acknowledges how influential this trinity has been, both in China and the west. One of the early references to the three was made by a scholar in sixth-century China, who wrote, "Buddhism is the sun, Daoism is the moon, and Confucianism the five planets." It is essential that we understand where these three names came from, who used them and under what circumstances, and what forms of religious practice are hidden or denied by adhering to these categories. Professor Teiser therefore begins with a detailed survey of Confucianism, Daoism, and Buddhism, setting forth the wide range of practices that have been gathered under those headings over the centuries. He goes on to discuss what often has been called, for want of a better term, Chinese popular religion, something that does not fit easily within or without the three religions of China. It encompasses such disparate practices as: funeral and memorial services, with their prescribed degrees of mourning and the ceremonial installation in the home of a wooden tablet inscribed with the name of the deceased; the annual New Year's festival when, on the twenty-third day, each family dispatches their God of the Hearth to the highest heaven to make his report to the Jade Emperor; and a consultation with a spirit medium, who invokes a deity to diagnose the cause of a recent misfortune, a nightmare, or an illness and then requests that the deity prescribe a cure in the form of an herbal remedy or an offering at a temple. Professor Teiser turns next to two social institutions that are not always considered "religious," but that are absolutely central to Chinese religious life, the family system and the government bureaucracy. He concludes with a discussion of "the spirits of Chinese religion," explaining the wealth of meaning to be derived from rendering the term in the plural.

My essay on the religions of Tibet follows a roughly chronological sequence, beginning with the royal cult of the pre-Buddhist period in which the king was said to ascend to heaven on a rope when his first son was old enough to ride a horse. It then turns to the introduction of Buddhism in the seventh century and the subsequent development of the Buddhist and Bön traditions. Rather than seeing Bön as a form of shamanism, as the pre-Buddhist religion of Tibet, or as simply a facsimile of Tibetan Buddhism, I argue that Bön should be seen as a central form of Tibetan religious practice that engaged in a rich and mutual exchange with Buddhism.

In addition to outlining those elements of Buddhist practice that are held in common with other Buddhist traditions, I examine those practices unique to Tibet. Perhaps the most famous of these is the institution of the incarnate lama. Like other adherents of Mahāyāna Buddhism, Tibetans believe that buddhas and bodhisattvas, beings dedicated to the salvation of others, return to the world in lifetime after lifetime rather than seeking their own solace in nirvana. It is also a tenet of Mahāyāna Buddhism that enlightened beings are not limited to the form of the Buddha with which we are familiar; a buddha is able to appear in whatever form, animate or inanimate, that is appropriate to benefit the suffering world. Tibetans believe not only that enlightened beings take rebirth in the world out of their infinite compassion, but that such beings can be identified at birth. These beings, called incarnate lamas or *tulkus*, are said to have complete control over their rebirth, choosing the time, the place, and the parents in advance, so that a dying lama will often leave instructions for his disciples on where to find the baby he will become. Since the fourteenth century, all sects of Tibetan Buddhism have adopted the practice of identifying the successive rebirths of a great teacher. The most famous incarnate lama is the Dalai Lama. But there are some three thousand other lines of incarnation in Tibet (the vast majority of whom are male). The institution of the incarnate lama came to be a central component of Tibetan society, providing the means by which authority and charisma, in all of their symbolic and material forms, were passed from one generation to another in a society where many of the most influential figures were celibate Buddhist monks.

In his essay on the religions of Japan, George Tanabe focuses on the ethical, ritual, and institutional practices, which are sometimes shared and sometimes contested both within and among the traditions of Japan, whether they be called Confucian, Shintō, or Buddhist. He examines, for example, the remarkable array of practices designed to bestow enlightenment in this life, or more precisely, designed to produce the realization that one is already enlightened. One practices in order to understand that there is no need for practice. But there is great contention over precisely what that practice should be: the chanting of a prayer, the posture of a meditation, or the name of a text. The debates over who was right and who was wrong were not merely a matter of scholastic inquiry, and religious truths were used to legitimize and enhance political institutions. Indeed, many of the major figures in the history of Japan have argued that the proper practice of their particular religion is essential to the welfare of the nation, protecting it both from natural disaster and foreign invasion. The Zen monk Eisai argued that the ruler should support Zen Buddhism because of the crucial role that Zen monks play in upholding society; by maintaining strict monastic purity, monks generate a power that protects the nation. Should there be a lapse in their discipline, the nation is placed at risk. But monasticism in Japan also served more immediate human needs: in Kamakura there was a nunnery that provided a sanctuary for women until their husbands could be convinced to send a letter of divorce. In the course of his essay, Professor Tanabe calls into question many of our presuppositions about Japanese religions, demonstrating the fluid relationship that exists between doctrine and practice. Indeed, his central image is one of rocks and tides, with the rocks establishing patterns in the flow of the water, while the water slowly, but inexorably, reshapes the rocks.

Taken together, the five essays in this volume provide a rich introduction to the history, doctrines, and practices of the religions of Asia. They describe the practices of the elite and the humble, practices designed to sustain the cosmos and the village. The essays also provide many occasions for reflection and discussion. They ask, for example, whether the lines between elite and popular practice in Asia are as clear as they are sometimes imagined to be; they ask whether the village is not, in important ways, also the cosmos, and the cosmos the village; they ask whether there is anything to be gained in speaking about "Asian religion" as if it were a singular entity; and they ask, finally, what we mean when we use the term "religion."

RELIGIONS OF INDIA IN PRACTICE

Richard H. Davis

Now Vidagdha, Śakala's son, asked him, "Yājñavalkya, how many gods are there?"
Following the text of the Veda, he replied, "Three hundred and three, and three thousand and three, as are mentioned in the Vedic hymn on the Viśvadevas."
"Right," replied Vidagdha, "but how many gods are there really, Yājñavalkya?"
"Thirty-three."
"Right," he assented, "but how many gods are there really, Yājñavalkya?"
"Six."
"Right," he persisted, "but how many gods are there really, Yājñavalkya?"
"Three."
"Right," he answered, "but how many gods are there really, Yājñavalkya?"
"Two."
"Right," Vidagdha replied, "but how many gods are there really, Yājñavalkya?"
"One and a half."
"Right," he agreed, "but how many gods are there really, Yājñavalkya?"
"One."
"Right," Vidagdha said. "And who are those three hundred and three, and three thousand and three gods?"

Bṛhadāraṇyaka Upaniṣad 3.9.1

In one of the world's earliest recorded philosophical dialogues, the Indian sage Yājñavalkya pointed to the multiplicity of theological views concerning the number of gods in India. He then went on to show how, following different ways of enumerating them, each of these views could make sense.

Much the same can be said about the religions of India. Some scholars and observers focus on the tremendous diversity of distinct schools of thought and religious sects that have appeared over the course of Indian history. Others prefer to specify the three or five "great" or "world" religions that have occupied the subcontinent: Hinduism, Buddhism, Islam, plus Jainism and Sikhism. And still others, of a more syncretic persuasion, maintain there is really just one religious tradition.

In the introduction I provide a brief account of the main periods, principal schools of thought, and most significant texts in Indian religions. Over the course of this account, I focus on certain key issues or points of controversy that appear and reappear through Indian religious history. I focus also on a set of terms—Veda, brahman, yoga, dharma, bhakti, Tantra, and the like—that constitute a shared religious vocabulary in India. As we will see, such terms were often considered too important to be left uncontested, and so different authors or traditions would attempt to redefine the terms to suit their own purposes.[1]

The Question of Hinduism

The dominant feature of South Asian religious history is a broad group of interconnected traditions that we nowadays call "Hinduism." Although other distinct non-Hindu religious ideologies (notably Buddhism, Islam, and Christianity) have challenged its dominance, Hinduism is now and probably has been at all times the most prevalent religious persuasion of the subcontinent. According to the most recent census figures, 83 percent of India's population is classified as Hindu, a total of perhaps 700 million Hindus.

It is important to bear in mind, however, that Hinduism does not share many of the integrating characteristics of the other religious traditions we conventionally label the "world religions." Hinduism has no founding figure such as the Buddha Śākyamuni, Jesus of Nazareth, or Muḥammad. It has no single text that can serve as a doctrinal point of reference, such as the Bibles of the Judaic and Christian traditions, the Islamic Qurʾān, or the Ādi Granth of the Sikhs. Hinduism has no single overarching institutional or ecclesiastical hierarchy capable of deciding questions of religious boundary or formulating standards of doctrine and practice.

This is not to say that Hinduism, lacking these supposedly "essential" attributes of other religions, is therefore not a religion. Rather, the historical process by which Hindus and others have come to consider Hinduism a unitary religious formation differs markedly from other traditions. In one respect, Hinduism is one of the oldest, if not the oldest continuous recorded religion, tracing itself back to a text that was already edited and put into final shape by about 1200 B.C.E. In another respect, though, it is the youngest, for it was only in the nineteenth century that the many indigenous Indian religious formations were collectively named "Hinduism." Before this, not only did these groups not have a name for themselves as a religious unity, but for the most part they did not consider that they were members of a single religious collectivity.

Since histories of names often tell us a good deal about the realities they signify, let us look more closely at the word "Hinduism." The term derives originally from the Indo-Aryan word for sea, *sindhu*, applied also to the Indus River. Persians to the west of the Indus picked up the term, modifying it phonologically to *hind*, and used it to refer also to the land of the Indus valley. From Persian it was borrowed into Greek and Latin, where *india* became the geographical designation for all the unknown territories beyond the Indus. Meanwhile, Muslims used *hindu* to refer to the native peoples of South Asia, and more specifically to those South Asians who did not convert to Islam, lending the term for the first time a reference to religious persuasion. Non-Muslim Indians did not commonly take up the terminology, however, until much later.

Only in the nineteenth century did the colonial British begin to use the word Hinduism to refer to a supposed religious system encompassing the beliefs and practices of Indian peoples not adhering to other named religions such as Islam, Christianity, or Jainism. This coinage, based very indirectly on the indigenous term *sindhu*, followed the Enlightenment reification of the concept "religion" and the scholarly attempt to define a series of distinct individual "world religions," each with its own essence and historical unfolding. "Hindu" was then incorporated into the Indian lexicon, taken up by Indians eager to construct for themselves a counterpart to the seemingly monolithic Christianity of the colonizers. As much as anything, it may have been British census taking, with its neat categories of affiliation, that spread the usage of "Hindu" as the most common pan-Indian term of religious identity. To specify the nature of this religion, Western scholars and Indians alike projected the term retrospectively, to encompass a great historical range of religious texts and practices.

Even though anachronistic, the term "Hinduism" remains useful for describing and categorizing the various schools of thought and practice that grew up within a shared Indian society and employed a common religious vocabulary. However, applying a single term to cover a wide array of Indian religious phenomena from many different periods raises some obvious questions. Where is the system? What is the center of Hinduism? What is truly essential to Hinduism? And who determines this center, if there is any? Scholars and Indians have largely adopted two contrasting views in dealing with these questions, the "centralist" and the "pluralist" views.

Centralists identify a single, pan-Indian, more or less hegemonic, orthodox tradition, transmitted primarily in Sanskrit language, chiefly by members of the brahmanic class. The tradition centers around a Vedic lineage of texts, in which are included not only the Vedas themselves, but also the Mīmaṃsā, Dharmaśāstra, and Vedānta corpuses of texts and teachings. Vedic sacrifice is the privileged mode of ritual conduct, the template for all subsequent Indian ritualism. Various groups employing vernacular languages in preference to Sanskrit, questioning the caste order, and rejecting the authority of the Vedas, may periodically rebel against this center, but the orthodox, through an adept use of inclusion and repressive tolerance, manage to hold the high ground of religious authority.

The pluralists, by contrast, envision a decentered profusion of ideas and practices all tolerated and incorporated under the big tent of Hinduism. No more concise statement of this view can be found than that of the eminent Sanskrit scholar J. A. B. van Buitenen in the 1986 *Encyclopedia Britannica*:

> In principle, Hinduism incorporates all forms of belief and worship without necessitating the selection or elimination of any. The Hindu is inclined to revere the divinity

> in every manifestation, whatever it may be, and is doctrinally tolerant. . . . Hinduism is, then, both a civilization and a conglomeration of religions, with neither a beginning, a founder, nor a central authority, hierarchy, or organization.

Adherents of this viewpoint commonly invoke natural metaphors. Hinduism is a "sponge" for all religious practices or a "jungle" where every religious tendency may flourish freely. Within the pluralist view, the Vedic tradition figures as one form of belief and worship among many, the concern of elite brahmans somewhat out of touch with the religious multiplicity all around them.

In India, various contending religious groups have vied to present a view of the cosmos, divinity, human society, and human purposes more compelling and more authoritative than others. One finds such all-encompassing visions presented in many Hindu texts or groups of texts at different periods of history: the Vedas, the Epics, the puranic theologies of Viṣṇu and Śiva, the medieval texts of the bhakti movements, and the formulations of synthetic Hinduism by modern reformers. The religious historian may identify these as the paradigmatic formations of Hinduism of their respective times. Yet such visions have never held sway without challenge, both from within and from outside of Hinduism.

The most serious challenges to Hindu formations have come from outside, from the early "heterodoxies" of Buddhism and Jainism, from medieval Islam, and from the missionary Christianity and post-Enlightenment worldviews of the colonial British. These challenges have been linked to shifts in the political sphere, when ruling elites have favored non-Hindu ideologies with their patronage and prestige. In each case, such fundamental provocations have led to important changes within the most prevalent forms of Hinduism. This introduction will follow this pattern of historical challenge and transformation.

The Indo-Aryans and the Vedas

The textual history of Indian religions begins with the entry into the subcontinent of groups of nomadic pastoralists who called themselves "Āryas," the noble ones. Originally they came from the steppes of south-central Russia, part of a larger tribal community that, beginning around 4000 B.C.E., migrated outward from their homeland in several directions, some westward into Europe and others southward into the Middle East and South Asia. These nomads were the first to ride and harness horses; they also invented the chariot and the spoked wheel and fabricated weapons of copper and bronze. Such material innovations gained them obvious military advantages, and they were able to impose themselves on most of the indigenous peoples they encountered as they migrated. Wherever they went they took with them their language, and it was this language that formed the historical basis for Greek, Latin, the Romance languages, German, English, Persian, Sanskrit, and most of the modern languages of northern India. We now call these pastoral peoples the Indo-Europeans, and those who migrated south into the Iranian plateau and the Indian subcontinent we call the Indo-Aryans.

As early as about 2000 B.C.E., Indo-Aryan peoples began to move gradually into the Indus River Valley in small tribal groups. In 1200 B.C.E.. they were still located primarily in the Punjab, the fertile area drained by the five rivers of the Indus system, but by 600 B.C.E. the Indo-Aryans had gained political and social dominance over the Gangetic plain and throughout much of northern India.

The Ṛg Veda

The religious beliefs and practices of this community are contained in a corpus of texts called the Vedas. Since the term *Veda* comes up frequently in all discussions of Indian religious history, it is helpful to consider briefly some of its meanings and usages. The term derives from the verbal root *vid*, "to know," and so the broadest meaning of *Veda* is "knowledge," more specifically knowledge of the highest sort, religious knowledge. It denotes several compendia of religious knowledge composed in an early form of Sanskrit (the "perfected" language) by the Indo-Aryan community, the four Vedic "collections" (*saṃhitā*): the *Ṛg Veda*, *Yajur Veda*, *Sāma Veda*, and the *Atharva Veda*. Supplementary compositions were attached to each of these four Vedic collections—namely, the Brāhmaṇas, Āraṇyakas, and Upaniṣads—and these too became part of the Veda. This entire corpus of sacred literature came to be portrayed by its proponents as revelation, something that was only "heard" and not composed by human beings. Additional texts were later added to the corpus: the Vedāṅgas or "limbs" of the Veda, auxiliary works that aimed to explain and extend the significance of the Vedas. These later texts did not have the same revelatory status as the Vedas themselves, but they did belong to the Vedic corpus in an extended sense. The Vedas constitute a huge, diverse, and fascinating corpus of texts composed over many centuries.

The earliest of the Vedic collections, and one of the world's oldest intact religious texts, is the *Ṛg Veda*. It consists of 1,028 hymns, numbering around 10,000 verses, roughly equal in size to the complete works of Homer. These hymns were composed over a period of several hundred years by different lineages or families of poet-priests, and then compiled into a single large collection sometime around 1200–1000 B.C.E. This great collection was carefully memorized and transmitted orally, virtually without alterations, for almost 3,000 years by generations of religious specialists.

The hymns of the *Ṛg Veda* reflect the religious concerns and social values of the Indo-Aryan community as it settled in the Punjab. Most often the hymns address and praise a pantheon of deities, of whom the most important is undoubtedly Indra. The hymns portray Indra as an active, powerful, unpredictable, combative god who leads the other gods in a series of antagonistic encounters with a competing group of superhuman beings, the demons. The poets honor and extol Indra for his courage and strength, and also supplicate him to be generous to his votaries. Moreover, they view him as a model chieftain: as Indra leads the gods in defeating their enemies, the poets proclaim, so may our leaders guide us to victory over our enemies.

Indra's paradigmatic status reminds us that the Indo-Aryans were not simply occupying uninhabited territory as they moved into the Indian subcontinent. They encountered other peoples there whom they regarded as posing a threat to their own well-being and expansion. These others, often referred to as *dāsas*, were described in the *Ṛg Veda* as dark-skinned, flat-featured stealers of cattle, speaking a different language and living in fortified citadels.

In fact, from around 2500 to 1700 B.C.E. a complex, urbanized, centrally organized civilization flourished in the Indus River Valley, with two capital cities and a host of other towns and smaller settlements. Although archeologists have excavated a great deal of evidence from the Indus Valley civilization, including several thousand brief inscriptions, much about its religious culture remains mysterious since no one has yet convincingly deciphered the Indus Valley script. Yet most linguists believe the language of this civilization was a member of the Dravidian family, which also includes the languages of southern India where the Indo-Aryan language did not penetrate. This suggests that the Indus Valley civilization was linked, in language and presumably in culture, with pre-Aryan peoples in other parts of the subcontinent.

Many elements of Indus Valley material culture suggest religious usage, and these have led scholars to postulate Indus Valley influence on the development of later Indian religion. For example, archeologists have interpreted the numerous terra-cotta figurines of fleshy women with accentuated breasts and hips and fabulous headpieces found in the Indus Valley cities as popular representations of a "Great Mother," whose domestic and rural cult would reappear in medieval Hindu literature. While such connections remain speculative, they do point to an important problem in Indian religious history. Much that appears as innovation in recorded Indian religious traditions may have been borrowed from nonliterate or undeciphered traditions that we do not yet know.

Although the urban civilization of the Indus Valley had largely collapsed prior to the arrival of the Indo-Aryans, the dāsas of the *Ṛg Veda* were probably the descendants of that culture, and they must have posed a significant obstacle to Indo-Aryan expansion. The *Ṛg Veda* shows us an Indo-Aryan culture primed for battle. Even the poets participated in battle, apparently, as singing charioteers, invoking Indra's strength on behalf of the warriors as they drove the horses.

If Indra was for the *Ṛg Veda* poets the divine prototype of the warrior, the second most important deity in the pantheon, Agni, can be seen as the model priest. Agni is fire, in its multiple forms: the sun, the hearth fire, the fire of the sacrifice, the digestive fire in one's belly, and the fire of poetic inspiration. But Agni's primary role in the *Ṛg Veda* pertains to sacrifice (*yajña*), the central ritual practice of Vedic society. Agni is the priest of the gods and yet is also accessible to humans, so he is most fit to serve in sacrifice as the primary intermediary, bringing gods and humans together. The poets of the *Ṛg Veda* know sacrifice to be a powerful ritual, one that enables the gods to defeat the demons and that likewise can assist the Aryans to overcome their earthly enemies. It brings a host of worldly results: wealth, cattle, victory, and ultimately order. Yet in the *Ṛg Veda* sacrifice remains rather loosely organized, inchoate, experimental; only later is it systematized and elaborated into a full-fledged worldview.

One other figure in the Ṛg Vedic pantheon deserves attention: the mysterious Soma, also closely associated with sacrifice. Soma is simultaneously a plant, a liquid made by crushing the stalks of that plant, and a god personifying the effects of ingesting this concoction. The identity of the botanical soma has proved to be a major scholarly conundrum, but the effects ascribed in the *Ṛg Veda* to drinking its juice are clear enough. It is a drink of inspiration, of vision, of revelation. At their sacrificial gatherings the poets pound and imbibe the soma juice, and through it they come to mingle with the gods. They perceive the resemblances and identities between things that we normally see as different and unrelated, weaving the world together in a fabric of connectedness. The revelations inspired by soma, moreover, are not regarded as mere hallucinations or dreams, but as more real, more true than the awareness of normal consciousness. This is the first example of a recurrent theme in Indian religions: what is ontologically most real is often not accessible through ordinary human experience but must be sought through some other means—whether it be soma, yoga, meditation, devotional fervor, or ritual.

Sacrifice and Society

If the Indo-Aryans entered India as nomads over the ruins of the urban civilization of the Indus Valley, during the period from 1200 to 600 B.C.E. they reinvented urban society on a new cultural basis. The later Vedic literature reflects the social transformations of this period, particularly the growing role of sacrifice in the religious life of the Indo-Aryans and the beginnings of criticism of sacrifice. By 600 B.C.E. the Indo-Aryan community had changed from a nomadic and pastoral tribal society into a predominantly agrarian one. The introduction of iron during this period facilitated the clearing of the heavily forested Gangetic plain and the development of plough agriculture. A more stable population and greater food resources led in turn to larger settlements, and the tribal organization of the Indo-Aryan nomads began to give way to an incipient class society based on occupational specialization and status distinction. Those outside the Indo-Aryan community, rather than being treated as threatening dāsas, were increasingly incorporated into society as laborers and social inferiors, śūdras. Larger political formations, primarily kingdoms, began to form, and with these early kingdoms came the rebirth of cities as capitals and centers of trade. By 600 B.C.E. there were a dozen substantial cities in northern India.

These changes naturally had their consequences for Vedic religion. Surplus production enabled society to support a nonproducing class of religious specialists, who could devote themselves to elaborating sacrificial ritual and articulating its significance. At the same time, the new rulers found in increasingly dramatic sacrifice a means to extend and legitimate their political authority over larger, mixed populations. The interests of nascent ruling and priestly groups thus converged in sacrifice. And with the defeat of the Indo-Aryans' primary autochthonous opponents, sacrifice came to be seen less as a way of defeating enemies than as a means of creating, maintaining, and stabilizing the order of the cosmos and of society.

One can already see this in some of the later hymns of the *Ṛg Veda*, most notably the famous Puruṣasūkta (*Ṛg Veda* 10.90), where the entire cosmos as well as human society come into being out of a primordial sacrifice. The sacrificial cosmology emerges still more clearly in the later Vedic texts devoted to prescribing sacrificial procedures (the *Yajur Veda*) and the interpretive texts known as the Brāhmaṇas. These texts outline a complex system of sacrificial practice, ranging in scale from modest domestic rites around home fires to elaborate public ceremonies sponsored by the wealthiest kings. The gods who figured so importantly in the *Ṛg Veda* seem to have been demoted; what is most important in the later Vedic period is the sacrifice itself.

As the role of sacrifice grew, so did the status of the new group of religious specialists who called themselves *brāhmaṇas* (Anglicized as "brahman" or "brahmin"). Like *Veda*, this is a crucial term in the history of Indian religions. The poets of the *Ṛg Veda* employ the term *brahman* primarily to refer to the Vedic hymns themselves, understood as powerful and efficacious speech. The notion that certain kinds of liturgical speech are inherently powerful is common to many schools of Indian religious thought. The Indian term most often used for such potent verbal formulae is *mantra*. The *Ṛg Veda* poets also used *brāhmaṇa* to refer by extension to those who fashioned and recited the hymns. At that time the brahman reciters did not constitute a hereditary or endogamous social group, but in later Vedic texts *brāhmaṇa* came to be defined, at least by the brahmans themselves, as a hereditary occupational social group, specializing in ritual matters and the teaching of the Vedas.

A crucial first step in the social institutionalization of the brahman class can be found in the Puruṣasūkta hymn. According to this hymn, four social classes emerged from the Puruṣa, the original sacrificial victim: the brahmans from his mouth, the kṣatriyas (warriors) from his arms, the vaiśyas (merchants) from his loins, and the śūdras (servants) from his feet. Thus the poem portrays the brahmans and other social classes not simply as social groups, but as an order of creation. Because the brahmans emerge from the mouth of the Puruṣa, they enjoy in this order the highest status.

The Puruṣasūkta hymn is the earliest depiction of what later became known as the fourfold *varṇa* scheme, a model of society as an organic hierarchized unity of classes or castes that was to have great persistence through Indian history. The word "caste" derives from *casta*, the Portuguese word for social class. Yet historically it was a flexible and contentious model, one that was just as often questioned and opposed as it was accepted and defended. One can get a taste of the kind of criticism and satire that was recurrently directed against brahmanic claims of privilege in Kabīr's poem, "The Sapling and the Seed", while a defense of the varṇa system appears even in such an unlikely setting as the "Dog Oracles" of the *Śarṅgadhara Paddhati*.

The Upaniṣads and the Renunciatory Model

Within the supplementary texts of the Vedic corpus composed around 900–600 B.C.E., one sees evidence both of a growing sophistication in reflection concerning the sacrifice and also the beginnings of an opposition to sacrifice. The texts called the Brāhmaṇas, arising from discussions and controversies that engaged the new class of brahman ritualists as they conducted the sacrifices, devote themselves particularly to explication of ritual action, providing a learned commentary on the myriad sacrifices of the Vedic system. The idea underlying these hermeneutical texts is that the most adept priest not only performs the actions of sacrifice, but also understands their inner meanings.

The Āraṇyakas (literally, "forest books") and especially the Upaniṣads ("sitting close to a teacher") took the sacrificial worldview in a different direction. As their names imply, these texts were intended for a more restricted audience, often recounting private discussions between teachers and students in the forest. The Upaniṣads pose themselves, and were later accepted by many Indians, as the "culmination of the Veda" (*vedānta*), its highest teachings. For example, in the *Bṛhadāraṇyaka Upaniṣad*, one of the earliest and most influential Upaniṣads, we learn of the brahman teacher Yājñavalkya, whom we have already met in his enumeration of the gods. At the conclusion of a royal sacrifice, Yājñavalkya claims that he is the most knowledgeable of all present in Vedic matters. A series of interlocutors—not only priests, but also a woman, a cart driver, and the king himself—question him, trying to rebuff his declaration and gain for themselves the thousand head of cattle he has claimed as his reward. Yet as Yājñavalkya substantiates his superior Vedic knowledge, he introduces several important ideas unknown to earlier Vedic tradition. So too the other Upaniṣads: together they introduce a set of new concepts that grow out of earlier Vedic thought while calling into question some of its central premises. These concepts, simultaneously old and new, proved to raise enduring issues for Indian religious and philosophical debate.

Yājñavalkya was the first recorded spokesman for the notion of transmigration, which holds that upon death a person is neither annihilated nor transported to some other world in perpetuity, but rather returns to worldly life, to live and die again in a new mortal form. This continuing succession of life, death, and rebirth is termed *saṃsāra* (circling, wandering) in the Upaniṣads. *Saṃsāra* comes to denote not just the individual wandering of a person from life to life, but also the entire world process seen as a perpetual flux. This cyclical worldview of the Upaniṣads grows out of an earlier Vedic concern with natural cycles of the moon, day and night, and the seasons, but projects it in a new direction.

Although transmigration answers the question of beginnings and ends, it also raises two new issues. What determines a person's subsequent form of rebirth? Is there anything other than eternal transmigration? To answer the first question, Yājñavalkya redefines the Vedic notion of *karman*. *Karman* (derived from the verb root *kṛ*, to do or to make, and usually Anglicized as "karma,") means action in a very broad sense; in the Vedas the term refers particularly to sacrificial actions, as the most efficacious kind of activity. In Vedic sacrifice, all ritual actions have consequences, leading to fruits (*phala*) that are often not apparent at the time but will inevitably ripen. Yājñavalkya accepts this extended notion of causality and gives it a moral dimension: the moral character of one's actions in this lifetime determines the status of one's rebirth in the next. Behave in this life as a god and you will become a god. But gods, in this view, are not immortal either, and may after a long period of heavenly hedonism be reborn as humans.

Yājñavalkya also suggests an alternative to this endless cycle of becoming. The release from the cycle of rebirth is most often called *mokṣa*, liberation or salvation. According to Yājñavalkya an individual may attain liberation through lack of desire, since desire is what engenders saṃsāra in the first place.

In postulating an alternative state superior to worldly life and attainable through individual conscious effort, mokṣa is perhaps the most consequential of all Upaniṣadic ideas for later Indian religious history. In contrast to the Vedic ideology of sacrifice, in which goals were as much social and collective as individual, the pursuit of mokṣa takes an individualist goal to be the highest attainment. If Vedic sacrifice was responsible for engendering and maintaining the world process, the search for mokṣa posed a direct abnegation of that process, an escape from saṃsāra into something transcendent. This division of aims forms a major point of contention throughout Indian religious history. It reappears centuries later in the life stories of two modern women renouncers, Mīrāṃ and Śrī Arcanāpuri Mā.

Although the Upaniṣads are not united in their views, the strategies they recommend to those seeking mokṣa most often include a regimen of renunciation and asceticism coupled with instruction in the higher forms of knowledge, namely, the world according to the Upaniṣads. If mokṣa is an escape from the world cycle, it makes sense that one would reach it through progressive abstention from worldly involvements. That is exactly what the renouncer (*sannyāsin*) does. He (or occasionally she) would leave home and family to live in relatively isolated and austere circumstances, sleeping on the ground, restricting the diet, practicing control of the breath, and bringing the senses under control—in short, withdrawing from all that might bind one to the world, with the ultimate goal of escaping from rebirth itself. Such psychophysical practices were not confined to adherents of the Upaniṣads, as we will see, but the logic of renunciatory practice was first articulated in Upaniṣadic texts such as the *Bṛhadāraṇyaka Upaniṣad*.

The Vedas, then, contained a large variety of religious ideas and practices, introducing a host of terms and questions that would recur throughout Indian religious history. In sacrifice, the Vedas provided a system of public and private rituals that engendered the order of cosmos and of society, and that was utilized by political powers to validate their own authority. The brahmans appeared as an endogamous class of religious and intellectual specialists claiming high social status, and through the articulation of the varṇa system they portrayed society as an organic unity of distinct ranked classes pursuing different occupational specialties. The renunciatory model presented by the Upaniṣads centered around the individual pursuit of liberation through austerity and knowledge.

In later times the Vedas became one gauge for Hindu "orthodoxy." Those who adhered most closely to the Vedic tradition claimed a superior status and judged others as either within or outside the Vedic fold, even though the actual language of the Vedic texts had become incomprehensible to most. Many new Hindu groups honoring new deities with new forms of worship claimed allegiance to the Vedas, or portrayed themselves as extensions of the Vedas. The epic *Mahābhārata*, for example, poses itself as the "fifth Veda," whereas the Vaiṣṇava devotional poetry of Nammāḻvār is said to constitute a "Tamil Veda." Nineteenth- and twentieth-century reformist movements like the Brāhmo Samāj and the Ārya Samāj sought to return Hinduism to what they claimed were its purer Vedic roots.

Proximity to the Vedic tradition, however, is not an altogether reliable criterion for defining Hinduism. Although non-Hindus like Buddhists and Jains define themselves by rejecting the authoritative claims of the Vedas, so too do many later religious teachers such as Kabīr and the Bengali Bāuls, whom most Hindus view as Hindu. Theistic Hindu schools often contested Vedic authority in a different manner. Rather than rejecting the Vedas outright, the Śaiva devotional poet Māṇikkavācakar, for instance, simply asserts that Śiva is "Lord over the Vedas." His strategy, typical of many, is to establish a new hierarchy of religious values, within which the Vedas are included but subsumed under the higher authority of his god, Śiva.

In the end, what is most striking about the Vedas is their longevity rather than their hegemony. In the shifting, changing, contentious discourse of Indian religious history, one hears over and over echoes of the concerns, the terms, the goals, and the practices first recorded in India in the ancient Vedas.

The New Religions of the Sixth Century B.C.E.

Upaniṣadic sages like Yājñavalkya were not the only renouncers in the seventh and sixth centuries B.C.E. From all indications, there were many peripatetic seekers wandering the fringes of Gangetic civilization during this period. The authors and teachers of the Upaniṣads allied themselves with the Vedas, recommending that renouncers continue reciting the Vedas and view their ascetic practices as "interior sacrifice." Other forest teachers of the same period, including some undoubtedly not of the Indo-Aryan community, were willing to dispense altogether with Vedic models. They developed new teachings and practices with no attempt to link them to the established ideology of sacrifice and the Vedas. A teacher named Ajita of the Hair-Blanket proclaimed a thoroughgoing materialism (later identified as the Cārvāka school), denying both ethical prescriptions and existence after death.

The Ājīvika school led by Makkhali Gosāla adhered to a doctrine of fatalism, claiming that human free will was an illusion; destiny was all.

Varied as they were, most teachers accepted a common intellectual foundation, not differing greatly from that taught by Yājñavalkya. With few exceptions, they accepted the notion of cyclical transmigration (*saṃsāra*), the causal connection between act and consequence (*karman*) as the moral determinant of one's rebirth, and the possibility of escape (*mokṣa*) from this cyclical existence. Within this broad consensus, disagreement and debate continued. What is the underlying cause of saṃsāra? What kinds of activities engender karma? What are the best means of avoiding or removing the consequences of one's actions? What is the character of mokṣa? What exactly is it that attains liberation?

The seekers also generally accepted certain kinds of psychological and physical practices as particularly conducive to the religious attainments they sought. The general Indian term for such practices is *yoga*, from the verbal root *yuj*, to bind together, as one harnesses animals to a yoke. In Indian religious discourse, *yoga* refers to all sorts of disciplined practices aimed at restraining one's unruly inclinations in order to attain a higher state of concentration or "one-pointedness." In the vivid metaphor of one Upaniṣad, the senses are wild horses hitched to the chariot of the body; the mind is the charioteer who must somehow bring them under control. Yoga is what one uses to do so.

The earliest systematic exposition of yoga is found in the *Yogasūtras*, a text composed by Patañjali in about the second century B.C.E. but systematizing a much older body of practices. Patañjali describes eight "limbs" of yoga, starting with physical restraints such as limiting one's food and practicing celibacy, proceeding through a mastery of physical postures, the control of the breath, gradual withdrawal of the senses from the outer world, and culminating in fixed meditative awareness. As the practitioner masters each limb, he or she gradually detaches from the physical world, reins in the wayward senses, and achieves a reintegration or unification of self.

Patañjali himself adhered to the dualistic metaphysics of the Sāṃkhya school, but the techniques he described and systematized were practical tools for all religious seekers, adaptable to various philosophical viewpoints. Later in Indian religious history, new groups developed new forms of yogic practice as well. Medieval devotional and tantric forms of yoga emphasize such practices as meditative visualization of deities, repetitive chanting of the name of God, and ritualized sexual intercourse, among many others. Alchemists incorporated yoga into their transformative practices, and non-Hindu religious specialists like Islamic Sufis also adapted yogic techniques to their own purposes.

Out of the questing milieu of the sixth century B.C.E. grew two new religious formations that have had a powerful and continuing impact on Indian religions—Jainism and Buddhism. Both were historically established in the Magadha region (present-day Bihar) by members of the warrior class who renounced their positions in society to find enlightenment: Vardhamāna (c. 599–527 B.C.E.) called Mahāvīra ("great hero"), and Siddhārtha Gautama (c. 566–486 B.C.E.) called the

Buddha ("awakened one"). Both advocated paths of monastic austerity as the most effective means of attaining liberation, and both were critical of the Vedic formation. Adherents of the Vedas, in turn, characterized followers of Jainism and Buddhism as "outside the Veda," and accordingly modern scholars often classify the two religions as heterodoxies in contrast to Vedic orthodoxy.

Jainism

The name Jains use to designate themselves, *jaina*, derives from the verbal root *ji*, to conquer, and points to the central religious concern of the Jain community. Jaina monks must fight an ascetic battle to conquer the senses and karma, seeking to attain a purity of soul that liberates them from all bondage. Those who have succeeded in this quest are Jinas, conquerors, and their followers are Jainas.

According to Jain tradition, Vardhamāna Mahāvīra was only the most recent in a succession of twenty-four Tīrthaṅkaras, or "path-makers." His most immediate predecessor, Pārśva, may well have founded an earlier Jain community, but Mahāvīra is the first clearly attested historical Jain leader. Born of royal parents, the traditional biographies relate, Mahāvīra left his family and home at age thirty, abandoned all possessions, stripped off his clothes, and pulled out his hair by the roots. With these dramatic renunciatory acts he began twelve years of severe austerities, until finally at the age of forty-two he attained mokṣa, and so became a Jina or Tīrthaṅkara. Gradually a large group of followers grew around him. The first disciple was Indrabhūti Gautama, a proud brahman and Vedic scholar; in fact, Vardhamāna's eleven primary disciples were all converted brahmans. According to one tradition, Indrabhūti's conversion occurred when Mahāvīra delivered a sermon on the virtues of nonviolence (*ahiṃsā*) at a Vedic animal sacrifice—pointing to a major issue on which the Jains would most pointedly criticize the Vedic order.

Mahāvīra was a human being born of human parents, but he was also, as all Jain accounts make abundantly clear, something more than human. They describe his conception and birth as surrounded by auspicious omens and marvels preordaining his spiritual career. After he was liberated, the supramundane quality of Mahāvīra became still more apparent. His body, free of all impurities, was said to shine like a crystal on all sides. According to the Jain texts, the Vedic gods themselves, far from condescending to Mahāvīra as a mere mortal, recognized that his powers, knowledge, and status were superior to their own and honored him accordingly. Later Jain reformers like Ācārya Vijay Ānandsūri argue that the Jina is God.

The Jain community, male and female, divided itself into two groups: lay followers and renouncers. For lay followers, Mahāvīra and later Jain preceptors advocated self-restraints and vows. A Jain layperson should avoid meat, wine, honey, and snacking at night. One should also give up falsehood, stealing, and especially violence. Jain texts also recommend fasting and distributing one's wealth to monks, nuns, and the poor as means of strengthening the discipline of a lay adherent.

Jains soon developed forms of devotional practice directed toward the Tīrthaṅkaras and other worthy figures. Most prominent among these rituals is devapūjā, in which followers worship the Jinas physically represented by statues depicting them in poses of deepest meditation. Worshipers approach and bow before the image, chant the Jina's names, circumambulate, bathe the image, make a series of physical offerings to it, and wave lamps before it. Considering the transcendent status of the liberated beings, strict-minded Jains do not regard the Jinas as actually present in their images, nor do they suppose that offerings have any effect on the Jina, but rather view devapūjā as a meditational discipline intended to remind worshipers of the ideal state achieved by the Jina and to inspire them to seek that state for themselves. However, Jain devotional hymns indicate that most Jains have looked to the Tīrthaṅkara for direct benefits, and have believed the Jina to inhabit the images they honored.

Jains also incorporated into their temple liturgy the worship of goddesses and other guardian deities, lesser beings who may intervene in worldly affairs on behalf of the votary. As the stories indicate, Jaina goddesses like Cakrā could grant practical rewards such as wealth and release from earthly prison, as well as helping their devotees on the way to escaping the prison of karma.

The ethical and ritual disciplines of the Jain laity were regarded as preparations for the more rigorous and more efficacious life of a Jain renouncer. Indeed, Jains organized their religion largely around the necessity of renunciation for attaining true purity of soul. This central theme emerges even in the didactic stories of medieval Jain collections, in which the narrator seeks to instill in his audience a feeling of revulsion toward the world and to nudge it toward renunciation through exaggeration and macabre humor.

When a lay person decides to relinquish worldly life, this is treated as a great event both in the prospective renouncer's own spiritual career and in the life of the Jain community. In the ceremony of renouncing social life and entering upon a new monastic life—a veritable death and rebirth—Jain initiates cast off all their former possessions, pull out their hair in large handfuls, and give up their own names. They are presented with the austere provisions of mendicants and with new monastic names. At this point the new monk or nun undertakes the five "great vows," abstaining from all violence, dishonesty, theft, sexual intercourse, and personal possessions, under the close supervision of monastic preceptors. Through self-restraint, careful conduct, physical austerities, and meditations, the anchorite gradually removes the karma that inhibits the soul's inherent powers and virtues, aiming always at the final victory. The Jain path of rigorous austerity may culminate most dramatically in sallekhanā, voluntary self-starvation, in which the Jain renunciant gradually abandons the body itself for the sake of the soul's ultimate purity.

One of the first major royal patrons of Jainism was the Mauryan emperor Candragupta I (r. 321–297 B.C.E.). According to Jain tradition, this ruler was also involved in the major schism of Jainism into two communities, named Śvetāmbara (white-clad) and Digambara (sky-clad—that is, naked) after the monks' characteristic robes or lack thereof. In the third century B.C.E., the Jain leader Bhadrabāhu apparently moved half the Jain community south to Karnataka in order to escape a famine in Candragupta's kingdom. Candragupta himself went along as Bhadrabāhu's disciple. Divided geographically, the two Jain communities began to diverge doctrinally, and eventually formalized those differences at the Council of Vallabhī in the fifth century C.E. The Śvetāmbaras were and continue to be based primarily in the western Indian regions of Rajasthan and Gujarat, whereas the Digambaras have always been most prominent in Karnataka, and were also influential for a time in Tamilnadu.

Throughout the early medieval period, Jain monks and advisers played prominent roles in the courts of many Indian rulers. During this period Jain authors produced a remarkable array of literary and scholarly works in virtually every field, and Jain patrons sponsored impressive Jain temples. In the later medieval period, with Islamic rulers powerful in northern India and the Hindu state of Vijayanagar dominating the south, Jains lost much of their public patronage and became a more self-sufficient, inward-looking community. They survived, however, and now number some four million adherents, mostly in India but with substantial groups of Jains in the United States, Canada, the United Kingdom, and other parts of the English-speaking world.

Buddhism

Buddhists are those who follow the way of the buddhas, beings who have fully "awakened" (from the root *budh*, to wake up) to the true nature of things. In our historical era, the Awakened One was a kṣatriya named Siddhārtha Gautama, born in the foothills of the Himalaya Mountains in about 566 B.C.E. According to traditional accounts, the future Buddha Siddhārtha spent the first twenty-nine years of his life ensconced in affluent family life before renouncing society to seek liberation as a wandering ascetic. After spending six years in austerities, study, and meditation, Siddhārtha sat down under a fig tree in the town of Bodh Gaya one night in 531 B.C.E. and vowed that he would not get up until he had gained enlightenment. That night he attained nirvāṇa and became a buddha. One may view the remainder of the Buddha's life, and indeed all of Buddhist religion, as an attempt to enable others to replicate for themselves what Siddhārtha accomplished that night under the Bodhi tree.

The Buddha delivered his first public discourse, the first "turning of the wheel of Buddhist doctrine (*dharma*)," to an audience of five ascetics outside Varanasi. As soon as he had gathered sixty disciples, he sent them out in all directions to spread his teachings. From its inception, Buddhism was a proselytizing religion, and within a few centuries it was successful not just in the Indo-Aryan society of northern India but throughout South Asia. Spreading the message still further afield, Buddhist missionaries soon traveled to Sri Lanka, Southeast Asia as far as Indonesia, China, Japan, Korea, and Tibet. From the second through the seventh centuries C.E., Buddhism was the major cosmopolitan religion throughout Asia and probably the predominant religious community in the world at that time.

As a pan-Asian religion, Buddhism receives a separate volume in this series. It would be redundant to attempt to outline the complex doctrines or practices of Buddhism here. But Buddhism was first a powerful religious movement in India, and it had a major impact on the development of other religions in India, so it is necessary to refer to a few of its salient features.

Like Mahāvīra and the early Jains, the Buddha considered that the most effective way for his disciples to work toward individual salvation was in small monastic groups. Although renunciation of society was necessary, it was desirable also to avoid the isolation of the hermit. Monastic cells would allow for instruction, support, and enforcement of moral precepts. Establishing mendicant orders, however, posed a challenge to the brahmanic religious specialists and the sacrificial order. After all, mendicants still depend on alms, and the surplus production available to support the various religious claimants was finite.

In this competitive situation the Buddha and his followers developed a penetrating critique of the Vedic religion, much as the Jains did. Not only did the Buddha denounce the public sacrifices advocated by brahman specialists as overly costly, violent, and uncertain in their results, but he also sought to undercut the brahmans' own claims to authority. Satirizing the creation myth of *Ṛg Veda* 10.90, in which the brahman class emerges from the mouth of the primordial male Puruṣa, he pointed out that anyone could see that brahmans in fact emerge from the same female bodily organ as everybody else. He questioned brahmanic claims that the Vedas were revealed texts, not human in origin, as well as their claims to a special inborn religious authority.

Even early followers in the Buddhist community, however, considered the Buddha Śākyamuni to be a superhuman figure. Buddhists preserved his bodily charisma in his ashes and relics, entombed in burial mounds called *stūpas*. Located within monastic settlements, stūpas became centers of Buddhist devotion, where votaries would circumambulate, present flower garlands, burn incense and lamps, serenade with music, and recite eulogies. By the first century C.E. if not earlier, Buddhists also began to use physical images of the Buddha and other important Buddhist figures as objects of devotion. These informal acts of homage toward the Buddha in the form of stūpa or image were later formalized as the ritual of pūjā. During this same period, bodhisattvas, those motivated by compassion to achieve enlightenment, became objects of veneration and emulation in a movement that came to be known as the Mahāyāna (great vehicle).

Buddhist monks and nuns often established their "retreats" on the outskirts of the largest cities of the time and actively sought the patronage of royalty and the wealthy urban merchant class. With the conversion of the great Mauryan ruler Aśoka in the third century B.C.E., Buddhism became the imperial religion of South Asia. Aśoka patronized Buddhist institutions lavishly and sent out missionaries to spread Buddhist teachings abroad. He also publicized his new policies with inscriptions carved on pillars or rock faces throughout the empire. In his epigraphs, Aśoka speaks of his pursuit of dharma, by which he means a common ethical code based on values of tolerance, harmony, generosity, and nonviolence. While proclaiming tolerance toward all religious seekers, he also emphasized nonviolence, thereby effectively ruling out the animal sacrifices that had been the heart of the Vedic system of sacrifice. Far better, he announced, to practice the nonviolent ceremony of dharma, by which he meant giving gifts to Buddhist monks and nuns and other worthies.

Though the Mauryan empire fell apart rather soon after Aśoka's death, he had established a model for Buddhist kingship. For several centuries, every successor dynasty seeking to claim imperial status in India would begin to patronize Buddhists as its primary, though never exclusive, religious recipients. By the time of Harṣavardhana, the seventh-century emperor of Kanyākubja, however, there were clear signs that the role of Buddhism in India was diminishing. It was at this time that the Chinese pilgrim Xuanzang toured South Asia, and he observed the dramatic ceremonies of Buddhist gift-giving that Harṣa held at his capital; but he also noticed many abandoned Buddhist monasteries and temples throughout the subcontinent. Patronage and support apparently were drying up, a trend that accelerated after Harṣa's demise. Only in eastern India, the Himalayan regions, and Sri Lanka did Buddhism continue to flourish in South Asia. By the time of the Turko-Afghan raids of the eleventh through thirteenth centuries, Buddhism in northern India was confined to a few rich monastic institutions and universities, which made ripe targets for plunder. Many of the monks fled to Tibet, and Buddhism was effectively exiled from its land of origin.

Since the 1950s, Buddhism has been revivified in India from unexpected sources. A reformer and leader in the struggle for Indian independence, B. R. Ambedkar, was a member of a Maharashtran untouchable community and spokesman for untouchables nationwide. After a lifetime fighting for social justice, Ambedkar decided that Hinduism as it existed would never allow full status to the lowest orders of society, and at a huge public ceremony in 1956 he converted to Buddhism. Many of his followers did also, and the latest census estimates nearly four million Buddhists in Maharashtra alone. During the same period, the Chinese takeover of Tibet forced many Tibetan monks and lay Buddhists to flee south. The Dalai Lama, spiritual head of the Tibetan people, established his new home in exile in India, where he leads a substantial and visible community of Buddhist refugees.

Hinduism Redefined

During the period of Buddhist initiative and imperial spread, those social and religious groups who remained loyal in some way to the Vedic tradition were not inactive. In fact, as one historian puts it, "in the face of this challenge Brahmanism girt itself up by a tremendous intellectual effort for a new lease on life."[2] This statement overstates the degree to which "Brahmanism" reacted as a cohesive entity; historical sources suggest rather a multiplicity of initiatives. Nevertheless, the intellectual and socio-political challenge posed by Buddhism, Jainism, and the other renunciatory groups did inspire many creative and fruitful responses, which collectively add up to a virtual transformation in "orthodox" circles, from the Vedic worldview to forms of classical "Hinduism" that explicitly maintained continuity with the Vedic tradition but effectively altered it into a new religious formation.

The literature of this period is extensive. There was continued production of texts within the Vedic corpus: new Upaniṣads, new auxiliary texts, and texts that styled themselves "appendices" to the Vedic corpus. During this period the formative texts of six major philosophical schools were first put together—the Mīmāṃsā, Vedānta, Sāṃkhya, Yoga, Nyāya, and Vaiśeṣika schools. Of these, the Mīmāṃsā school occupied itself primarily with the interpretation of the Vedic sacrificial texts and ritual, whereas the Advaita Vedānta reformulated some of the teachings of the Upaniṣads into a consistent monist metaphysics. Sāṃkhya developed an alternative dualist philosophy, and Yoga systematized the psychophysical practices of the ascetics in accord with Sāṃkhya teachings. Nyāya was most concerned with the logic and rhetoric of philosophical disputation and the nature of reality, and Vaiśeṣika sought to develop a realist ontology of substances.

Another major genre of religious literature was the Dharmaśāstra, whose central concern, as the name implies, was the definition and delineation of dharma. The term *dharma* comes from the root *dhṛ*, to uphold, to maintain, and dharma may well be defined as "that which upholds and supports order." Yet different parties could hold very different ideas of what constitutes "order." In the Vedas the term *dharma* referred to the sacrifice as that which maintains the order of the cosmos. In Buddhist texts it meant the teachings of the Buddha, and Jain sources spoke of a Jaina dharma. Aśoka employed the term to describe his own religio-political policies. In the Dharmaśāstra literature, dharma referred to an overarching order of the cosmos and society, and to a person's duties within the world so constituted. It determined specific duties for all groups belonging to Indo-Aryan society, varying according to sex, class, family, stage of life, and so on. The Dharmaśāstras addressed themselves especially to the male brahman householder, directing him to live a life of austerity, purity, Vedic learning, and ritual observance.

The Epics

If the early Dharmaśāstras represent the response of one important social group to the new situation, the immense epic poems formulated during this period constitute a still more significant corpus of texts explicitly meant for all Hindu society. There are two great epics: the *Mahābhārata* (at 100,000 verses, roughly six times the length of the Christian Bible) and the *Rāmāyaṇa* (a mere 25,000 verses), plus an "appendix" to the *Mahābhārata* (as if 100,000 verses weren't enough) called the *Harivaṃśa*. "Whatever is here may be found elsewhere," admits the *Mahābhārata* (1.56.34), "but what is not here is nowhere else." Not only do the epics claim to be comprehensive in depicting the world, but they also intend to be of continuing relevance. The *Rāmāyaṇa* (1.2.35) predicts, "As long as mountains and streams shall endure upon the earth, so long will the story of the *Rāmāyaṇa* be told among men." Together the epics illustrate with remarkable thoroughness and rich detail a Hindu world in transition.

Although the *Mahābhārata* was later claimed as a "fifth Veda," the Sanskrit epics developed outside the Vedic corpus. They originated as the oral literature of bards who told and retold stories of heroic battles of the past, primarily for audiences of kṣatriya chieftains and warriors. The *Mahābhārata* tells the story of a great war between two rival clans and their allies that may have taken place around 900 B.C.E. Unlike the Vedas, however, the bardic literature was never meant to be preserved and transmitted verbatim. Over the generations storytellers reworked their narratives of the great war, expanding and supplementing them with all sorts of other stories and teachings, until the tales assumed a more or less final form around the fourth century C.E.

The epics center around great battles and wars, reflecting their origins as oral literature of the warrior class. The narratives begin with family conflicts leading to disputes over royal succession. Developing this theme to an extreme, the *Mahābhārata* uses the rivalry between two related kṣatriya clans to characterize the entire warrior class as quarreling, contentious, and increasingly deviating from dharma. With the ruling classes in such disarray, disorder and violence threaten society itself. The dire situation is mirrored throughout the cosmos, where (in the *Rāmāyaṇa*) the demon Rāvaṇa has overcome Indra, the divine representative of the Vedic order, and new heroes and deities must intervene to reestablish dharma. The crises lead with tragic inevitability to great battles, involving all the warriors of India in the *Mahābhārata*—and not just humans but also demons, monkeys, bears, and vultures in the *Rāmāyaṇa*. Through war the ancient order is purged and the demonic forces are subdued. The epics conclude with victorious kings restoring the social order.

While focusing on human conflict, the epics also present a new theophany. As the Vedic gods appear unable to contend with the demons and threatening chaos of a new age, these texts introduce a deity who can overcome these threats: Viṣṇu.

Viṣṇu is not an entirely new deity. In fact, he appears even in the *Ṛg Veda*, which associates him with three steps that mysteriously stretch over the whole world; later Vedic texts relate a myth linking Viṣṇu's three steps to the sacrifice. The myth relates how the gods trick the demons, who foolishly agree to allow the gods only as much ground for their sacrificial enclosure as the dwarflike Viṣṇu can cover in three steps. The demons should have realized the danger from the name Viṣṇu, which means "the one who pervades." As the gods sacrifice at their altar, the dwarf grows to become as large as the entire world, and in three steps covers the three worlds of heaven, earth, and the netherworld. Likewise, by the time the epics were put into final shape, Viṣṇu's religious role had grown from its diminutive appearance in the *Ṛg Veda* to a position of superiority over all other gods.

The epics present Viṣṇu as a divinity with clearly heroic qualities, who takes over Indra's role as primary vanquisher of demons. Other gods have begun to recognize Viṣṇu as their superior and pay homage to him. He continues to associate himself with the sacrifice, and actively maintains the order of society. Most importantly, and paradoxically, the epics identify Viṣṇu both as the supreme deity and as an active, embodied, finite god who intervenes directly in human affairs. On the one hand, the epics assert that Viṣṇu is identical with the Puruṣa of *Ṛg Veda* 10.90, the *Brahman* of the Upaniṣads, and other previous formulations of a transcendent Absolute. Yet he also retains features of a more anthropomorphic divinity, particularly when he takes on human forms or incarnations (*avatāra*, literally a "crossing down" to human form) and intervenes directly in human society to kill demons and restore dharma.

In the *Harivaṃśa*, Viṣṇu incarnates himself as Kṛṣṇa in order to destroy the tyrannical demon Kaṃsa, who has usurped the throne of Mathura. Though born of royal parentage, Kṛṣṇa is raised among a tribe of cowherds, who only gradually become aware of his superhuman character. When Kṛṣṇa has grown to manhood, he returns to Mathura and puts an end to Kaṃsa and the other demons of his coterie. In the *Mahābhārata*, Viṣṇu appears again as Kṛṣṇa, ruler of Dwaraka and a loyal friend of the Pāṇḍava hero Arjuna. Here too the divinity of Kṛṣṇa is only occasionally revealed, though in many ways Kṛṣṇa acts as a hidden, inscrutable instigator and manipulator of events throughout the epic.

Viṣṇu takes on a different human embodiment in the *Rāmāyaṇa*, as Rāma, the young prince of Ayodhya, whose primary mission is to rid the world of Rāvaṇa and other demons. Rāvaṇa has gained a divine blessing making him invulnerable to other gods and demons, and this enables him to defeat Indra and to insinuate himself as sole recipient of sacrificial offerings. Yet he has arrogantly neglected to request invincibility from humans as well. Rāvaṇa's ruin comes about after he abducts Sītā, the beautiful and chaste wife of Rāma, and imprisons her in his palace in Lankā. With the aid of an army of monkeys and bears, the warrior-prince Rāma, divine and human, defeats Rāvaṇa's army, rescues Sītā, and finally returns to Ayodhya to rule as its king.

The concept of *avatāra*, one can imagine, offered important advantages to an expanding community of Viṣṇu worshipers. It enabled the Vaiṣṇavas to maintain their identification of Viṣṇu as the Absolute, yet also incorporate other local or regional deities and their cults as incarnations of an encompassing Viṣṇu. Historically speaking, Kṛṣṇa no doubt originated as a human hero, the warrior leader of a pastoral tribe in the Mathura region. Folkloric aggrandizement turned him into a legendary hero with godlike qualities, and finally in the *Harivaṃśa* he was revealed to be a divinity incarnate, the avatāra of Viṣṇu.

Of all portions of the Sanskrit epics, none is considered more significant to the development of Indian religions than the *Bhagavad Gītā*, the "Song of the Lord Kṛṣṇa," a part of the *Mahābhārata* composed around 200 C.E. Placed at the dramatic climax of the epic's narrative, the *Gītā* also provides the central ideological and theological vision of the epic. Just as the great battle is about to begin, with huge armies facing one another across the battlefield of Kurukṣetra, the most powerful warrior on the Pāṇḍava side, Arjuna, suffers from a paroxysm of doubt and anxiety. Why should he fight, particularly when his opponents include relatives and former teachers? Acting as Arjuna's charioteer, Kṛṣṇa responds to his doubts by offering a sustained discourse on the moral and religious propriety of war, the nature of human action, and the most effective means of attaining liberation. Kṛṣṇa argues that worldly action in support of dharma is not incompatible with mokṣa, as the various renunciatory orders had suggested. One should accept one's personal dharma as a guide to proper conduct, he avers, but without regard to the fruits of that conduct.

To clinch his argument, Kṛṣṇa also progressively reveals himself to Arjuna as a deity, indeed as the highest, supreme divinity. The teaching culminates with an overwhelming vision. Granted "divine eyes" by Kṛṣṇa, Arjuna is suddenly able to see Kṛṣṇa's complete form, the awesome, all-inclusive Viśvarūpa. Kṛṣṇa acknowledges that previous methods of self-transformation such as sacrifice and yoga may be efficacious, but in light of his self-revelation he also recommends a new and superior method of religious attainment, which he calls *bhakti* (devotion). The most efficient way to reach the highest state, he tells Arjuna, is to dedicate one's entire self to Kṛṣṇa, a personal god who is simultaneously the Absolute.

With Arjuna's vision of the embodied Absolute and Kṛṣṇa's advocacy of bhakti we are initiated into the world of Hindu theism.

The Purāṇas and Hindu Theism

Throughout the period loosely labeled as the "Gupta" and "post-Gupta" ages, 300–700 C.E., Buddhism remained a powerful religious force in India, but new groups devoted to Viṣṇu and Śiva gained in visibility and resources. The Gupta rulers themselves satisfied both sides by lavishly patronizing Buddhist institutions while also declaring themselves followers of Viṣṇu. Throughout history Indian rulers have usually diversified their religious patronage as a means of integrating multiple religious communities within their kingdoms. The earliest Hindu temples built in permanent materials appeared during this period. Images of Hindu gods increased in scale and quality of workmanship. Reflecting and consolidating this growth in the religious orders of Viṣṇu and Śiva, another genre of texts, the Purāṇas, articulated more fully the theistic worldview outlined in the epics.

The Purāṇas (literally, ancient traditions) constitute another huge corpus of texts, numbering eighteen "major" Purāṇas, eighteen "sub-major" ones, and countless others. The major Purāṇas alone run to something like 400,000 verses. Like the epics, the Purāṇas were composed orally over many centuries, so that earlier and later teachings are regularly juxtaposed in the same texts. Bards put the earliest Purāṇas into final shape by about the fifth century C.E., while other texts kept incorporating new materials. The *Bhaviṣya Purāṇa* (or "Future Purāṇa," an oxymoron), the most open-ended of the major Purāṇas, contains sections from the fifth century or earlier, yet also "predicts" such late medieval figures as Akbar, Kabīr, Caitanya, and Guru Nānak, and even foretells the coming of British rule to India.

Comprehensive and encyclopedic in scope, the Purāṇas discuss cosmology, royal genealogies, society and dharma, the sacred geography of pilgrimage sites, yogic practices, town planning, even grammar and poetics. For the religious history of South Asia, however, the most significant aspect of the Purāṇas is their presentation of the theology, mythology, and ritual of the two primary gods Viṣṇu and Śiva.

Already in the epics, proponents of Viṣṇu were advancing him as the highest lord of the cosmos. The Vaiṣṇava Purāṇas advocate this with greater confidence and fuller cosmological breadth. The cyclical epochs of creation and dissolution of the universe, we now learn, are none other than Viṣṇu's alternating periods of activity and rest. The Purāṇas flesh out the incipient notion of Viṣṇu's intervening incarnations and gradually systematize it into a list of ten embodiments, including not only Kṛṣṇa and Rāma, but also zoomorphic forms (fish, tortoise, boar, man-lion), anthropomorphic ones (the dwarf who took three steps, Paraśurāma), a future incarnation (Kalkin), and even the Buddha. As the *Viṣṇu Purāṇa* relates, once when the demons had become too powerful through sacrifice, Viṣṇu took form as the Buddha and also as a naked Jain mendicant to dissuade them from sacrificing, so that the gods could overcome them and restore the proper order of things. Generally, all his incarnations reinforce Viṣṇu's essential attributes: benevolence, a desire to preserve order in the world, and a paradoxical capacity to be simultaneously infinite and finite.

Like Viṣṇu, Śiva appears in a rather minor role in the *Ṛg Veda*, but gradually advances in status until the Śaiva Purāṇas single him out as the Absolute. In the *Ṛg Veda*, Rudra ("the howler") is a peripheral divinity. Dwelling outside society in the forests or mountains, he is associated with the destructive forces of nature and rules over undomesticated animals. Since Rudra is not numbered one of the auspicious gods, he is excluded from the soma sacrifice, and instead is offered tribute to avert his wrath. Although he is characteristically destructive in his actions, Rudra may also become beneficent if properly praised and propitiated. When Rudra shows this kinder, gentler nature he is called Śiva, the "auspicious" one.

Already in this early appearance, we can observe two traits central to Śiva's later personality. In contrast to the sociable Viṣṇu, Śiva is an outsider. Residing typically in the highest Himalayan Mountains, he is the lord and role model for yogis, less concerned with instituting dharma on earth than with leading souls toward mokṣa. Second, Śiva has a dual nature, conjoining what are to us antithetical attributes. Not only is he both malevolent and benevolent, he is also both ascetic and erotic, hermit and family man, an immobile meditator and an unruly dancer. In one iconographic form, Śiva appears simultaneously male and female, an integral hermaphrodite.

In the epics, Śiva's character remains ambiguous, capricious, fierce, and sometimes wrathful. He continues to live outside society, and if he intervenes at all it is usually to disrupt things. Though they are predominantly Vaiṣṇava in orientation, the epics nevertheless recognize Śiva's growing power and his increasing claim to certain ritual prerogatives. In one famous episode, King Dakṛa organizes a large public sacrifice but declines to invite Śiva since, after all, Śiva is rather unruly. Learning of this slight, Śiva sends a swarming horde of emanations to break up the sacrifice, and then appears in person to demand that from now on he be the primary recipient of all sacrificial offerings.

One early Upaniṣad, the *Śvetāśvatara*, had identified Rudra-Śiva as the transcendental Absolute, identical with Puruṣa and the Upaniṣadic Brahman. The Śaiva Purāṇas reassert this claim and link it with a fully developed mythology of Śiva's doings. Unlike Viṣṇu, Śiva does not incarnate himself as a human being for an entire lifetime; rather he occasionally manifests himself physically in a body to carry out his varied intentions. In the Purāṇas, Śiva's manifestations most often demonstrate his superiority over other contestants, defeat demons, and grant grace to his followers.

Viṣṇu and Śiva are not the only deities in the world of the Purāṇas. In fact, these texts present a complex, inclusive pantheon, populated with divine families, animal mounts for each deity, Vedic divinities (now cast exclusively in supporting roles), and hosts of lesser semi-divinities such as celestial dancers, musicians, titans, sages, magicians, and many more. Among them two deserve special note: Brahmā and the Goddess.

The god Brahmā, with roots in the late Vedic and Dharmaśāstra literature, appears in the Purāṇas as the god of creation and as the patron of Vedic and orthodox brahmans. Sometimes the texts portray him comically as a senile grandfather who causes trouble by indiscriminately rewarding even demons for their austerities; at other times he shows better judgment in recognizing the preeminence of Viṣṇu and Śiva. Some Purāṇas of a more integrationist tendency, however, stress the interdependence of the three principal male divinities in performing distinct cosmic functions: Brahmā creates the world, Viṣṇu protects and sustains it, and Śiva destroys it. In modern times this has become known as the "Hindu trinity."

The Goddess presents a more complex picture. In the literature of the fifth through seventh centuries, several important female deities gain a new importance. Three are consorts or wives of the principal male deities: Lakṣmī is the consort of Viṣṇu, Pārvatī of Śiva, and Sarasvatī of Brahmā. These goddesses often take on significant responsibilities in their own rights, as Lakṣmī becomes the goddess of prosperity and domestic good fortune. Some Puraṇic texts, most notably the *Devīmāhātmya* section (c. 600 C.E.) of the *Mārkaṇeya Purāṇa*, go further to present a single great Goddess not as a wife, but as the Supreme Lord, appropriating for her all the common epithets of the Absolute. In her most famous incarnation she appears as Durgā, a warrior goddess. A buffalo demon, having gained nearly invincible powers through austerities, is running rampant through the cosmos and none of the male gods can subdue it. Durgā is born from the collective anger and frustration of all the gods. She receives a weapon from each of them and then rides forth on her lion mount to confront and finally destroy the demon.

Like Viṣṇu and Śiva, this female Absolute has an absorbing personality. She incorporates many local and regional cults and manifests herself in a plethora of distinct guises and forms. Only occasionally in the major Purāṇas does she appear in full force, but these glimpses point to the existence during this period of a significant school of thought that identified the fundamental force of the cosmos as feminine in nature and devoted itself to her praise and worship. This religious sensibility reappears in new forms among the tantric schools of medieval India and the Kālī bhakti of eighteenth-century Bengal.

The rich and varied religious literature of the Purāṇas created a compelling portrayal of the theistic Hindu cosmos. Moreover, these narratives of divine characters and their supernatural doings became part of the cultural literacy of Indian audiences from this period on. Medieval poets composing epigraphic eulogies and devotional verses could take this knowledge for granted and use it as a basis for literary allusion, exploration, and satire in their own verse. Temple sculptors rendered the puranic stories visible in their iconographic figures and narrative reliefs. Still today, hymns of praise recited in domestic and temple worship reiterate the mythic deeds and attributes of the Hindu deities much as they were first spelled out in the Purāṇas.

Temple Hinduism

By 700 C.E., the religious transformation first envisioned in the epics was complete. A new form of Hindu theism, focusing upon the gods Viṣṇu and Śiva as supreme deities but incorporating as well a host of other lesser gods and goddesses, now dominated the public sphere. Harṣavardhana was the last emperor to follow the Aśokan model by converting to Buddhism and supporting the Buddhist establishment with ostentatious gifts. No longer did sovereigns proclaim their performance of Vedic sacrifices as the principal way of asserting their authority to rule. Instead, they increasingly chose to articulate royal claims in a more concrete and lasting form, by constructing massive stone Hindu temples. These mountainlike structures, rising up to two hundred feet high and covered with sculptural representations of the Hindu pantheon, assumed a conspicuous and commanding presence in the Indian religious and political landscape during the early medieval period. During the half millennium from 700 to 1200 C.E., temple Hinduism dominated the public religious life of India.

The inscriptions of the seventh-century south Indian king Mahendravarman exemplify this shift in royal patronage. Although his Pallava predecessors had performed sacrifices as their primary ritual means of establishing royal legitimacy, Mahendravarman switched dramatically to temple sponsorship. He viewed his lordship over rival rulers as directly linked to Śiva's own cosmic overlordship. By constructing temples for Śiva, he brought God into his own territory and also proclaimed his authority over defeated rivals and their territories. Similarly, the succeeding rulers and dynasties of early medieval India sought to outbuild one another in conspicuous devotion to their chosen deity, Viṣṇu or Śiva.

A Hindu temple is primarily a home or residence for a god. Located in the main sanctum of the temple is an image or icon, a physical form that serves as a support within which Viṣṇu, Śiva, or some other principal deity may make himself physically present and accessible, enabling worshipers to enact a direct personal relationship with that divinity. At the same time, the temple offers through its physical structure a vision of the orderly cosmos presided over by that deity, with hierarchical ranks of subordinate deities, semi-divinities, devotees, and other auspicious entities all finding their proper places. Finally, in its layout the temple provides a map of the spiritual path a worshiper must follow toward participation with the deity ensconced in the "womb-room" at the center. The temple is thus a place of crossing, in which god descends from transcendence and devotee moves inward from the mundane.

Anyone may build a temple, but its size will naturally depend on the resources available to the patron. From small home shrines meant for private devotions to village temples, and on up in scale to the imposing edifices put up by Hindu kings with imperial aspirations, all serve basically the same purposes. Temple liturgy centers around physical and spiritual transactions between the incarnate deity and worshipers, mediated in the case of public temples by priests. These transactions are called *pūjā*. "How to Worship at the Abode of Śiva," a nineteenth-century pamphlet instructing pious Śaiva worshipers in proper temple conduct, provides a concise and reliable account of south Indian pūjā based on early medieval formulations.

The historical origins of pūjā are uncertain. In Vedic texts, the term refers to the respectful treatment of brahman guests. Jains and Buddhists, as we have seen, developed forms of pūjā to images and stūpas quite early. Small but recognizable images of the Hindu divinities, probably employed in simple household pūjā ceremonies, have been found dating back to the early centuries C.E. It is likely that all these forms of pūjā among the written traditions derive from earlier informal practices of image worship by autochthonous peoples outside the Indo-Aryan society. Hindu texts of the medieval period, however, see this new form of worship as the result of the god's own direct intervention and instruction, as in the puranic episode of the "Origin of Liṅga Worship." There, Śiva guides a group of renunciatory sages from their earlier Vedic-based rites to the new practice of worshiping Śiva's liṅga. Pūjā replaces sacrifice, but at the same time it incorporates select portions of the Vedic repertoire of mantras and ritual gestures, much as Śiva advises the sages to recite Vedic texts when offering pūjā.

In the context of large-scale royal temples, pūjā developed into an elaborate, rule-bound, priestly activity. New genres of liturgical guides were composed—Vaiṣṇava saṃhitās, Śaiva āgamas, and Śākta tantras—claiming to be the direct teachings of the deities concerning the metaphysical organization of the cosmos and how humans ought best to worship them. Pan-Indian Hindu theological orders, such as the Pāñcarātra and Vaikhānasa schools directed toward Viṣṇu and the Pāśupata and Śaiva Siddhānta schools dedicated to Śiva, employed these texts to maintain the temples as centers of community worship.

While priests and their texts emphasized proper ritual performance as a means of religious attainment, others began to assert that emotional enthusiasm, or bhakti, played a more crucial role in worshiping god. The term *bhakti* is usually translated as "devotion," but its meaning is more complex than our English equivalent would suggest. *Bhakti* comes from the verb root *bhaj*. In its earliest usage, *bhaj* means to divide or share, as one divides and partakes of the sacrificial offerings. *Bhaj* can also denote experiencing something, as one enjoys food or relishes music. It signifies waiting upon someone, as an attendant serves a king. It can mean to make love in a very corporeal sense and to adore in a more disembodied, spiritual manner. As its Indian adherents define it, *bhakti* partakes of all these shades of meaning. It is a way of participating or sharing in divine being, however that is understood, of tasting and enjoying a god's presence, of serving and worshiping him, of being as intimate as possible, of being attached to him above all else.

As a religious attitude or way of relating to a being one takes as superior, bhakti is widespread throughout Indian religions. One finds hymns of devotion throughout the Purāṇas and the liturgical texts of temple Hinduism, and similar genres of eulogistic poetry are common in Buddhist and Jain literature. Historians also use the term in a more restricted sense, however, to refer to a series of regional movements in medieval India that stressed intense personal devotion to god or goddess, the leadership of exemplary poet-saints, and the importance of a community of devotees. The earliest of these bhakti movements date from the seventh through ninth centuries, in the southern region of Tamilnadu, and are represented by the poetry of Māṇikkavācakar. Later bhakti movements occurred in the Deccan and throughout northern India from the twelfth century through the seventeenth centuries; these will be discussed in the context of Hindu responses to Islam.

The groups of devotees to Śiva and to Viṣṇu of early medieval Tamilnadu were closely allied with the spread and growth of Hindu temples in the region. Itinerant poets traveled from village to village singing hymns of praise to their gods as they saw them in each new place of worship. Although they did not overtly criticize the temple priests or their ritualism, the bhakti poets of Tamilnadu proposed what they saw as a more satisfying and accessible means of reaching the divine. Whereas priests performed ritual invocations to bring Śiva or Viṣṇu into visible material supports, the bhakti saints used their poetry to evoke each deity in full and sensuous detail. Reiterating the god's activities, they often placed themselves as participants in those mythical scenes. They stressed the importance of establishing a close relationship with the god conceived in a personal and particularized manner. Using a trope that would become common among bhakti poets, Tamil devotees often spoke in the poetic voice of women infatuated with the alluring male deity, drawing on the conventions of secular love poetry and transforming the erotic into a religious allegory of soul and God. Women saints like Āṇṭāḻ did not require this metaphoric step. According to her hagiography, Āṇṭāḻ's single-minded love led her to reject all human suitors and unite with Viṣṇu himself, in the form of a temple image.

Yet at the same time, as Māṇikkavācakar's poetry shows, the poets recognized the paradox inherent in conceptualizing the divine this way. However anthropomorphically the poets might portray their god, Śiva and Viṣṇu remained ultimately beyond, and unknowable as well. The tensions between god's immanence and his transcendence (or, as Vaiṣṇava theologians phrased it, his simultaneous "easy accessibility" and his "otherness"), and between the devotee's mixed feelings of intimacy and alienation provide central themes that run throughout Indian devotional literature.

While temple Hinduism centered around Viṣṇu and Śiva held sway in the public sphere in early medieval India, many other religious formations were present, as well. As we have seen, Hindus never sought to develop a pan-Indian "church" structure nor did they establish a clear ecclesiastical hierarchy. Even the brahmans, seemingly the religious elite, formed a very diverse and permeable social group, with new priestly groups sometimes successfully claiming brahmanic status for themselves.

Vedic schools continued their intellectual activities even though sacrifice was no longer a significant public form of ritual. The Mīmāṃsā school developed elaborate means of interpreting the Vedic texts, and scholars of Dharmaśāstra applied these principles to the reading of dharma texts. Groups of brahmans loyal to the Vedic traditions often received special land grants called *agrahāras*, where they were able to maintain small-scale Vedic sacrificial programs free from economic need.

Other orthodox writers with a more philosophical bent developed and systematized the metaphysical monism implicit in some portions of the Upaniṣads, culminating in the ninth-century writings of Śaṅkara, a brilliant author and philosophical disputant of the Advaita Vedānta school. Śaṅkara's writings demoted temple image worship to the status of a useful but decidedly lower form of religious attainment, and reserved the highest place for intellectual realization of the oneness of Brahman. The other principal Vedānta school, the "qualified nondualist" system of Rāmānuja (c. 1050 C.E.) gave a more prominent role to devotion and engaged itself more directly in the doings of temple Hinduism. Rāmānuja even served as monastic superior in one of the largest south Indian Viṣṇu temples.

During this period, Buddhism was still strong in the areas of Kashmir and northeastern India, and such celebrated universities as Nālandā in Bihar served as international centers for Buddhist study. Communities of Jains were numerous in Gujarat and Karnataka, maintaining their own traditions of scholarship and asceticism, and not infrequently placing Jain ministers in the royal courts of those areas. We must assume the existence of many other forms of religious thought and practice during this period which, because they were esoteric or domestic or nonliterate, did not leave behind texts or other historical evidence.

The diversity of indigenous Indian religions was supplemented by religious and ethnic communities who migrated from elsewhere and settled in India, especially along the western coast. Jewish traders and Syrian Christians arrived in India at least as early as the fourth century, and from the seventh century Arab Muslim merchants set up a trading network around coastal India. Starting in the tenth century, the Parsees ("Persians"), who adhere to the ancient Iranian religion of Zoroastrianism, fled their homeland for the safer terrain of India. Each of these groups maintained itself as an autonomous, insular, and largely unthreatening religious minority within Hindu-dominated society.

In such a pluralistic setting, members of many religious persuasions articulated their differing positions and debated their views in public and at court. The stakes were sometimes high. Although some modern scholars and Hindus have portrayed the pre-Islamic period of Indian history as one of overriding religious tolerance, this was not entirely the case. The hymns of the south Indian poet-saints, for instance, included an often bitter polemic against Jains and Buddhists, and in the later biographies of these saints we hear of intentional destruction of Buddhist images and of a pogrom carried out against the eight thousand Jains of Madurai. Whatever the historicity of such later accounts, they clearly reflect an atmosphere in which religious concerns were taken as serious and consequential, not a matter of unobstructed personal choice.

Islam in India

Around 610 C.E. Muḥammad, a member of the Arab tribe ruling Mecca, began to receive revelations. By 622 his criticisms of Arab paganism and of the injustice of Meccan society had aroused considerable opposition. When residents of another city to the north invited him to come and act as arbiter, he led a few followers in an exodus to build in Medina a new society based on divine law. Muḥammad had embarked on his career as the Prophet of Islam. Revelations continued until his death in 632, and were later collected into the foundation text of Islam, the Qur'ān. These distant events held immense consequences for the history of Indian religions.

For the first 150 years of its existence, Islam was the most dynamic, expanding religious movement the world had ever seen. Imbued with a theological and ethical directive to transform the "house of unbelievers" into the "house of submission (*islam*)" through "righteous struggle" (*jihād*), the military forces of the early Muslim leaders conquered first the Arab peninsula, then the surrounding West Asian regions of Syria, Iraq, Iran, and Afghanistan, and the countries of North Africa. By the early part of the eighth century, Muslim armies had expanded into Spain and were pushing into the southern parts of France in the West; in the East they had reached as far as Sind, in present-day Pakistan. This success came at a price, though. The religious quest of Muḥammad's companions was stifled by disputes, and although the leaders of the Muslim community legitimated their regimes through Islamic law, they soon adopted the Roman Caesar and the Persian Shāh as their models of sovereignty, much to the disgust of Islamic religious scholars.

Over the next few centuries an Indian frontier was defined and gradually pushed back as Arab, Persian, and Turkish armies invaded and conquered Afghanistan, Kashmir, and the Punjab. Despite continued resistance by indigenous rulers, the more centralized and organized tactics of the invaders eventually proved successful. In the early eleventh century, Maḥmūd, the Turko-Afghan ruler of Ghazna (in Afghanistan), mounted eighteen campaigns into northern India. He conquered and incorporated the Punjab into the Ghaznavid empire and then enriched his state by sacking many of the Buddhist monasteries and Hindu temples of northern India, and transporting the loot back to Ghazna. Though he temporarily disrupted the existing Indian political and religious order, Maḥmūd did not seek to establish a permanent Islamic polity centered in the subcontinent. That was left to a successor dynasty also based in Afghanistan, the Ghūrids.

In 1193 Mu'izzuddīn Muḥammad of Ghūr and his general Qutb al-Dīn Aibak defeated the Cāhamāna ruler of Delhi, then the most powerful north Indian king, and in 1026 Qutb al-dīn declared himself Sultan of Delhi. The Delhi sultanate lasted some 320 years, under six different Turko-Afghan dynasties, and dominated much of north India. Other Islamic polities were established in the Deccan and southern India during this period. The sultanate was in turn supplanted by the Mughal empire, founded by the Central Asian adventurer Bābar in 1526. The Mughal empire held sway over much of India into the early part of the eighteenth century. Thus for roughly five hundred years of late medieval Indian history, from 1200 to 1700, rulers adhering to Islam prevailed in northern India. With these rulers came a conservative clerical elite who sought, with mixed success, to maintain Islamic social and legal order in the urban centers of India.

The face of the conqueror, however, was not the only visage of Islam in India, nor even the most common one. With Islamic rule in India, itinerant Muslim Sufi teachers came to till the fertile religious fields of India. *Sufism* is the generic term for Islamic mysticism. Already sharing features with some forms of Hinduism, Sufis found it relatively easy to acclimatize their messages and concerns to the Indian environment. Indeed, they came to regard themselves as a kind of spiritual government of India, responsible for the religious welfare of the people, parallel to but separate from the political government of the sultans. The Sufis taught an esoteric form of Islam aimed at an elite, and they were not consciously interested in attracting non-Muslim masses to Islam. They used their Indian mother tongues to compose mystical poetry, however, and their tombs became centers of a cult of saints that increasingly attracted both Muslims and non-Muslims.

In a history of Indian religions, it is necessary to recognize both sides of Islam in India. The conquests of the Turkic, Afghan, and Central Asian Muslim warriors and their continuing struggles for power both among themselves and with Hindu warrior elites like the Rajputs had significant repercussions not only for Indian political history but also for the development of Indian religions, continuing to the present. At the same time, the more conciliatory and assimilative activities of the Sufis played a greater role in implanting Islam as an indigenous Indian religious formation in South Asia. In this anthology most of the readings emphasize the role of Sufism in Indian Islam.

Orthodox Islam and Political Authority

Al-Bīrūnī, one of the great medieval Muslim scholars, accompanied Maḥmūd on his military forays into India in the early eleventh century, and wrote of the Indians he encountered there: "They differ from us in everything which other nations have in common. In all manners and usages they differ from us to such a degree as to frighten their children with us, our dress, and our ways and customs, and to declare us to be the devil's breed, and our doings as the very opposite of all that is good and proper." The response he observed was perhaps not surprising, considering that the Ghaznavids were plundering their way across northern India at the time. Yet al-Bīrūnī points to very real differences between the various ruling Islamic groups of late medieval India and the predominantly Hindu society they ruled.

The book of Allah's revelations to Muḥammad, the Qur'ān, specifies five basic constituents or "pillars" of the Islamic faith: the profession of faith, regular prayer, giving of alms, fasting during the month of Ramadān, and pilgrimage.

Islam is based on a simple, shared creed, in which the Muslim believer acknowledges his or her submission to a single supreme God and recognizes Muḥammad as the Prophet. Orthodox Islam is rigorously monotheistic. Allah's transcendence excludes all other claims to divinity. Medieval Hinduism, by contrast, was hierarchically pluralistic in its theological outlook, admitting a host of immanent divinities and semi-divinities who participate in every sphere of the cosmos. A Hindu might well regard one of these deities as the highest "God of gods," but this did not prevent recognition of many other divinities appropriate for other persons or purposes. To the orthodox Muslim, this divine multiplicity of the Hindus appeared as a clear case of polytheism, which would diminish the adoration due to Allah alone.

The Allah of the orthodox is all-powerful and transcendent. While acting as the creator of all things, Allah never takes on physical form in the world. Hindu deities like Viṣṇu and Śiva, we have seen, do intervene directly in the world, often in human or even animal bodies. They also enter into the physical forms of icons and images, and this makes possible the institution of temples and their liturgies of worship. For orthodox Muslims, the Qur'ān and other authoritative traditions contain strong prohibitions against any adoration of physical idols.

Relations between the Muslim faithful and Allah are best expressed in prayer, a nonreciprocal and nonmaterial communication from believer to God. All believers should pray five times daily while facing Mecca, the geographical center of the Islamic community. Early in its history, the Muslim community institutionalized public prayer as a regular collective act, and the mosque grew to accommodate this activity. The Islamic mosque provides a large, mostly open area for congregational prayer, an egalitarian space enclosed by a surrounding wall to separate believers from nonbelievers. Though there can be no central image or icon representing Allah, the mosque does provide a spatial focus in the form of a wall indicating the direction toward Mecca.

The fifth pillar, pilgrimage, indicates another important aspect of Islam. At least once in a lifetime, the Muslim believer ought to make a pilgrimage to Mecca. From its earliest decades Islam was a universalistic and international religion, spread out geographically from Spain through northern Africa, across the Middle East, and into southern Asia. In different regions Islam naturally took on various regional characters, but it always maintained the ideal of a single unified community of believers. The institution of pilgrimage brought about an annual assembly of Muslims from all over the Islamic world, and thereby strengthened this unity. Islam in India had a dual identity. While grounded in the distinctive social and cultural realities of India, it was also part of the wider world of international Islam.

As Islamic warrior elites from Turkey and Central Asia established their authority in new parts of India there was inevitably conflict. At the frontiers of contested control, the conquerors sometimes symbolized their victories through a physical metaphor: the destruction of Hindu temples (as well as Jain and Buddhist sites, equally "polytheistic"), often followed by the construction of mosques on the leveled sites. Hindu chieftains, in response, might reconsecrate these same religious sites as a way of claiming independence from Delhi's political overlordship. In this way temples sometimes became indices of political control.

Within areas of settled rule, however, Muslim authorities adopted a more lenient attitude toward their Hindu subjects. Early in Islamic history, Muslims had formulated an intermediate category for those who could not be classified as either "believers" or "heathens." Christians and Jews, sharing the Abrahamic lineage with Muslims, were labeled "people of the book," and treated as tolerated religious communities within the Islamic state. The Hindus of India were idolaters and polytheists, admittedly, but brahmans could be regarded as the equivalent of Christian monks, and so could be left largely to their own religious customs. Hindu subjects might even construct temples, so long as these structures did not pose a threat to the dominating Muslim institutions. Indeed, Turkish and Mughal rulers even gave endowments of land and granted tax exemptions for certain Hindu, Jain, and Zoroastrian religious foundations. Reciprocally, Hindu rulers sometimes facilitated the construction of mosques for the benefit of their Muslim subjects.

Sufism

Sufism stresses the personal relationship between believer and Allah. The word *Sufi* (Arabic *ṣūfī*) derives from the Arabic for wool, alluding to the coarse woolen garments favored by early Muslim mystics. As with Ajita of the Hair-Blanket and countless other Indian ascetics, early Sufis chose to represent their austerity and renunciation of worldly concerns through a conspicuous rejection of comfortable clothing.

Despite its mystical and renunciatory tendencies, Sufism should not be seen as outside the mainstream of Islam. Sufis ground their teachings firmly in Muḥammad's revelation, but they draw on different portions of the Qur'ān than do more conservative exegetes. Whereas conservative Muslims focus on passages emphasizing Allah's almighty, awesome, and ineffable character, Sufi interpreters stress the sections that speak of Allah's pervasive presence in the world and in the hearts of his believers. Significantly, Sufis speak of a "jihād of the heart" as a more important religious struggle than the "jihād of the sword." In the medieval Islamic world, far from being a peripheral movement, Sufism engendered some of the most powerful and influential theological writings, such as that of Ibn al-ʿArabī, and the most moving and popular Muslim poetry, as that of the thirteenth-century Jalāl al-Dīn Rumi. To a considerable extent Islam in medieval India took on a Sufi coloring.

Sufis arrived in India early. They were already in the Punjab during the Ghaznavid period. Once the Delhi sultanate was established, Sufis of the Chishti and Suhrawardi orders began to settle throughout northern India. Two other formal Sufi orders, the Naqshbandi and Qādiri, arrived during the Mughal period and became influential within the Mughal court. At court and in the urban centers, Sufis vied with the more orthodox Islamic scholars for status and influence, and needed to maintain a degree of respectability themselves. Even so they occasionally suffered persecution for their hubris, as when the Mughal ruler Jahāngīr imprisoned Sirhindi. Others held aloof as much as possible from the court and its secular ways. Certain Sufis became more involved with local culture, and adopted the local language and customs. In some cases they took on the deliberately unconventional character of the qalandar, the activist ascetic dropout who flouted the authority of respectable Muslim society.

The most basic relationship among Sufis is that of master and disciple. The master, known as a *shaykh* or *pīr*, is first and foremost a teacher, instructing his or her followers in proper ethical and spiritual conduct. As in the folk imagery of Sulṭān Bāhū's laudatory poem, the master is a "washerman" for the heart, endeavoring to "shine up those begrimed with dirt, leaving them spotless." Disciples often recorded the teachings of masters as a way of perpetuating and disseminating their cleansing wisdom. "Conversations of the Sufi Saints" provides examples of this popular genre of Sufi literature.

Notable masters came sometimes to be regarded as "saints," figures possessing extraordinary capacities who could act as virtual intercessors with God on behalf of their followers. The hagiographies of these saints depict them performing a variety of miracles such as levitation, mind reading, and physical transformations. As in Indian religious discourse generally, miracles serve in these stories as visible confirmations of inner states of attainment and as criteria for determining religious powers. Tombs of Sufi saints often became pilgrimage centers, much as the stūpas and miracle sites of the Buddha had earlier. They perpetuated the charisma of the saint enshrined there and served as centers for the transmission of Sufi teachings and practices.

The saints were all subordinate to the Prophet Muḥammad. Concomitant with the rise of Sufi orders in the medieval Islamic world was an increasing veneration of the Prophet and his family expressed through ritual and song. A few puritan critics, forerunners of modern fundamentalists, objected to this reverence as idolatry, but most of the Islamic community came to see Muḥammad as a figure of loving devotion and miraculous powers. In domestic ceremonies honoring Muḥammad's birth, Muslim women speak of the miracles surrounding his birth and childhood, and request his intercession in solving their everyday difficulties. In the various genres of devotional verse addressed to him, Muḥammad appears as a guide, benefactor, miracle worker, and a lover, the supremely desirable bridegroom. Adapting a convention common to Hindu bhakti poetry, and employed also in Jain and Sikh poetry of the period, Indo-Muslim poets represented themselves as young women tormented by separation from their beloved, in this case the Prophet. Such mutual borrowings and recyclings of poetic themes were common in the close encounters between Sufism and Hindu devotionalism in medieval India.

Religious practice within Sufi circles centered around "recollection" (*dhikr*) and "listening" (*sama'*). The Qur'ān instructs Muslims to remember Allah frequently, and Sufis developed various techniques to evoke and intensify the recollection. Most commonly, the practitioner would rhythmically chant the one hundred names of God, and often enhance the chanting through bodily postures and breath control. Much like indigenous Indian forms of yoga, these disciplines are meant to bring the body, senses, and mind under control so they would not obstruct union with the divine. Though willing to borrow useful techniques from yogic traditions, Indian Sufis were certainly not uncritical advocates or borrowers of all Hindu practices, as Chirāgh-i Dihlī shows in his vivid denunciation of image worship, reiterating a core Islamic tenet.

Sufi poetry such as that of the two Punjabi poets Sulṭān Bāhū and Bulleh Shāh grows out of the musical assembly. Emphasizing their rural origins, these poets employ the vernacular language in preference to religious Arabic or courtly Persian, and draw their images from the everyday world of village Punjab. Reiterating common Sufi themes, they advocate love of Allah as the supreme virtue, and they often figure themselves as brides entreating their bridegroom Allah. From the austere and utterly transcendent God of the conservatives, these poets render him personal and accessible. They stress the importance of inner purity and criticize religious formalism, particularly ritual and intellectual approaches to the divine, in favor of an intuitive, personal approach. Again one sees here striking parallels with existing Indian traditions, in this case with the thematic repertoire of medieval Hindu bhakti poetry.

Sufism unquestionably germinated within the earliest phases of Arab Islam and flourished throughout the medieval Islamic world, but it was uniquely suited to the Indian religious setting. From the monist cosmological formulations of Ibn al-'Arabī to the personalizing of Allah in Sufi poetry, from the familiar renunciatory appearance of Sufi masters to their use of yogalike meditative techniques, this form of mystical Islam could seem both familiar and yet new to India. Adapting to their surroundings, Sufi teachers were able to bring the message of Islam to an Indian audience that the more conservative scholars of the urban centers could never reach. In this sense, the Sufis of late medieval South Asia deserve the greatest credit in making Islam a truly indigenous Indian religion.

Although Islam did originate historically as an extraneous religious formation, it is important to bear in mind the counterargument offered in "India as a Sacred Islamic Land." Whether migrating from other parts of the Islamic world or adapting Islam through conversion, most Indian Muslims did not regard themselves as foreigners in India. Rather, from the very start they sought to integrate their homeland, India, into the larger sacred topography of the world of Islam. Indeed, in the view of Āzād, the first man—Adam—descended to earth in South Asia, and so South Asia figures as the site of the first revelation and the first mosque. For Indian Muslims no less than Hindus, Jains, or Buddhists, India is a religious terrain, a place where the divine, in whatever form, can indeed manifest itself to all.

Hinduism under Islam

Prior to the thirteenth century, as we have seen, temple Hinduism had offered a pan-Indian theory and legitimation of political authority, with royal claimants articulating their sovereignty through personal and ceremonial devotion to the Hindu deities Viṣṇu and Śiva. Subsequently, however, the most powerful rulers in Delhi and many other parts of South Asia grounded their dominion in a very different theo-political system. Hindu ruling elites were largely confined to southern India and peripheral regions. Not only was the political sphere transformed by this shift in rulership, but the growing presence in the subcontinent of new religious teachers with competing and often compelling messages, most notably the Sufis, also posed a serious challenge to the authority of existing forms of Hindu thought and practice.

Hindus responded to the presence and political sway of Islam in late medieval India in complex, diverse, and creative ways. As in any period of social change, there were many in medieval India who sought mainly to defend and hold on to what they had. Hindu warrior elites might signal their independence from Islamic overlordship by reconstructing or reconsecrating a desecrated temple. In the religious sphere this attitude manifested itself in efforts to collect, maintain, and reassert already existing aspects of Hindu traditions. By collecting and commenting on the older textual genres such as the Vedas and Dharmaśāstras, brahman scholars made a conscious attempt to recreate past formations in altered conditions. The scholarly work of orthodox brahmans at this time, aimed at conserving and reasserting what they saw as traditional Hindu values, also had a large and generally unrecognized effect. They were the first to assemble what later scholars of the nineteenth and twentieth centuries would reassemble as a Hindu canon of sacred books.

However, the eclipse of temple Hinduism as the prevailing ideological formation in northern India also set new and innovative directions in the development of Indian religions. What is most apparent in late medieval Hinduism is the vitality of forms of religion that are devotional, esoteric, or syncretic, and a corresponding deemphasis on the role of religion in constituting the political and social order.

Devotional Movements

Hindus sometimes personify bhakti as a beautiful woman, born in southern India, who grew to maturity in the Deccan. In twelfth-century Karnataka, a group of devotees called the Vīraśaivas coalesced around the Kalacuri minister Basavaṇṇa, and from the late thirteenth through seventeenth centuries, the Maharashtrian pilgrimage center Paṇḍarpur was the center of Marathi devotionalism toward the god Viṭhobā, a form of Kṛṣṇa. Tukārām was the last of the great Marathi poet-saints. Finally, according to the metaphor, the woman reached her finest flourishing in the north. Bhakti movements appeared in northern India by the fourteenth century, and from then on were a major force in north Indian Hindu life, from Kashmir and Gujarat to Bengal.

It is somewhat misleading, however, to speak of a single organic bhakti movement. Different groups used the various regional languages in their poetry, directed themselves toward different deities, and assumed distinct theological standpoints. Some poet-saints were profoundly inward and mystical in their lives and song, while others adopted a more outward, socially critical orientation to the world around them. Some north Indian poets and bhakti groups appeared oblivious to the presence of Islam, but for others this was a cardinal reality. Yet virtually all considered emotional "participation" with God as a core value. Whether devotees direct themselves toward Śiva, Kṛṣṇa, Rāma, or the goddess Kālī, they seek always to develop a personal relationship with that divine figure. For bhakti theologians mokṣa consists more in attaining or reattaining closeness to God than in gaining liberation.

The deities of medieval bhakti bring with them the mythical narratives of theistic Hinduism that had previously been set forth in the epics and Purāṇas. The Kṛṣṇa of the sixteenth-century Gauḍīya Vaiṣṇavas, for instance, is the same Kṛṣṇa whose story is told in the *Harivaṃśa* and *Bhāgavata Purāṇa*. But most bhakti poets shift the cosmic scope of the Purāṇas and temple Hinduism to the background. There is less concern with God as creator and ruler of the cosmos, and more with God as humanly alive and embodied on earth. So with Kṛṣṇa, devotional poets and theologians tend to play down his earlier identity as an incarnation of Viṣṇu and instead focus on the pastoral life of his youth among the cowherds of Vraja. At the same time, they emphasize the inward presence of God in the heart and his loving regard for the faithful. Even when they do acknowledge the deity's role in creating and sustaining the world, devotionalists often portray God as playful, inscrutable, and sometimes downright devious in his or her activities. How else could one explain the bad state of things?

Not all devotionalists, however, comprehend God as an anthropomorphic form. Although most, like the Gauḍīyas, orient themselves to a God "with attributes" (*saguṇa*) like the eminently embodied Kṛṣṇa, others like Kabīr prefer to conceptualize God "without attributes" (*nirguṇa*). For the nirguṇa poets, any attempt to characterize or comprehend God is doomed ultimately to fail, and all the mythical and ritual ways we humans seek to relate to God are distractions or delusions.

According to the sixteenth-century devotional theologian Rūpa Gosvāmī, it is possible to enjoy various relationships with God. Rūpa specified five predominant ones, largely based on analogies with human relationships. One may relate to God as an insignificant human relates to the supreme deity, as a respectful servant relates to his lord and master, as a mother relates to her child, as a friend relates to his friend, or as a lover relates to her beloved. Devotional groups explore all these modes of relationship, and particularly the latter three, through their poetic and ritual practices. In the south Indian devotional genre of piḷḷaittamiḻ, for example, poets address their chosen deities in the form of a child, employing a domestic idiom and redirecting parental love toward religious figures. Gauḍīya Vaiṣṇavas envision themselves as cowherd friends of Kṛṣṇa to participate in his divine sports. Of all forms of association, Rūpa claims, the erotic is the highest, and much bhakti poetry explores the passionate love between the cowherd women of Vraja, who represent all human souls, and the enchanting young Kṛṣṇa. Arguing against other more conventional Hindu ways of conceptualizing one's relationship with God, Rūpa values emotional intensity over the meditative stasis of the yogis or the intellectual comprehension of the Advaitins as the highest goal.

The bhakti movements engendered various forms of devotional yoga, techniques for evoking and focusing the devotee's participation with God. According to the Gauḍīya followers of Caitanya, the simplest technique, and therefore the one most suitable for the present age of decline, consists in repetitive chanting of God's name. Since Kṛṣṇa's name is more than just an arbitrary signifier—it is itself a portion of his reality—chanting his name as a mantra makes Kṛṣṇa himself actually present. The Gauḍīyas institutionalized chanting combined with ecstatic dancing as a collective practice, similar to the musical sessions of the Sufis. The tale of Haridāsa illustrates how these public displays of congregational revelry could provoke suspicion and suppression by civil authorities. At the same time, Haridāsa's miraculous fortitude in the face of adversity provides a metaphor for the resistant powers of inner bhakti against outward social pressure.

The practice most characteristic of medieval bhakti, though, was song and poetry. In contrast to Indian courtly traditions of poetic composition, poet-saints of north India sang in vernacular languages and drew their imagery from everyday life. They adopted highly personal poetic voices to speak of the tribulations and joys of the devotional life. The poetry of medieval bhakti in Hindi, Bengali, Marathi, and other vernacular languages of India is quite likely the richest library of devotion in world literature, distinguished not only by its religious intensity but also by the great variety of psychological states and emotional responses it explores. These medieval songs of devotion remain very much alive in contemporary

India. Few of us indeed can recite as much of any author as the average Hindi speaker can reel off from Kabīr, Sūrdās, or Mīrābāī.

For devotionalists, the poetic invocation of God often supplanted ritual invocation and physical images. Although the earliest devotional movements in south India treated temples as an important locus of religiosity, some later bhakti groups dispensed with the temple as superfluous or criticized it as a place of purely formal religious observances, where priests and the dull-witted could go through the motions of worship. Bhakti poet-saints often broadened this skeptical attitude toward temple ritualism into a critique of all aspects of what they considered conventional or orthodox Hindu practice: Vedic recitation, pilgrimage, and the social hierarchy of the caste system.

The critical perspective of medieval bhakti reached its apogee in the writings of Kabīr. Raised in a poor community of Muslim weavers, Kabīr was initiated into bhakti by a Vaiṣṇava guru, and later attracted a following among both Muslims and Hindus. Throughout his poetic utterances he drew from the many religious traditions around him—Sufis, devotionalists, tantrics, Buddhists, and others. Yet, as in his poem "Simple State," Kabīr was quite happy to dish out equal scorn for the orthodoxies of Islam and Hinduism, urging instead a spiritual path of merging with an indescribable Absolute outside, or perhaps equally within, those verbose schools of thought. The historical irony is that both Hindus and Muslims later claimed this irascible skeptic and mocker of formal religions, and his verse was also incorporated into the canon of a third religion, the *Ādi Granth* of the Sikhs.

Tantra

Like devotionalism, the developments we now classify as tantra originated when temple Hinduism still dominated the public sphere. It developed from older and largely unrecorded practices of yoga, medicine, folk magic, and local goddess cults. From about the seventh century, Hindu and Buddhist tantra texts begin to appear, as do descriptions, often satirical, of recognizable tantric adepts. Beginning around the time of Maḥmūd's raids into north India, Hindu tantric groups and literature began to proliferate throughout the subcontinent. Reaching its greatest influence during the period of Islamic dominance, tantra continues in varied forms in present-day India, albeit much diminished, and has made itself known and notorious in the West through such international gurus as Bhagwan Shree Rajneesh.

The word *tantra* does not admit to a single unequivocal definition. Drawn from the vocabulary of weaving, where it may refer to the threads, the warp, or the entire loom, the term *tantra* was extended to signify texts as things spun out and threaded together, both physically (since palm-leaf manuscripts require strings) and verbally. Later the word came to refer especially to one genre of texts directed to the Goddess, the Śākta tantras, and to the adherents of its teachings.

Historians of Indian religions use the word *tantra* primarily in two ways. In a broad sense they employ *tantra* to identify a whole series of ritual and yogic practices not found in the Vedic lineage of texts, such as visualization, geometrical designs, impositions of mantra powers, and Kuṇḍalinī yoga. The word *tantra* in this sense refers more to a shared repertoire of techniques than to any religious system. Many religious groups in medieval India made use of these techniques, and so there were Buddhist tantra, Jain tantra, and many "tantric elements" incorporated in the rituals of the temple Hindu schools. In a more restricted sense, tantra is taken as a system of thought and practice, based on a few shared premises and orientations. In this anthology, we use tantra primarily in this narrower definition.

Hindu tantric groups most often recognize the female goddess Śakti ("energy"), Śiva's consort, as the fundamental creative energy of the cosmos, and therefore as the Absolute. Tantrics view the human body as a microcosm of the universe, and focus on it as the only vehicle for attaining powers and liberation. Through yogic practices and ritual activities the tantric adept seeks to inculcate knowledge physically. Rather than seeking a disembodied escape from bondage or a devotional relationship with divinity, tantrics set as their highest goal the transformation of the body itself into divinity.

Tantra is often promulgated away from society, within small circles of initiates clustered around preceptors. Tantric groups often compose their texts in "intentional" or "upside-down" language, making them deliberately unintelligible to those outside the initiated group. Some tantrics intentionally transgress social proprieties and consume forbidden meat and wine, in order to escape what they consider conventional reality and proceed directly to the ultimate. Though practiced by only a few tantric circles, this antinomian tendency, combined with the esoteric and ritualistic orientation of tantra, led to its widespread condemnation as a degenerate form of Hinduism by many Western scholars and by punctilious Indians, as well.

One of the most distinctive characteristics of tantra is the role played by the Goddess. Worship of goddesses is undoubtedly very ancient in South Asia. The *Devīmāhātmya* proclaimed a single pan-Indian Goddess as the Absolute. Medieval Śaiva theologians often bifurcated the godhead into male and female. They postulated an inactive but transcendent male Śiva who carries out all his worldly activities through an immanent energetic female Śakti. From this cosmic division of labor, tantra took the next logical step: if Śakti is doing everything anyway, why not focus upon her as the real force of the universe? Tantra thereby subverted Śiva's superior role and located Śakti—identified as Pārvatī, Durgā, Kālī, and all female divinities—at the top of the divine hierarchy, indeed as the animating energy of all.

As in bhakti, tantric groups paid close attention to the erotic, but they viewed it from a different perspective. Devotional poet-saints most often directed themselves toward male divinities, figured themselves as female lovers, and used human romance and sexuality as metaphor for the complex personal relationship between soul and God. According to tantric cosmology, the world itself comes into being through the primordial, recurrent coupling of Śiva and Śakti. Since the human body in tantra is a concentrated microcosm, an embodiment of the cosmos, it makes sense to view sexual union as a way of reenacting creation, bringing the practitioner in harmony with the forces of the cosmos. Detached from the romantic narratives of bhakti and given an impersonal cosmic significance, ritualized sexual union enabled the tantric adept to transcend all dualities. Ultimately, most devotionalists did not wish to overcome duality. For them, Rāmprasād Sen's observation rang true: "I like the taste of sugar, but I have no desire to become sugar."

Tantra, like bhakti, sometimes took a skeptical view of the social categories of merit and demerit, right and wrong, promulgated by the orthodox. Followers of bhakti might be led by their passionate attachment to God to transgress normal social boundaries, much as the cowherd women of Vraja willingly left their husbands and children to rendezvous with Kṛṣṇa in the forest. Some tantric groups prescribed a more deliberate, ritualized overturning of conventional mores. For the Kaula school, five normally forbidden offerings—the famous "Five Ms" of liquor, meat, fish, parched grain, and sexual intercourse—were regularly consumed or enjoyed as part of pūjā. Here too transgression acknowledged the superior claims of religious attainment over the everyday rules of social conduct. But by no means did all tantra groups accept this antinomian attitude. The eleventh-century tantric alchemical treatise *Rasārnava*, for instance, strongly criticized the Five-M mode of tantra. As in every other religious formation we have looked at, there was always internal debate among tantric proponents over the ultimate ends and the best means to reach it.

Guru Nānak and Sikhism

When conservative proponents of two seemingly irreconcilable religious systems were struggling to gain ideological supremacy, one religious option was to declare both equally wrong. Alternatively, one could consciously adopt whatever seemed most worthwhile from both traditions. In medieval India this unitarian strategy sought a domain of spiritual peace outside the pervasive disagreement between orthodox Muslims and orthodox Hindus. The most influential of medieval Indian syncretists, Guru Nānak (1469–1539) ended up founding a new religion, Sikhism.

Born in a Hindu merchant family in the predominantly Muslim Punjab, Nānak worked as an accountant until, at age twenty-nine, he had a transformative experience. He fell into a bathing pool and disappeared from sight. Unable to find him, friends and family finally gave him up for dead. When Nānak returned to society three days later, his first utterance was, "There is no Hindu; there is no Muslim." He spent the remainder of his life traveling, teaching, singing, and gathering a band of followers. The name "Sikh" is derived from the Sanskrit word for pupil, *śiṣya,* indicating the relationship first adopted by Nānak's followers toward their guru.

In his teachings and songs, Nānak gently but firmly repudiated the external practices of the religions he saw around him—the oblations, sacrifices, ritual baths, image worshiping, austerities, and scriptures of Hindus and Muslims. For Nānak, the all-pervasive and incomprehensible God must be sought within oneself. The nirguṇa Absolute has no gender, no form, no immanent incarnations or manifestations. Despite God's infinitude and formlessness, Nānak proposed a very simple means of connecting with the divine. One must remember and repeat the divine Name. Nānak rigorously refused to specify what that Name was, though he sometimes called it "Creator of the Truth," equating truth with godliness.

During his own lifetime Nānak began to organize his followers into a community of the faithful. He set up informal procedures for congregational worship centering around collective recitation. Most important, he chose one of his disciples, Aṅgad, to follow him as preceptor and leader of the group, its guru. By choosing a single successor, Nānak established a precedent of group leadership that would last through ten gurus and nearly two hundred years. Nānak's followers collected anecdotes of his life that illustrated his central teachings and located his songs within biographical events, whether factual or imagined. Hagiography became an important genre of early Sikh literature, as it was among Sufis and devotionalists.

Nānak most often identified himself as a Hindu by virtue of birth, but as his followers consolidated their own practices they gradually distinguished themselves from both Hindu and Muslim communities. The fifth guru, Arjan, collected the writings of the first five leaders and other like-minded poet-saints into the *Ādi Granth*, the foundation text of the Sikh religion. In Sikh ceremonial this book came to occupy the central place on the altar, where Hindus would place an image. Guru Arjan rebuilt the temple at Amritsar and set himself up as lord of the Sikhs. With the Sikh community now a formidable social group, its Gurus began to play a more active role in north Indian political conflicts. They took sides in Mughal dynastic disputes and sometimes suffered the consequences of backing the losing side.

In the late seventeenth century, the time of the tenth and last guru, Gobind Singh, many Sikhs identified themselves still more visibly and decisively as a separate religious community. A determined opponent of Mughal rule, Gobind Singh instituted the Khālsā fellowship (the "army of the pure"), a group of Sikh initiates who accepted a code of conduct that included five insignia: uncut hair, a dagger or sword, a pair of military shorts, a comb, and a steel bangle. Gobind Singh required initiates to renounce all previous religious affiliations and to repudiate all gods, goddesses, and prophets other than the one Name recognized by the Sikhs.

Under Gobind Singh, the Sikh community solidified both its socio-religious identity and its military strength. By the beginning of the nineteenth century a Sikh kingdom led by Ranjīt Singh posed the last major independent opposition to British rule in South Asia. Though finally defeated in the late 1840s, Ranjīt Singh's kingdom left a memory of a separate Sikh state, a Khalistan or "land of the pure," that would be evoked at the time of Partition, when the departing

British divided India along religious lines into Muslim Pakistan and Hindu India, and again in the 1980s. Though they form a relatively small religious community of around 13 million in India, roughly 2 percent of the population, the Sikhs today constitute the most visible and in many ways one of the most prosperous communities in South Asia. Large numbers of Sikhs have emigrated to the U.K., Canada, and other parts of the Commonwealth.

The British Period

From 1757 on, British traders with the East India Company gradually increased their role in South Asia until, by the time British armies defeated the Punjabi kingdom of Ranjīt Singh in 1849, they ruled most of India. And so, from the late eighteenth century until 1947, Indians were dominated by a foreign power whose seat of authority was halfway around the world in London. These foreigners brought with them not only a new language and philosophy of rule and a different set of religious beliefs but also a worldview grounded in the secular, modernizing ideology of the Enlightenment. The encounter of existing religious formations of India with new forms of Christianity and with post-Enlightenment modes of knowledge within this colonial milieu ushered in another period of challenge, debate, and dynamism within South Asian religions.

Christianity was not completely new to the subcontinent. Syriac Christian trading communities had inhabited the Malabar coast of southern India from as early as the fourth century, and continued as autonomous groups of high status integrated within the largely Hindu society around them. The Portuguese, who established themselves on the western coast in the sixteenth century, carried out Christian missionary work with rather mixed results. Some lower-class communities realized the advantages that could result from forming religious bonds with a colonizing power and converted en masse, gradually developing their own indigenized forms of Christianity. The Portuguese were unable, however, to make much headway with the large majority of Indians they proselytized. Unlike Islamic Sufism, the Catholicism of the Counter-Reformation did not seem particularly compatible with the Indian religious environment.

British administrators took a decidedly ambivalent attitude toward missionary activity in their colonial territories, fearing it might "stir up the natives," whom they wished mainly to pacify. Under pressure from evangelicals in England, though, they eventually allowed Protestant missionaries to pursue their work on a limited scale. The missions did not achieve the conversions of great masses that they hoped for, but their incisive and often hyperbolic critiques of indigenous religion in India did have the important effect of inspiring some spirited defenses from the indigens. The Tamil Śaivite Āṟumuga Nāvalar, for instance, studied and worked for many years in a Methodist school before setting out on a personal mission to refortify the Śaiva Siddhānta religion and defend it against Christian attacks. Religious apologetics, defending one's own religion against outside attack, often has the effect of altering precisely that which one seeks to defend, giving it a definition or fixity it did not have previously, and this occurred repeatedly among Indian religions during the colonial encounter.

More challenging to the self-esteem of educated Indians were the Western scholars who for the first time began to study the religions of India as historical entities. The Western concern with delineating the various religions of the world was given tremendous impetus in India through the inspiration and organizational work of William Jones, an exemplary man of the Enlightenment. Jones was the first to publicize the linguistic connection of Sanskrit with classical Greek and Latin, enabling scholars to reconstruct the Indo-European family of languages and laying the basis for the field of historical philology, an important intellectual discipline of the nineteenth century. In Calcutta, where he served as a judge, Jones organized a small group of British civil servants who had become enamored with India's classical literature into the Asiatick Society, the first scholarly organization devoted to comprehending the religions, history, and literatures of India from a Western perspective. These officials were responsible for the earliest attempts to translate what they considered to be the most important Indian texts—all ancient and Sanskrit—into English, making them available to the West and engendering a kind of "Oriental Renaissance" among educated Europeans in the late eighteenth and early nineteenth centuries.

These classical Indiaphiles, also called "Orientalists," felt less affectionate toward the present-day Indians among whom they were living. They judged contemporary Indian religions to be debased from their lofty origins in the classical past. The Orientalists' high valuation of classical antiquity, coupled with a condescending dismissal of modern India, led to a long-standing prejudice in the Western study of India, whereby the oldest, elite Sanskrit works were valued above all others.

An alternative position, still less sympathetic to the Indians, soon took shape in England and was then exported to India. Inspired by Jeremy Bentham's utilitarian philosophy, James Mill, an official with the East India Company based in London, wrote his *History of British India* in the 1820s without needing to set foot in India. Mill's *History*, an immense and thorough indictment of the Indian peoples, tried to justify the need for British rule among a population supposedly unable to govern itself. Mill especially condemned Hinduism, blaming it for much of what was wrong with India. Hinduism is ritualistic, superstitious, irrational, and priest-ridden, Mill charged, at each step implicitly contrasting it with the deist version of Christianity that he believed to be the highest form of religion. For several decades the East India Company provided a copy of Mill's tome to new Company officials embarking for India, to sustain them in their sense of racial and cultural superiority while in the colony.

The attitudes the British held toward India had far-reaching effects on the Indians who came in contact with them. While some were satisfied to reiterate what they saw as the traditional, time-tested, and therefore superior forms of Indian religiosity, other Indians, more deeply affected by Western forms of knowledge and British criticisms of Hinduism, became highly circumspect and self-critical. From this spirit of cultural self-reproach came the widespread religious reformism of colonial India.

The prototype of the Hindu reformer was Rammohan Roy (1774–1833), a Bengali brahman who received a wide education in Persian and Arabic (languages of the Indo-Muslim court culture), Sanskrit (language of his own religious background), and then English (the emerging language of commerce and administration in colonial India). Taking advantage of new moneymaking opportunities as the British expanded their operations, Roy was able to retire young as a wealthy landlord to pursue his intellectual and religious interests. Roy valued British "progress" and Western modernity, and believed there was an urgent need to modernize Hinduism, which he had come to see as a stagnant tradition. To do this, he urged a reappraisal and selective redefinition of Hinduism. Of course, Indian religious thinkers had been doing exactly this for centuries, but never before with such a historicist self-awareness. In many cases Roy accepted British and Christian judgments as valid. He agreed, for example, that Hindu "polytheism" and "idolatry" were primitive and debased, and he joined in British efforts to outlaw and suppress satī, the practice of widow self-immolation. Concurring with the Orientalists' notion that current Hinduism had degenerated from a more glorious past, Roy recommended that Hindus return to earlier, purer beliefs and practices, and he sought to advance the ancient Upaniṣads with their idealism and monotheism as the foundation texts for a new Hinduism. In 1828 he founded the Brāhmo Samāj, a voluntary religious organization, to help put his ideas into effect.

Rammohan Roy was the first but not the only religious reformer of colonial India. Reform movements arose in every region of South Asia under British control, and while each reflected its own local culture and religious tradition, all shared the fundamentalist attitude of the Brāhmo Samāj in criticizing contemporary forms of religiosity and in seeking to return to some presumed state of purity located in the past. The Ārya Samāj, founded in 1875 by Svāmī Dayānanda Sarasvatī in western India, likewise advocated returning to the Vedic texts. From the standpoint of the Vedas, Dayānanda argued, one should oppose not only religious corruption but also what he saw as the evils of contemporary Indian society, such as caste, untouchability, and the subjugation of women. Many Hindu reform movements saw their task as reforming both Hinduism and Indian society.

Among the Sikhs, the Nirankāri movement called for a rejection of existing Sikh practices and a return to the "formless" worship of the founder, Guru Nānak. The Śvetāmbara Jains had their own reform movement led by the mendicant Vijay Ānandsūri, and even the Syriac Christians experienced millenarian revivalist movements during the nineteenth century.

The Muslim-controlled areas of northern India were the last to come under direct British control, and the Muslim elite, nostalgic for the lost glories of Mughal imperium, initially resisted British learning and remained aloof from British administration. Nevertheless, by the late nineteenth century colonial reformism took shape among Indian Muslims as well. Syed Ahmed Khan set out to purge contemporary Indian Islam of what he considered its extraneous and unnecessary practices and to return to a pure Islam, while at the same time he attempted to harmonize Islamic ideology with modern science. In the early twentieth century, Mohamed Ali envisioned the reestablishment of a pan-Islamic polity centered in Ottoman Turkey. By this time religious reformism had begun to take on a more overt anti-colonial dimension among Muslim and Hindu elites as well, and Ali's call for a Turkish Khilafat was simultaneously an appeal for ending British rule.

Perhaps the most renowned nineteenth-century Hindu reformer was Svāmī Vivekānanda. He was a young member of the Brāhmo Samāj when he first met Rāmakṛṣṇa, a charismatic ascetic and devotee of the goddess Kālī. Eventually Vivekānanda became Rāmakṛṣṇa's disciple, and sought to integrate within a single religious outlook the experiential devotionalism of Rāmakṛṣṇa, the social agenda of the Brāhmo Samāj, and the nondualist philosophy of Śaṅkara and the Advaita Vedānta. As a spokesman for Hinduism in 1893 at the World's Parliament of Religions in Chicago, he created a sensation. Building on this success, he toured the United States for three years, attracted many Western followers, and set up the Vedanta Society. Returning to India, Vivekānanda founded the Ramakrishna Mission, an organization dedicated to education and social service much like Christian missions in India. Vivekānanda is still celebrated as a teacher of "practical Vedānta," which scholars sometimes label "neo-Vedānta," a significant version of modern Hindu ideology. He was also the prototype of a new breed of cosmopolitan Hindu gurus who would bring their teachings to Western audiences.

As the movement for Indian independence took shape in the late nineteenth and early twentieth centuries, activists drew upon and reworked elements from the Hindu tradition for explicitly political purposes. The Maharashtrian leader B. G. Tilak, for example, instituted a public festival to the elephant-headed god Gaṇeśa, celebrating Hindu popular culture as a means of regaining "self-rule," and not incidentally attracting large crowds for his political speeches. In Bengal the ferocious goddess Kālī lent her fierce energy to the independence struggle, and the new goddess Bhārat Māta ("Mother India") appeared, iconographically modeled on Lakṣmī, as a national focus for devotion and sacrifice. Literary and political figures alike rewrote and reinterpreted old texts like the *Bhagavadgītā* and the *Rāmāyaṇa*, making them speak to the colonial situation. Although reintroducing Hindu deities and rituals to make political statements was nothing new in India, and it certainly helped extend the politics of anticolonialism beyond the educated urban elite, in the colonial setting it also had the unfortunate effect of identifying the independence movement as a largely Hindu enterprise, alienating Muslims and other non-Hindu communities.

Throughout the colonial period, the British viewed India as a society made up of distinct, identifiable religious communities: Hindus, Muslims, Sikhs, Jains, "tribals," and so on. British administrators soon learned the advantages of "divide and rule," and often promoted religious divisions as a conscious strategy to weaken those who might oppose them. Even in seemingly nonpolitical administrative activities like census taking, the British use of unequivocal categories to classify a religious reality that was complex and mingled promoted a clarification and hardening of religious distinctions.

Indians themselves increasingly employed the same classifications, and many of the reform movements, with their weekly meetings, membership lists, and search for the essence of their traditions, also helped define and solidify community boundaries. By the early decades of the twentieth century, religious conflict increased in Indian society. The outcome of this "communalization" was that, when the English finally quit India in 1947, they felt it necessary to divide their colony along religious lines into two nation-states, Islamic Pakistan and Hindu India. This tragic decision led to terrible violence and suffering among Muslims, Hindus, and Sikhs alike during the Partition, and its consequences are still felt powerfully in the politics of modern South Asia.

Religions of Home and Village

One important dimension of Indian religions that is too often lost sight of in historical summaries like this one is the religion of the domestic sphere. Historians have frequently overlooked domestic religious traditions because the activities of the household are generally transmitted orally, from woman to woman over the generations, and do not receive the textual documentation accorded more public, male-dominated domains of religion. Only with the work of recent anthropologists and folklorists have these traditions begun to receive the attention they deserve. Several readings in this volume exemplify this new scholarly focus on the home as a locus of religiosity.

Transmitted orally, domestic religious traditions show marked local and regional diversity, but certain themes are common. Domestic forms of Indian religions directly address the concerns of women, but not only those of women. Successful marriage, healthy offspring, domestic accord, and prosperity of the home are values shared by all members of the household. Domestic rites seek to ward off the various calamities—disease, family dissension, poverty, death—that threaten the well-being of the family and lineage. Though one finds little interest here in the attainment of mokṣa that looms so large in other Indian religious traditions, these domestic concerns certainly are not trivial or parochial. Other forms of divine salvation, such as marriage or motherhood to a god, are recognized, and the world of the kitchen may even be identified with the cosmos itself, as in the Tamil poem addressed to the child-goddess Mīnāṭci, "Sway back and forth."

Female divinities figure strongly in domestic religion. Some are decidedly benign, like Mother Ten and the basil-shrub goddess Tulsī, worshiped for their capacities to bring sustenance and health. But there are other goddesses of a more uneven temperament, such as Mother Ten's opposite number, "Bad Ten," or the Bengali Śītalā, goddess of smallpox. Quick to take offense, Śītalā requires careful mollifying to insure that her wrath does not come down on one's own family. In

Rajasthan, women sing devotional songs also to satīs, exemplary women who overcame the inauspiciousness of their husbands' deaths through extraordinary adherence to purity, and who have become protector spirits of the lineage.

Although domestic religions often take a different perspective from the public traditions, they nevertheless share with them a single language of Indian religious discourse. The domestic goddess Tulsī, for instance, is linked with Kṛṣṇa, and her stories explore the jealous rivalry that may arise among co-wives attached to this famously promiscuous male god. The Rajasthani regional goddess Mother Ten, we find, is identified as Lakṣmī, the pan-Indian Sanskritic goddess of good fortune. Likewise, when Muslim women worship at moments of domestic crisis, they focus on the miraculous birth of Muḥammad, connecting their concerns about procreation and healing with the most public figure of the Islamic tradition. Domestic ceremonies, too, draw upon the common Indian repertoire of ascetic and ritual practices, such as fasting, bathing, purification rites, pūjā, and the maintenance of vows (*vrata*) to bring about the desired ends.

An earlier generation of anthropologists and Indianists spoke of the ongoing relationships between public, literary, pan-Indian traditions and localized, oral traditions in terms of the "great" and "little" traditions, and those terms may still be useful provided one observes some precautions. One should not imagine a single normative "great tradition," and one should not use the distinction to verify a hierarchical separation between two insular domains, such that the pan-Indian enjoys an assumed dominance over the local. Likewise, the little traditions of village and household are not unchanging. Although some of the concerns and aims of these traditions are grounded in the relatively constant struggles of rural and village populations of India, the stories, rituals, and deities may change.

In ongoing two-way cultural traffic, elements of local traditions may be selectively drawn into public, literate traditions, while other elements from those pan-Indian cultural traditions may be selectively drawn upon to enhance or reformulate religious practices at the level of village or household. We may take the Mother Ten story of the amazing cow with its magical dung as an illustration of one direction in this traffic. When the remarkable cow is brought to the royal court, the "little tradition" figure of Mother Ten receives the public recognition that incorporates her into a regional "great tradition." This kind of dynamic interchange has been going on in India for centuries.

The Contemporary Scene

A modern-day Vidagdha might ask, "What are Indian religions like now?"

In a cultural area as large and diverse as India, with its 800 million people, eighteen official languages, and strong regional traditions, it is never easy to get a fix on contemporary religion. Instead, one finds oneself returning to Yajñavālkya's Upaniṣadic perspective, from which a single question requires multiple answers.

Yes, but what do religions in India look like now?

In a trip around contemporary India, a religious sightseer will certainly encounter many characters made familiar by a study of the history of Indian religions, but they are often dressed in new clothes. One may see Buddhist monks chanting Buddha's teachings at the site of his enlightenment in Bodh Gaya, but then notice that they are political refugees dressed in the vermillion robes of Tibetan Buddhism. One will find ash-smeared yogis in their Himalayan ashrams discoursing in English to audiences of young Germans, Japanese, and Australians. In south Indian temples one can follow priests and devotees as they worship Viṣṇu and Śiva according to liturgical models set down in early medieval guidebooks, and then pause outside to purchase a brightly colored lithographic reproduction of the temple deity or to arrange an international pūjā by airmail. One may encounter street performances retelling the epic stories of Rāma, Kṛṣṇa, and the Pāṇḍavas, interspersed with Hindi film songs. Those epic narratives have also been reanimated for a nationwide television audience, the most widely followed television series ever in India. The devotional songs of Māṇikkavācakar and Tukārām are available on cassette and compact disk, and during festival seasons one cannot avoid them as they blare from loudspeakers outside seemingly every tea and coffee stall. One will read in the newspapers of "Hindutva" (Hinduness) and a new form of conservative political Hinduism, centering on a dispute over the birthplace of Rāma in Ayodhya and a mosque built by the Islamic Mughal conqueror Bābar, allegedly atop the ruins of the medieval Hindu temple.

Though historically grounded, Indian religions remain alive to their modernity—to their new political settings, the new international audiences, and the new possibilities of technology in the modern world. And in turn they are changed by them, sometimes subtly and sometimes profoundly.

Yes, but how can we best characterize the religions of India?

The collectivity of Indian voices will bring us closer to its complex reality, no doubt. It offers a sampling of perspectives rather than any authoritative collection or canon, and in this way approximates more closely the living texture of Indian religious thought and practice. It is important when attending to these voices, however, not to hear them as isolated, self-standing statements. One should place them in conversation with one another, and listen in on their discussions of mutual religious concerns. At times they share insights while at others they disagree over fundamental premises.

If we have seen debate as a central feature in the history of Indian religions, it would be wrong to imagine that somehow those controversies have ended. Indeed, over the past decade debates about the nature and role of religion in contemporary Indian society have taken on a renewed urgency. How does one define Hinduism? Or for that matter, Islam? Sikhism? Who gets to do the defining? Should Hinduism be defined at all? What are the key texts and narratives of the Indian tradition? How relevant are the normative works of the past—Vedas, epics, Dharmaśāstras, Qur'ān, *Ādi Granth*, and the like—to present-day concerns? How should Hindus relate themselves to other religious communities in India? How clear are the boundaries between them? What are the proper roles for religious groups and institutions in the modern secular state of India? Should Indians understand their national identity in terms of a dominant Hindu heritage, or view Hinduism as one among many threads in the cultural fabric of India? And looking beyond national borders, how may Hinduism, Islam, Sikhism, and Jainism best be reformulated to meet the new social settings and needs of Indian immigrants in the United States, United Kingdom, and around the world?

These are serious discussions not likely to end any time soon. They make the study of the religions of India, that land of ancient sages and age-old scriptures, a matter of great contempory significance.

Notes

1. I would like to thank all those who offered helpful suggestions and encouragement on drafts of this essay: Pravin Bhatt, Carl Ernst, Phyllis Granoff, Valerie Hansen, Lindsey Harlan, Norvin Hein, Donald Lopez, Rita McCleary, Sandhya Purohit, Paula Richman, Phil Wagoner, and Irene Winter.

2. U. N. Ghoshal, *A History of Indian Political Ideas* (London: Oxford University Press, 1959), p. 157.

BUDDHISM IN PRACTICE

Donald S. Lopez, Jr.

There is a remarkable diversity and range among the practices of persons who over the course of 2,500 years have been identified, by themselves or by others, as Buddhists. In this diversity there are often contradictions, such that the practices of a Buddhist community of one time might seem strange or unfamiliar to a Buddhist community elsewhere. Indeed, one of the questions that must be raised is whether one can accurately speak of something called "Buddhism" or "the Buddhist tradition," or whether those terms are better rendered in the plural. At the same time, there is evidence of often surprising parallels among the practices of Buddhist cultures widely separated by both history and topography, parallels to be accounted for in large part by a constant retrospection to the figure of the Buddha, making Buddhism less the inevitable unfolding of a distinct and self-identical entity and more a dynamic process of borrowing, conflict, and interaction between and within traditions that have been identified as Buddhist.

This introduction is meant to serve two purposes. First, it will provide a brief historical sketch of the history of Buddhism. Second, it will provide a description of some of the Buddhist doctrines that have come to be considered fundamental by the tradition of scholars, both Buddhist and Western.

The life and teachings of the Buddha as they recorded in traditional sources are recounted in some detail below.[1] After the death of the Buddha, the community of his followers is said to have met in a series of councils, each sponsored by a different king, to settle disputes regarding what the Buddha had taught and what rules the monastic order should follow. The Buddha had preached for over forty years to a wide variety of audiences, and there was a concern that those teachings be remembered and preserved before they could be forgotten. This preservation was done orally, with different groups of monks responsible for the memorization and retention of what evolved into a variety of oral canons. None of these was committed to writing until the last decades before the common era, and not in India but in Sri Lanka, some four hundred years after the Buddha's death. Despite the sophisticated mnemonic devices that Buddhist monks employed in preserving these teachings, there can be little certainty as to which of them, if any, were actually the words of the Buddha; there remains debate even about which language the Buddha spoke. Thus, it is no longer tenable to accept the assumption shared by both early Western scholars of Buddhism and Buddhist figures in Southeast Asia (often under Western influence) that what is known as the Theravāda tradition (the tradition of the Elders) found in the Pāli language represents an original Buddhism from which all other forms of Buddhism derived (and sometimes deviated). The original teachings of the historical Buddha are extremely difficult, if not impossible, to recover or reconstruct.

The Buddhist community flourished in India during the Mauryan dynasty (324–187 B.C.E.), especially during the reign of the emperor Aśoka, whose rule extended over most of the Indian subcontinent and who, in a series of rock edicts, professed his faith in the Buddha, his teaching, and the monastic community. Although Aśoka's edicts set forth a generalized morality that allowed him to support many religious groups in his vast kingdom, he is remembered in Buddhist legends as the ideal Buddhist king, deeply devoted to the propagation of the Buddha's teaching and to the support of the monastic community. By the end of Aśoka's reign, Buddhist monks and nuns were established in monasteries throughout the Indian subcontinent, monasteries that were often located near cities and that relied on state support. From this point on, the fortunes of Buddhism in India waxed and waned largely in dependence on the policies of local rulers.

In the first centuries of the common era, a movement, or series of movements, occurred in India that came to be referred to as the *Mahāyāna,* the Great Vehicle. This seems to have begun as a disparate collection of cults centered around newly composed texts and their charismatic expositors, the dharmabhāṇaka. These texts, although composed centuries after the Buddha's death, were accepted by their devotees as sūtras (discourses attributed to the Buddha or spoken with his sanction). Some of the texts, like the *Lotus Sūtra* (discussed below), in addition to proclaiming their own unique potency as the means to salvation, would also praise the veneration of stūpas, the reliquaries in which the remains of the Buddha were enshrined. Other texts, like much of the early Perfection of Wisdom (*prajñāpāramitā*) corpus, would proclaim their superiority to stūpas, declaring themselves to be substitutes for the body and speech of the absent Buddha, equally worthy of veneration and equally efficacious.

It is perhaps best to regard the Mahāyāna as a social movement of monks, nuns, and lay people that began in reaction against the controls exercised by a powerful monastic institution. This movement was responsible for the production and dissemination of a body of literature that challenged the authority of that institution by having the Buddha proclaim a superior and more inclusive path and a more profound wisdom. In subsequent centuries, during which sūtras continued to be composed, the Mahāyāna became not merely a collection of cults of the book but a self-conscious scholastic entity. Adherents of the Mahāyāna devoted a good deal of energy to surveying what was by then a rather large corpus and then attempting, through a variety of hermeneutical machinations, to craft the myriad doctrines into a philosophical and doctrinal system. In short, it is in this later period that the sūtras, which seem at first to have been recited and worshiped, became the object also of scholastic reflection. The fact that these treatises commonly contain a defense of the Mahāyāna as the authentic word of the Buddha—even treatises composed a millennium after the composition of the first Mahāyāna sūtras—may provide evidence of the minority status of the Mahāyāna in India.

These new movements came to designate themselves by the term "Mahāyāna," the "Great Vehicle" to enlightenment, in contradistinction from the earlier Buddhist schools who did not accept their new sūtras as authoritative (that is, as the word of the Buddha). They disparagingly referred to these earlier schools with the term "Hīnayāna," often rendered euphemistically as the "Lesser Vehicle," although *hīna* means also "inferior," "base," and "vile." Members of these earlier schools, of course, never thought of or referred to themselves as passengers on the Hīnayāna. It has thus become common in Western writing about Buddhism to avoid this term by replacing it with "Theravāda." But the terms "Hīnayāna" and "Theravāda" do not designate the same groups; there is a traditional list of some eighteen Hīnayāna schools with diverse doctrines, only one of which has survived into the present, the Theravāda of Sri Lanka and Southeast Asia, whose works are preserved in the Pāli language.

The term "Mahāyāna" is less objectionable for the reason that it was used self-referentially. Most anthologies provide selections from the Pāli texts followed by a sampling from Mahāyāna sūtras, suggesting that with the rise of the Mahāyāna the earlier traditions were both superseded and eclipsed. This is, however, historically inaccurate. The reports of Chinese pilgrims to India in the seventh century indicate that followers of the Mahāyāna and the "Hīnayāna" lived together in monasteries (*vihāras*) and that they all maintained the same "Hīnayāna" monastic vows. The reports further indicate that in many monasteries adherents of the Hīnayāna outnumbered those of the Mahāyāna. Thus, as an alternative to the polemical "Hīnayāna," the term "foundational Buddhism" may be used, referring to the members of Buddhist monastic communities and their supporters who did not accept the legitimacy of the new scriptures composed by followers of the Mahāyāna. As the seventh-century Chinese pilgrim Yijing observed about India, "those who worship bodhisattvas and read Mahāyāna sūtras are called Mahāyāna, while those who do not do this are called the Hīnayāna." The foundational nature and persistence of the Hīnayāna schools in India is often forgotten because of the domination of the Mahāyāna in China, Japan, Korea, Mongolia, and Tibet.

Some five centuries after the rise of the Mahāyāna, another major movement occurred in Indian Buddhism, which was retrospectively designated as the Vajrayāna (the Thunderbolt or Diamond Vehicle). Its origins are even less clearly understood than those of the Mahāyāna. Like "Hīnayāna" and "Mahāyāna," "Vajrayāna" is a retrospective designation, in this case coined to describe a rather disparate set of practices by which the long path to buddhahood could be traversed more quickly than was possible via the Mahāyāna, a path on which various supernormal powers were gained in the process. Some of these practices, such as engaging in behaviors that broke caste taboos, appear to have been borrowed from ascetic movements current in India at the time. Others were developments of themes long present in Buddhist texts, such as the possibility of coming into the presence of the Buddha through visualization practices. Despite the efforts of generations of Buddhist thinkers, it remains exceedingly difficult to identify precisely what it is that sets the Vajrayāna apart. And this difficulty of identifying distinguishing features applies more generally to the issue of distinguishing the Buddhist vehicles, the Hīnayāna, the Mahāyāna, and the Vajrayāna. Adherents of this or that vehicle have much invested in claims to uniqueness. However, these three vehicles share more than is usually assumed.

Anthologies of Buddhist texts have often been organized according to vehicle. One difficulty with such an approach is the almost unavoidable propensity to see the Hīnayāna-Mahāyāna-Vajrayāna sequence as a value-laden development of one kind or another, in which one member of the triad is exalted above the others. According to one view (found especially among European scholars of Buddhism in the nineteenth century), the Hīnayāna (what they called "original Buddhism") was a simple ethical creed of self-reliance, free of ritual elements. In the rise of Mahāyāna, they saw a concession to the masses, in which the Buddha was deified and became an object of worship, and salvation became possible not through diligent practice but through faith in a dizzying pantheon of buddhas and bodhisattvas. The Vajrayāna was an even later development in which, they believed, debased Hindu practices polluted Buddhism until any kind of licentious behavior became accepted.

Another view (found particularly among scholars of Chinese and Japanese Buddhism) also sees the Hīnayāna as an ethical creed, which became an institution of self-satisfied and complacent monks who cared only about their own authority. The Mahāyāna, they believe, was a popular lay movement that sought to restore to the tradition the Buddha's original compassion through the ideal of the bodhisattva, the person who sacrifices his or her own welfare in order to lead all sentient beings in the universe to nirvāṇa. The bodhisattva path is a long one, and requires many millions of lifetimes of practice. According to this view, the Vajrayāna was again a late development, coming at a time when people were no longer interested in dedicating themselves to this protracted path to enlightenment for the sake of others, and imagined that the Vajrayāna provided a shortcut.

Finally, there is the view that sees the Vajrayāna as the pinnacle in the evolution of Buddhism, moving from the austere individualism of the Hīnayāna to the relatively simple compassion of the Mahāyāna, which sees salvation only in the ever-distant future, and finally to the culmination in the Vajrayāna, where buddhahood is possible in this very body and in this very lifetime, not through a suppression of desire and the sensual but through the discovery of ultimate reality even there.

The processes by which Buddhist practices developed through Asia are far more complex than any of these three models suggests. For example, the first model ignores the wealth of rituals and devotional practices found in the Theravāda. The second model ignores the important role played by monks and nuns throughout the history of the Mahāyāna. And the third model places far too much emphasis on the claim of buddhahood in this very lifetime, an important but hardly universal claim of tantric texts. Beyond these specific errors, a more general problem with such an evolutionary (or devolutionary) model is that it suggests that one vehicle ceases or dies out before the next becomes fully formed. Such a suggestion is supported in those anthologies that only provide works from the Pāli "canon," the early collection of works considered by the Theravāda to represent the authentic teachings of the Buddha and his early followers. These anthologies ignore the great mass of literature composed in subsequent centuries in both Pāli and the vernaculars of Southeast Asia, as if the Buddhism of this region essentially ceased its literary output after the fifth century of the common era.

Buddhist institutions had disappeared in India by the thirteenth century. The reasons for this demise remain much debated. The overt cause was a series of Muslim invasions, beginning in the eleventh century, during which the major monastic centers of northern India were destroyed. There had been persecutions of Buddhism by various Hindu kings in the past, but these had been localized and short-lived, often followed by an infusion of support under another dynasty. In this case, however, no such dynasty arose. It also appears that by the end of the first millennium, the locus of Buddhism in India had become the large monastery, which depended on royal rather than local patronage; the most famous of these was Nālandā, said to have housed ten thousand monks. When such centers were destroyed (as Nālandā was by Turkic troops in 1197), the power and influence of the monastic institutions quickly dissipated. Some scholars argue as well that by this time many Buddhist practices had been incorporated into Hinduism and that the local functions fulfilled by Buddhist monks in the past were being performed by Hindu priests. Historians no longer subscribe to the further claim that Buddhism was already weak during this period due to the degenerating influence of tantra. Indeed, tantric Buddhism has survived in Nepal until the present day in a tradition of Mahāyāna devotionalism officiated by a saṅgha of married priests.

Buddhism is often described as the only pan-Asian religion, the only Asian religion to spread beyond the boundaries of its native culture. This is not entirely accurate. Confucian thought has had a profound influence on Korea and Japan, for example, and Hindu epics, with their gods, demons, and social ideals have shaped the cultures of Southeast Asia. It is true, however, that Buddhism spanned both the Indian and Chinese cultural domains of Asia. But it is important to think not so much of a disembodied dharma descending on another culture from above, but rather of a more material movement—of monks, texts, relics, and icons—along trade routes and across deserts, mountains, and seas.

The Buddha is reported to have exhorted his monks to "go and travel around for the welfare of the multitudes, for the happiness of the multitudes, out of sympathy for the world, for the benefit, welfare, and happiness of gods and humans. No two should go in the same direction." Although this last admonition seems not to have been heeded, it is true that Buddhist "missions" were not large and well-organized movements, and instead often took the form of itinerant monks (or groups of monks) traveling by land and sea in the company of traders and royal emissaries. According to traditional accounts, the first foreign mission was to the island of Sri Lanka, and was led by the son of Aśoka.

In descriptions of Buddhism outside of India, one sometimes encounters the term "Southern Buddhism" to describe the Buddhism of Sri Lanka, Thailand, Cambodia, Burma, Laos, and parts of Vietnam, and the term "Northern Buddhism," used in reference to China, Japan, Korea, Tibet, and Mongolia. It is often said that Southern Buddhism is Theravāda and Northern Buddhism is Mahāyana. This is not historically accurate. Theravāda has been the dominant school of Buddhism in most of Southeast Asia since the thirteenth century, with the establishment of the monarchies in Thailand, Burma, Cambodia, and Laos. Prior to that period, however, many other strands of Buddhism were also widely present, including other Hīnayāna sects, as well as Mahāyāna and tantric groups. The great monument at Borobudur in Java reflects Mahāyāna doctrine, and there are reports of Indian monks traveling to Sumatra to study with Mahāyāna and tantric masters there. Indeed, Buddhists texts, icons, and institutions (Hīnayāna, Mahāyāna, and Vajrayāna) were just some of the Indian cultural forms introduced into Southeast Asia by traders and travelers, beginning as early as the fourth century. Buddhist Bengal exerted a strong influence from the ninth through thirteenth centuries, and Sanskrit Mahāyāna and tantric texts were donated to Burmese monasteries as late as the fifteenth century. It was only after the demise of Buddhism in India that the Southeast Asian societies looked especially to Sri Lanka for their Buddhism, where by that time Theravāda was established as the orthodoxy. The monarchs of the kingdoms of Thailand, Burma, Cambodia, and Laos found an effective ideology in Theravāda notions of rulership, often invoking the model of Aśoka.

Just as Southeast Asian Buddhism was not always Theravāda, so "Northern Buddhism" was not always Mahāyāna. The monastic codes practiced in China, Japan, Korea, and Tibet were all derived from the Indian Hinayāna orders. Furthermore, several of these orders flourished in Central Asia (including parts of modern Iran and Afghanistan), whence Buddhism was first introduced into China via the silk route.

Buddhist monks came to China from the northwest sometime during the first century of the common era. China was the most advanced of the civilizations to encounter Buddhism, as measured in terms of literary culture and the organization of social and political institutions. Unlike Tibet and areas of Southeast Asia, for example, China was not a place to which Buddhist monks brought Indian cultural forms, such as writing, which would powerfully shape the future history of the society. It is sometimes argued that if China had not been suffering a period of political disunity in the first centuries of the common era, Buddhism would never have taken hold. It is also argued that Buddhist institutions tended to be strongest in China when the central government was weakest and that Buddhist institutions existed in a state of atrophy after the Tang. Indeed, the first patrons of the dharma were the leaders of the foreign or "barbarian" dynasties in northern China. However, such claims can be overstated, for the influence of Buddhism on a wide range of Chinese cultural forms, such as vernacular literature, has been and remains profound. It is also often stated that Buddhism did not truly take hold in China until it had been fully "sinified," that is, made Chinese. It is important to consider the degree to which Chinese Buddhism is Chinese and the degree to which it is Buddhist, as well as to ponder the bases upon which such judgments might be made.

Contacts with China brought Buddhist monks into the Korean peninsula in the late fourth century. As elsewhere in Asia, these monks did not simply carry texts and icons, but brought with them many of the products of their own civilization, in this case, that of China. Buddhist institutions thrived especially after the unification of the Korean peninsula under the Silla Dynasty in 668. As had been the case in China and would be the case of Japan, part of the appeal of Buddhism to kings was the claim that worshiping the Buddha, promoting the dharma, and supporting the monastic community would protect the state from foreign invasion and calamity, a view set forth in apocryphal works such as the *Sūtra for Humane Kings*. During this period, a number of Korean monks became influential figures in China, Japan, and even in Tibet.

As in China, Buddhism has been both embraced and condemned in Japan as a foreign religion. In the sixth century, monks from Korea first introduced Buddhist texts and teachings into Japan, which, according to traditional accounts were received with enthusiasm at court. Just as Buddhist monks had served as carriers of Indian cultural forms to Southeast Asia, so they brought the products of Chinese civilization to Japan. The Japanese have since looked to China as the source of their Buddhism, and for centuries Japanese monks made the often perilous journey to China to retrieve texts and teachings. These monks, such as the founders of the Tendai and Shingon schools of the Heian period (794–1185), were generally rewarded with imperial support upon their return. During the Kamakura period (1185–1333), when the nation was ruled by a series of military dictators, the shoguns, new sects came to prominence with their patronage. The foremost of these were Zen, Pure Land, and Nichiren, which came to eclipse the previous schools in popular support. In contrast to the more eclectic approach of the Heian sects, each of these three claimed that their single practice offered the only effective means to salvation.

According to traditional accounts, Buddhist monks did not come to Tibet until the seventh century. As was the case with Japan, Buddhism was initially introduced to the court. Indeed, the Tibetan king is said to have been converted to Buddhism by two princesses—one from China and one from Nepal, but both Buddhists—whom he received in marriage as the result of treaties. The dissemination of Buddhist teachings and institutions in Tibet took place in two waves. The first, during the seventh and eighth centuries, saw royal support for the founding and maintenance of Buddhist monasteries, the invitation of Buddhist teachers from India, and the beginnings of a massive project to translate Buddhist texts from Sanskrit into Tibetan. The Tibetan script is said to have been invented for this purpose. Around 838, a king who was not kindly disposed to the dharma closed the monasteries. He was assassinated four years later by a Buddhist monk, thus ending the Tibetan monarchy. A revival of Buddhism took place in western Tibet almost two centuries later. One of the signal events of this second wave was the invitation of the Indian monk Atiśa. There followed a period of extensive contact with India, when Tibetans went to study at the great monasteries of northern India, often inviting their teachers to come back with them. By the end of the fourteenth century, most of the work of translation had been completed. The Tibetans were able to avoid invasion by the Mongols by serving as preceptors to a succession of Mongol khans, who were the first in a series of foreign patrons for the sects of Tibetan Buddhism. In the seventeenth century, the head of one of these sects, the fifth Dalai Lama, was able to consolidate political power over Tibet with the help of his Mongol patron. A succession of Dalai Lamas (or their regents) continued to rule Tibet until 1959, when the current Dalai Lama was forced to flee to India after the invasion and occupation of his nation by China.

In the history of Buddhism in each of these cultures, it is usually possible to discern two general periods. The first is one of assimilation in which Buddhist practices were introduced, with much attention devoted to the translation of texts, the founding of monasteries (with state support), the establishment of places of pilgrimage, often centered on a relic or icon, and close contact with the culture from which Buddhist cultural forms were being received (for example, India in the case of Tibet, Central Asia in the case of China, China in the case of Japan, Sri Lanka in the case of Thailand, and Tibet in the case of Mongolia). In most cases, the period of assimilation lasted for several centuries. This was followed by a period of adaptation, in which Buddhist forms were more fully integrated into the society and made more distinctively its own. It is during this period that schools developed that did not have precise analogs in Indian Buddhism, local deities were incorporated into the Buddhist pantheon, and Buddhist deities were incorporated into the local pantheon. Of course, the adherents of these new schools and devotees of these local cults would reject the suggestion that their practices could not be traced back directly to the Buddha. This concern with the authentic source of the teaching is evinced in the pan-Asian practice of pilgrimage to Bodhgayā, the site of the Buddha's enlightenment. The history of Buddhism in Asia continues to the present day.

Buddhism has a vast literature dealing with what we term logic, epistemology, and ontology—works that are (depending on one's perspective) as profound or as impenetrable, as rich or as arid, as anything produced in the West. However, like philosophical works in other cultures, Buddhist treatises are the products of a tiny, highly educated elite (largely composed of monks in the Buddhist case) and their works rarely touch the ground where the vast majority of Buddhists have lived their lives.

It is important to recall, however, that the Buddhist philosopher was also a Buddhist and, in most cases, a Buddhist monk. He was thus a participant in rituals and institutions that provided the setting for his work. The authors of Buddhist philosophical treatises do not, therefore, fulfill our traditional image of the philosopher engaged in a quest for knowledge "for its own sake," with an overarching concern with logic, rationality, and theoretical consistency. Although these enterprises find an important place in Buddhist traditions, it is also true that for many Buddhist scholastics the faculty of reason provides a relatively superficial awareness, insufficient to the task of directly apprehending the truth. All endeavors in the realm of what might be termed "philosophy" were theoretically subservient to the greater goal of enlightenment, and the ultimate task of the philosopher, at least in theory, was to attain that enlightenment. The Tibetan authors who are regarded as preeminent scholars, for example, devoted great efforts to the performance of tantric rituals or to various sophisticated forms of meditation, in an effort to manifest a fantastic world of benign and malevolent forces, propitiating deities and repelling demons. What we term "philosophy" was but one concern of these authors; a perusal of the titles in the collected works of any of Tibet's most erudite thinkers reveals that among the commentaries on Indian logical treatises and expositions of emptiness are myriad works devoted to tantric ceremonies and visualizations, along with instructions on techniques for drawing maṇḍalas, making rain, stopping smallpox, and manufacturing magical pills. The biographies of the most famous Buddhist philosophers are replete with the most extraordinary events. Thus, although there is a large and significant body of Buddhist literature devoted to such issues as the validity of sense experience and inference as sources of knowledge, the study of such texts must be undertaken with careful attention to their contexts, in the broadest sense of the term, so that the ideas and arguments are not regarded as denizens of a free-floating world, whether that world be the history of ideas or the dharma.

Buddhist texts speak often of the three jewels: of the Buddha, the dharma, and the saṅgha, that is, the Buddha, his teachings, and the community of his followers. In Buddhist texts, a Buddhist is defined as someone who takes refuge in these three, and the refuge ceremony is the most widely performed ritual in the Buddhist world. The Buddha, dharma, and saṅgha are called jewels because they are precious and rare. It is said that it is difficult to encounter them in the cycle of rebirth and when they are encountered they are of great value. The notion of refuge suggests two points fundamental to the Buddhist worldview. The first is that sentient beings are in need of protection, of a place of refuge where they can escape from the sufferings of saṃsāra, the cycle of rebirths. The second point is that the three jewels can provide such protection, that they themselves are free from the dangers and vicissitudes of saṃsāra, and thus can offer refuge to others. In the medical metaphor of which Buddhists are so fond, the Buddha is the doctor, the dharma is the medicine, and the saṅgha are the nurses. It is the Buddha who finds the path to liberation and shows it to others. The dharma is the path itself, and the saṅgha are one's companions who offer assistance along the way.

Before discussing the three jewels in more detail, it would be useful here to outline some of the doctrines most basic to Buddhist practices, as they have been understood by Buddhist authors and by Western scholars. Although there are significant variations among Buddhist cultures, Buddhists in Asia generally accept a view of the universe and of the afterlife that originated in India. Some elements of this cosmology seem to have been current in India at the time of the Buddha, whereas others are the results of elaborations by Buddhist thinkers, perhaps including the Buddha himself. The most standard cosmology divides the universe into three realms, called the realm of desire (*kāmadhātu*), the realm of form (*rūpadhātu*) and the formless realm (*arūpyadhātu*).

The realm of desire is the universe inhabited by humans. Its topography is symmetrical, with four islands surrounding a central mountain, Mount Meru (or Sumeru). Ours is the southern island, called Jambudvīpa (Rose-Apple Island). The other three islands are also inhabited by humans (although of different height and lifespan), but are generally regarded as inaccessible; a buddha can become enlightened only in Jambudvīpa. Mount Meru is the abode of a class of beings called *asuras,* often translated as "demigod" or "titan." They are usually depicted as mean-spirited lesser deities who can bring harm to humans. At a higher elevation on and above Mount Meru is the abode of six classes of gods (*deva*) who inhabit increasingly pleasant realms for increasingly long lifespans. The first two godly realms are on Mount Meru itself. The lower is that of the four royal lineages, ruled by the guardians of the cardinal directions. Next is the "Heaven of the Thirty-Three," on the flat summit of Mount Meru, where thirty-three gods abide. Here, as elsewhere, we see Buddhists assimilating elements from rival groups or other cultures, because thirty-three is the traditional number of gods in the *Ṛg Veda.* Although early Buddhists rejected any ultimate power for Vedic deities, such as Indra, they nonetheless incorporated them into their pantheon, acknowledging their worldly powers but placing them on the second lowest rung of their heavenly hierarchy. Indeed, throughout Buddhist cultures, the worship of local deities is not proscribed, unless that worship involves animal sacrifice. Gods are honored for the boons they can bestow. The thirty-three gods live very long lives: their lifespan is one thousand years, but each of their days is equal to one hundred human years. Yet they are not immortal; they are also subject to rebirth. The remaining four heavens of the realm of desire float in the sky above the summit of Mount Meru. It is in the fourth of the six godly realms, called Tuṣita (Joyous) that the future Buddha, Maitreya, waits.

Also inhabiting the realm of desire are, of course, all manner of animal and insect life, as well as a pitiful class of beings called *pretas,* usually translated as "ghosts" or "hungry ghosts." These beings—some of whom are visible to humans, some of whom are not—are depicted iconographically with huge, distended bellies and emaciated limbs. Their throats are said to be the size of the eye of a needle, rendering them constantly hungry and thirsty and forcing them to search constantly for food and drink. The feeding of these beings was seen as a special responsibility of Buddhist monks and nuns. Located far below Jambudvīpa (usually measured from Bodhgayā, the place in India where the Buddha achieved enlightenment) in the realm of desire is an extensive system of hells, some burning hot, others freezing cold. The beings there undergo a variety of tortures, often depicted in gruesome detail in Buddhist texts and paintings.

The realm of form is situated above the realm of desire and is regarded as superior to it. The beings here are gods who experience the pleasures of sight, sound, and touch, but not taste and smell. They are distinguished from the gods of the realm of desire by their greater powers of concentration, which provide deep states of mental bliss. There are four major levels within the realm of form, categorized by the increasing power of concentration of its inhabitants. Even more sublime is the formless realm, where gods exist in states of pure consciousness, without bodies and sense organs. This is considered the most blissful of abodes, yet it does not receive a great deal of attention in Buddhist literature outside the psychological treatises.

This universe has no beginning, although its physical constituents pass through a fourfold cosmic cycle of evolution, stasis, devolution, and vacuity. Mount Meru and its surrounding islands are said to have evolved over a period of eons, during which, according to one of the Buddhist creation myths, they came to be populated. At the beginning of this process, the lifespan of humans is said to have been immeasurable. Human life had an Edenic quality about it: there was no need for food and humans illuminated the world with their own inner light. As the result of curiosity and desire (to taste the milky froth that covered the surface of the earth), humans began to eat, which required that they expel waste. Their bodies developed accordingly, leading eventually to sexual intercourse. Their natural light faded, the sun and moon appeared, and they began to hoard food for themselves, creating private property for the first time; the eventual result was human society. The human lifespan also gradually diminished until it reached an average of one hundred years, at which point the Buddha appeared in the world to teach the dharma. The quality of human life and the human life span will continue to decline until it reaches ten years of age, coinciding with a time of pestilence, poverty, and warfare. All memory of the Buddha and his teaching will have disappeared from the world. The human lifespan will then begin to increase once more, until it reaches eighty thousand years again, at which point the next buddha will appear. At the end of twenty such cycles, this universe will gradually be destroyed and will then enter into a long period of vacuity, after which a new universe will be created. As the current Dalai Lama has said, Buddhists do not believe in one Big Bang, they believe in many Big Bangs.

The realm of desire, the realm of form, and the formless realm are not only locations in the Buddhist universe, they are also places of rebirth. Buddhists conceive of a cycle of birth and death, called *saṃsāra* (wandering), in six realms of rebirth: those of the gods, demigods, humans, animals, ghosts, and hell beings (although sometimes the realm of demigods is omitted). The entire cycle of rebirth in which the creations and destructions of universes is encompassed has no ultimate beginning. The realms of animals, ghosts, and hell beings are regarded as places of great suffering, whereas the godly realms are abodes of great bliss. Human rebirth falls in between, bringing as it does both pleasure and pain. The engine of saṃsāra is driven by karma, the cause and effect of actions. Like adherents of other Indian religions, Buddhists believe that every intentional act, whether it be physical, verbal, or mental, leaves a residue. That residue, like a seed, will eventually produce an effect at some point in the future, an effect in the form of pleasure or pain for the person who performed the act. Thus Buddhists conceive of a moral universe in which virtuous deeds create experiences of pleasure and nonvirtuous deeds create experiences of pain. These latter are often delineated in a list of ten nonvirtuous deeds: killing, stealing, sexual misconduct, lying, divisive speech, harsh speech, senseless speech, covetousness, harmful intent, and wrong view. Wrong view can mean many things in Buddhist thought, but here refers especially to the belief that actions do not have effects. Buddhist texts provide extensive discussions of the specific deeds that constitute these ten nonvirtues and their respective karmic weight. The ten virtues are the opposites of this list: sustaining life, giving gifts, maintaining sexual decorum, and so on.

These deeds not only determine the quality of a given life but also determine the place of the rebirth after death. Depending on the gravity of a negative deed (killing being more serious than senseless speech and killing a human more serious than killing an insect, for example) one may be reborn as an animal, a ghost, or in one of the hot or cold hells, where the life span is particularly lengthy. Among the hells, some are more horrific than others; the most tortuous is reserved for those who have committed one of five heinous deeds: killing one's father, killing one's mother, killing an arhat, wounding a buddha, and causing dissent in the saṅgha.

Rebirth as a god or human in the realm of desire is the result of a virtuous deed, and is considered very rare. Rarer still is rebirth as a human who has access to the teachings of the Buddha. In a famous analogy, a single blind tortoise is said to swim in a vast ocean, surfacing for air only once every century. On the surface of the ocean floats a single golden yoke. It is rarer, said the Buddha, to be reborn as a human with the opportunity to practice the dharma than it is for the tortoise to surface for its centennial breath with its head through the hole in the golden yoke. One is said to be reborn as a god in the realm of desire as a result of an act of charity: giving gifts results in future wealth. Rebirth as a human is said to result from consciously refraining from a nonvirtuous deed, as when one takes a vow not to kill humans. The vast majority of Buddhist practice throughout Asia and throughout history has been directed toward securing rebirth as a human or (preferably) a god in the next lifetime, generally through acts of charity directed toward monks and monastic institutions. Despite repeated admonitions that birth as a god is a temporary state from which one must eventually fall, to be reborn in a lower realm—admonitions such as those made by the twentieth-century Thai monk Buddhadāsa—a happy life and an auspicious rebirth have remained goals more sought after than escape from saṃsāra into nirvāṇa. Indeed, much Buddhist literature intended for both monks and lay people has promoted a social ideal, defining the good life and explaining how to lead it.

Rebirth as a god in the realm of form or formless realm is achieved somewhat differently. Because these realms are characterized by deep states of concentration, one must achieve one of those states in this life through the practice of meditation in order to be reborn there in the next. For example, one must reach the third level of concentration in order to be reborn as a god in the third level of the realm of form. Because these states require a specialized and sustained practice, they have been little sought as places of rebirth. The formless realm in particular seems to have been more important as an abode to which non-Buddhist meditation masters could be consigned. For example, such a master may have wrongly imagined that he had achieved the ultimate state and liberation from rebirth, when in fact he was only in the realm of infinite consciousness of the formless realm, from which he would eventually be reborn into a lower abode; liberation is possible only by following the teachings of the Buddha.

In the Mahāyāna sūtras, a further cosmic wrinkle is provided by the description of buddha fields (*buddhakṣetra*) or "pure lands," worlds created by buddhas and presided over by them. Through a variety of pious acts, humans can be reborn in these blissful abodes, where the conditions are ideal for rapid progress on the path to enlightenment. The marvels of the pure lands are described in elaborate detail in certain Mahāyāna sūtras, which tell of every variety of jewel growing from trees, streams of variable temperature for bathing, and soothing breezes that carry sermons appropriate to each listener. Rebirth in one of these lands became a prominent goal of Buddhist practice in India, China, and Japan, where it seemed to serve as either a replacement or a temporary substitute for the purportedly greater goal of buddhahood. In some Mahāyāna sūtras, the notion of the buddha field was given a somewhat different twist with the claim that this benighted world in which humans now live is in reality itself a buddha field; it need only be recognized as such. This view was to be important in tantric Buddhism.

A brief description of the Buddha, the dharma, and the saṅgha follows below, organized under these three headings both to reflect this most traditional of Buddhist categories and to call these categories into question by demonstrating the myriad ways in which Buddhists have answered the questions: Who is the Buddha? What is the dharma? And who belongs to the saṅgha?

The Buddha

Scholars are increasingly reluctant to make unqualified claims about the historical facts of the Buddha's life and teachings. There is even a difference of opinion concerning the years of his birth and death. The long accepted dates of 563–483 B.C.E. have recently been called into question with the suggestion that the Buddha may have lived and died as much as a century later.

The traditional accounts of the Buddha's life are largely hagiographic and tend to include the following narrative. It tells of the miraculous birth of a prince of the warrior (*kṣatriya*) caste in a kingdom in what is today southern Nepal. Astrologers predict that the prince, named Siddhārtha ("He Who Achieves His Goal") will be either a great king or a great religious teacher. His father the king, apparently convinced that dissatisfaction with the world is what causes one's mind to turn to existential questions and the spiritual quest, is determined to protect his son from all that is unpleasant, and keeps him in a palace where he is surrounded by beauty and all forms of sport and delight. Only at the age of twenty-nine does the prince become sufficiently curious about the world beyond the palace walls to venture forth on four chariot rides. During the first he sees an old person for the first time in his life, and is informed by his charioteer that this is not the only old man in the world, but that old age eventually befalls everyone. On the next tour he sees a sick person, on the next a corpse. It is only then that he learns of the existence of sickness and death. On his final chariot ride he sees a religious mendicant, who has renounced the world in search of freedom from birth and death. He decides to follow a similar path and, against his father's orders and leaving behind his wife and infant son, goes forth from the life of a householder in search of liberation from suffering.

Over a period of six years he engages in a number of the yogic disciplines current in India at the time, including severe asceticism, and concludes that mortification of the flesh is not conducive to progress toward his goal of freedom from birth, aging, sickness, and death. He eventually sits beneath a tree and meditates all night. After repulsing an attack by the evil deity Māra and his armies, at dawn he comes to a realization that makes him the Buddha ("Awakened One"), forever free from future rebirth. Exactly what it was that he understood on that full-moon night has remained a source of both inspiration and contention throughout the history of Buddhism. Some accounts say that the content of the enlightenment was so profound that the Buddha was initially reluctant to try to teach it to others, and decided otherwise only after being beseeched by the great god Brahmā, himself subject to rebirth and hence desirous of liberation. In this volume, the life of the Buddha and the content of his enlightenment is recounted in a Thai ritual for consecrating (that is, animating) a statue of the Buddha, and in the lament of the wife he deserted.

The Buddha was one of an infinite series of buddhas, all of whom reached their exalted state in the same manner, at exactly the same spot in India under one or another species of bodhi tree. When the Buddha gained enlightenment (*bodhi*), he did so all at once, in an instant, and his realization of the truth was perfect. He also made his momentous discovery by himself, without the aid of a teacher. It was this fact above all that distinguished the Buddha from his enlightened disciples, called *arhats,* in the early tradition. The disciples had to rely on his teachings to realize nirvāṇa, and typically did so only in stages. The Buddha was able to reach his enlightenment on his own and in a single night of meditation because he had previously devoted himself to the practice of virtues such as generosity, patience, and effort over countless previous lifetimes. In one of his previous lives, in the presence of a previous buddha, he had made the firm resolution to become a buddha himself at a future time when the path to liberation had been lost; he had dedicated his practice of virtue over the next eons of rebirth to that goal.

Seven weeks after his enlightenment, the Buddha is said to have walked to th city of Varanasi (Banaras) and to a deer park on its outskirts, where he encountered five renunciates with whom he had previously practiced asceticism. To them he gave his first teaching, usually referred to as the "four noble truths." However, it is not the truths that are noble. The term is perhaps less euphoniously but more accurately rendered as the "four truths for nobles." The term "noble" or "superior" in Sanskrit is *āryan,* the term with which the Indo-European invaders of India had described themselves and which Buddhism appropriated to mean one who is spiritually superior, that is, who has had a vision of a state beyond birth and death. The four things that the Buddha set forth to the five ascetics are known to be true by such people, not by others. Although some Mahāyāna texts dispute that this was the Buddha's very first teaching after his enlightenment, all agree that the teaching of the four truths was of great importance. Over the centuries it has received numerous renditions, the general contours of which follow.

The first truth is that life is inherently unsatisfactory, qualified as it inevitably is by birth, aging, sickness, and death. Various forms of suffering are delineated in Buddhist texts, including the fact that beings must separate from friends and meet with enemies, that they encounter what they do not want, and do not find what they want. The fundamental problem is presented as one of a lack of control over future events; a person wanders constantly from situation to situation, from rebirth to rebirth without companions, discarding one body to take on another, with no certainty or satisfaction, sometimes exalted and sometimes debased. Briefly stated, the problem is change or, as more commonly rendered, impermanence (*anitya*). Because suffering can occur at any moment without warning, even pleasure is in a sense a form of pain, because it will eventually be replaced by pain; there is no activity in which one can engage that will not, in the short or long term, become either physically or mentally painful.

The second truth is the cause of this suffering, identified as action (*karma*), specifically nonvirtuous action, and the negative mental states that motivate such action. As described above, the experience of pleasure and pain is the direct result of actions performed in the past. These actions are motivated by states of mind called *kleśas* (often translated as "afflictions" or "defilements"), the most important of which are desire, hatred, and ignorance. The exact content of this ignorance is again the subject of extensive discussion in Buddhist literature, but it is represented as an active misconception of the nature of reality, usually described as a belief in self (*ātman*). There is, in fact, no permanent and autonomous self in the mind or the body, and to believe otherwise is the root cause of all suffering. It is this imagined self that is inflamed by desire and defended by hatred. As long as one believes in the illusion of self, one will continue to engage in deeds and accumulate karma, and will remain in the cycle of rebirth. This belief in self, in short, is not merely a philosophical problem, but is the cause of the egotism and [illegible] others now and oneself in the future through the negative

[illegible] s the truth of cessation, the postulation of a state beyond [illegible] g is caused by negative karma, and karma is caused by desire and hatred, and desire and hatred are caused by ignorance, it follows that if one could destroy ignorance then everything caused by ignorance, directly or indirectly, would also be destroyed. There would be a cessation of suffering. This state of cessation is called *nirvāṇa* ("passing away") and, again, a remarkable range of opinion has been expressed concerning the precise nature of this state beyond suffering—whether it is the cessation also of mind and body or whether the person persists in nirvāṇa.

The postulation of a state beyond suffering would be of little interest if there were not some means to achieve it. The fourth truth, then, is the path, the technique for putting an end to ignorance. One useful way to approach the topic is through the traditional triad of ethics, meditation, and wisdom. Ethics refers to the conscious restraint of nonvirtuous deeds of body and speech, usually through observing some form of vows. Meditation (*dhyāna*), in this context, refers to developing a sufficient level of concentration (through a wide variety of techniques) to make the mind a suitable tool for breaking through the illusion of self to the vision of nirvāṇa. Wisdom is insight, at a deep level of concentration, into the fact that there is no self. Such wisdom is said not only to prevent the accumulation of future karma but eventually to destroy all past karma so that upon death one is not reborn but passes into nirvāṇa. A person who has achieved that state is called an *arhat* ("worthy one"). Two paths to becoming an arhat were set forth. The first was that of the *śrāvaka* ("listener"), who hears the Buddha's teachings and then puts them into practice. The second was the *pratyekabuddha* ("privately awakened one") who becomes an arhat in solitude.

It is important to reiterate that although many Buddhists throughout history have known the teaching of the four truths in more or less detail, not very many have actively set out to destroy the ignorance of self and achieve nirvāṇa through the practice of meditation. Lay people tended to see this as the business of monks, and most monks tended to see it as the business of the relatively few among them who seriously practiced meditation. Even for such monks, the practice of meditation should be understood as a ritual act in a ritual setting, replete with devotions to the three jewels.

If the Buddha taught the four truths, he also must have taught many other things over the course of the four decades that followed his enlightenment. He is renowned for his ability to teach what was appropriate for a particular person, for adapting his message to the situation. Indeed, in the more spectacular descriptions of his pedagogical powers it was said that the Buddha could sit before an audience and simply utter the letter *a* and each person in the audience would hear a discourse designed specifically to meet his or her needs and capacities, in his or her native language. What he taught was represented as a truth that he had not invented but discovered, a truth that had been discovered by other buddhas in the past and would be discovered by buddhas in the future. Importantly, this truth, whatever it may be, was portrayed as something that could be taught, that could be passed on from one person to another, in a variety of languages. It is in this sense that we may speak of a Buddhist tradition. At the same time, the emphasis on the flexibility of the Buddha's teaching helps to account for the remarkable range of practices described as "Buddhist."

According to traditional accounts, at the age of eighty the Buddha died, or passed into nirvāṇa. He is said to have instructed his followers to cremate his body and distribute the relics that remained among various groups of his followers, who were to enshrine them in hemispherical reliquaries called stūpas. For all Buddhist schools, the stūpa became a reference point denoting the Buddha's presence in the landscape. Early texts and the archeological records link stūpa worship with the Buddha's life and especially the key sites in his career, such as the site of his birth, enlightenment, first teaching, and death. A standard list of eight shrines is recommended for pilgrimage and veneration. However, stūpas are also found at places that were sacred for other reasons, often associated with a local deity. Stūpas were constructed for past buddhas and for prominent disciples of the Buddha. Indeed, stūpas dedicated to disciples of the Buddha may have been especially popular because the monastic rules stipulate that donations to such stūpas became the property of the monastery, whereas donations to stūpas of the Buddha remained the property of the Buddha, who continued to function as a legal resident of most monasteries in what was called "the perfumed chamber."

The Mahāyāna stūpa later became a symbol of buddhahood's omnipresence, a center of text revelation, a place guaranteeing rebirth in a pure land. By the seventh century, the practice of enshrining the physical relics of the Buddha ceases to appear in the archaeological record. Instead, one finds stūpas filled with small clay tablets that have been stamped or engraved with a four-line verse that was regarded as the essence of the Buddha's teaching: "The Tathāgata has explained the cause of all things that arise from a cause. The great renunciate has also explained their cessation." Although this pithy statement is subject to wide interpretation, we can see here an intimation of the four truths: the Buddha has identified that suffering arises from the cause of ignorance and he has also identified nirvāṇa, the cessation of suffering. It is said that the wisest of the disciples, Śāriputra, decided to become the Buddha's follower upon simply hearing these words spoken by a monk, in the absence of the Buddha. But of perhaps greater importance in this context is the fact that this statement functions as a slogan, a mantra, and as a substitute for the relics of the Buddha to be enshrined in a stūpa. The teaching has become the teacher.

Stūpas were pivotal in the social history of Buddhism: these monuments became magnets attracting monastery building and votive construction, as well as local ritual traditions and regional pilgrimage. The economics of Buddhist devotionalism at these centers generated income for local monasteries, artisans, and merchants, an alliance basic to Buddhism throughout its history. At these geographical centers arrayed around the symbolic monument, diverse devotional exertions, textual studies, and devotees' mercantile pursuits could all prosper. The great stūpa complexes—monasteries with endowed lands, a pilgrimage center, a market, and support from the state—represent central points in the Buddhist polities of Central, South, and Southeast Asia.

The Buddha was also worshiped in paintings and statues. The production and worship of Buddhist icons—whether images of buddhas such as Śākyamuni and Amitābha, or bodhisattvas such as Avalokiteśvara and Maitreya—has been a central feature of Buddhist religious life throughout Asian history. The worship of Buddhist icons was promoted by sūtras, and sponsoring the production of an icon was considered an act of great merit, as was bathing an image, a practice that continues in Southeast Asia, China, and Japan. A common goal of both devotional and ascetic Buddhist practice was to recollect the good qualities of the Buddha, which sometimes led to seeing the Buddha "face to face." Images of the Buddha seem to have been important aids in such practices, in part because, far from being a "symbol" of the departed master, images of the Buddha were ritually animated in consecration ceremonies intended to transform an inanimate image into a living deity. Icons thus empowered were treated as spiritual beings possessed of magical powers, to be worshiped with regular offerings of incense, flowers, food, money, and other assorted valuables. Buddhist literature from all over Asia is replete with tales of miraculous occurrences associated with such images.

The Buddha was thus the object of elaborate ritual devotions, often accompanied by recitations of his myriad virtues and powers. These devotions were later incorporated into a larger liturgy that included the visualization of vast offerings and the confession of misdeeds. But not all buddhas were so extraordinary. Indeed, the Japanese Zen master Dōgen went to some lengths to explain why the extraordinary telepathic powers that were supposedly a standard byproduct of enlightenment were not necessarily possessed by enlightened Zen masters in China. The true Zen master is utterly beyond all such categories of Buddhist doctrine.

The question arose early as to the object of devotion in the universal practice of taking refuge in the three jewels: the Buddha, the dharma, and the saṅgha. In some formulations, the Buddha was regarded as having a physical body that was the result of past karma; it consisted of his contaminated aggregates (*skandha*), the final residue of the ignorance that had bound him in saṃsāra until his last lifetime. Because that body was the product of ignorance and subject to disintegration, it was not considered suitable as an object of veneration, as the Buddha-jewel. The Buddha was at the same time said to possess certain qualities (also called *dharma*) that are uncontaminated by ignorance, such as his pure ethics, his deep concentration, his wisdom, his knowledge that he has destroyed all afflictions, and his knowledge that the afflictions will not recur. The qualities were later categorized as the eighteen unshared qualities of a buddha's uncontaminated wisdom. This "body of [uncontaminated] qualities" was deemed the true object of the practice of refuge. Thus, the term "body" came to shift its meaning from the physical form of the Buddha, corporeal extension in space and over time, to a collection of timeless abstract virtues. In addition, the early community had to account for those fantastic elements in the Buddha's hagiography such as his visit to his mother, who had died shortly after his birth and been reborn in the Heaven of the Thirty-Three. The Buddha is said to have made use of a "mind-made body" for his celestial journey. These notions were later systematized into a three-body theory encompassing the physical body (*rūpakāya*), the body of uncontaminated qualities (*dharmakāya*), and the mind-made or emanation body (*nirmāṇakāya*).

In Mahāyāna literature also there is a doctrine of the three bodies of the Buddha. There we find references to the dharmakāya as almost a cosmic principle, an ultimate reality in which all buddhas partake through their omniscient minds. After the dharmakāya comes the enjoyment body (*saṃbhogakāya*), a fantastic form of a buddha that resides only in the highest pure lands, adorned with thirty-two major and eighty minor physical marks, eternally teaching the Mahāyāna to highly advanced bodhisattvas; the enjoyment body does not appear to ordinary beings. The third body is the emanation body (*nirmāṇakāya*). It is this body that appears in the world to teach the dharma. Thus we can discern an important change in the development of the conception of the Buddha in India: whereas in the earlier tradition, the nirmāṇakāya had been that specialized body employed by the Buddha for the performance of occasional supernormal excursions, in the Mahāyāna there is no buddha that ever appears in the world other than the nirmāṇakāya. All of the deeds of the Buddha are permutations of the emanation body—they are all magical creations, the reflexive functions of the dharmakāya. These functions are by no means random. Indeed, the biography of the Buddha is transformed from the linear narration of a unique event into a paradigm, reduplicated precisely by all the buddhas of the past, present, and future in twelve deeds: descent from the Joyous Pure Land, entry into his mother's womb, being born, becoming skilled in arts and sports as a youth, keeping a harem, taking four trips outside the city that cause him to renounce the world, practicing austerities for six years, sitting under the bodhi tree, defeating Māra and his hosts, attaining enlightenment, turning the wheel of doctrine, and passing into nirvāṇa.

The effects of this final deed have long been felt by Buddhist communities. Their sense of loss was not limited to the direct disciples of the Buddha but has been expressed by generations of future followers, often in the form of the lament that one's negative karma caused one to be reborn someplace other than northern India during the lifetime of the Buddha, that one's misdeeds prevented one from joining the audience of the Buddha's teaching. A standard part of Buddhist rituals became the request that other buddhas not pass into nirvāṇa but remain in the world for an eon, which they could do if they wished.

The absence of the Buddha has remained a powerful motif in Buddhist history, and remedies have taken a wide variety of forms. In Burma, secret societies, with possible antecedents in tantric traditions, concentrate their energies on kinds of supernormal power that the mainstream tradition regards with some suspicion. Specifically, they engage in longevity practices to allow them to live until the coming of the next buddha, Maitreya. In China and Japan, rituals constructed around the chanting of the name of the buddha Amitābha offer a means of being delivered at death into the presence of a buddha who is not present here but is present now, elsewhere, in the western paradise of Sukhāvatī.

With the absence of the historical Buddha, a variety of substitutes were conceived to take his place. One such substitute was the icon, as we already noted. Another was the written text of his teaching, the sūtra, described below. In the absence of the Buddha, the transcendent principle of his enlightenment, sometimes called the buddha nature, became the subject of a wide range of doctrinal speculation, devotion, and practice. This impersonal principle, which made possible the transformation of Prince Siddhārtha from an ignorant and suffering human being into an omniscient and blissful buddha, was most commonly referred to as the *tathāgatagarbha. Tathāgata,* "One Who Has Thus Come [or Gone]" is one of the standard epithets of the Buddha. *Garbha* has a wide range of meanings, including "essence" and "womb," which were exploited in works like the *Tathāgatagarbha Sūtra*, a popular and influential Mahāyāna work which declared that this seed or potential for buddhahood resides equally in all beings, and it needs only to be developed. A related work states that everything in the universe contains in itself the entire universe, and that, therefore, the wisdom of a buddha is fully present in each and every being. Such an impersonal principle was not only an important point of doctrine but could also be the object of devotion and praise, prompting the Japanese monk Myōe to address an island as the Buddha. In so doing, Myōe, who had desired to go to India, was able to find the Buddha in Japan.

There is a vacillation in the metaphors and similes employed in these texts as if between two models of the means of making manifest the buddha nature, of achieving enlightenment. One model regards the buddha nature as something pure that has been polluted. The process of the path, therefore, is a gradual process of purification, removing defilements through a variety of practices until the utter transformation from afflicted sentient being to perfect buddha has been effected. Other tropes in these texts, however, do not suggest a developmental model but employ instead a rhetoric of discovery: buddhahood is always already fully present in each being. It need only be recognized. It was this latter model that exercised particular influence in the Chan and Zen schools of China and Japan, which were at least rhetorically dismissive of standard doctrinal categories and traditional practices. And in Tibet, the most ancient Buddhist school spoke of a first buddha, a primordial buddha who is the fundamental embodiment of enlightenment.

One of the earliest substitutes for the Buddha was the wisdom by which he became enlightened and, by extension, the texts that contained that wisdom. This wisdom was called the "perfection of wisdom" (*prajñāpāramitā*). In part because it was this wisdom that metaphorically gave birth to the Buddha and, in part, because the word *prajñāpāramitā* is in the feminine gender in Sanskrit, this wisdom was anthropomorphized and worshiped as a goddess, referred to sometimes as Prajñāpāramitā, sometimes as "the Great Mother." But not all of the important female figures in Buddhism have been anthropomorphized principles. The eighth-century queen of Tibet is identified as a female buddha, and the tantric symbolism of her vagina as the source of enlightenment is set forth. The story is told of Gotamī, not the Buddha's metaphorical mother, but his aunt and foster-mother (his own mother died shortly after his birth). She was instrumental in convincing the Buddha to establish the order of nuns, and her life story has served as a female parallel to the life of the Buddha. The account of her passage into nirvāṇa clearly mimics the story of the Buddha's death.

Perhaps the most popular substitute for the absent Buddha, however, was the bodhisattva. The Buddha is said to have been able to remember all of his past lives, and he is said to have employed his prodigious memory to recount events from those lives. The Buddha's remarkable memory provided a scriptural justification for the appropriation of a diverse body of folklore into the canon. The Jātakas ("Birth Stories"), of which there are over five hundred, were transformed from an Indian version of Aesop's Fables into the word of the Buddha by a conclusion appended to each story, in which the Buddha represents the tale as the recollection of one of his former lives and inevitably identifies himself as the protagonist ("in that existence the otter was Ānanda, the jackal was Maudgalyāyana, the monkey was Śāriputra, and I was the wise hare"). In these tales, the Buddha is referred to as the *bodhisattva,* a term widely etymologized in later literature, but which generally means a person who is intent on the attainment of bodhi, enlightenment. If very few Buddhists felt that they could emulate the Buddha in his last life by leaving their families, living the life of an ascetic, and practicing meditation, the stories of the Buddha's previous lives provided a more accessible model. Stories of the Bodhisattva's deeds of generosity, morality, patience, and perseverance against great odds have remained among the most popular forms of Buddhist literature, both written and oral, and both in the Jātaka tales and in another genre called Avadāna.

In the early Mahāyāna sūtras, the bodhisattva's deeds were represented not merely as an inspiration but as a model to be scrupulously emulated. Earlier in the tradition, the goal had been to follow the path set forth by the Buddha and become liberated from rebirth as an arhat. But in the Mahāyāna, the goal became to do not what the Buddha said but what he did: to follow a much, much longer path to become a buddha oneself. It seems that, at least in the time of the Buddha, it had been possible to become an arhat in one lifetime. Later Mahāyāna exegetes would calculate that, from the time that one made buddhahood one's goal until buddhahood was achieved, a minimum of 384×10^{58} years was required. This amount of time was needed to accumulate the vast stores of merit and wisdom that would result in the omniscience of a buddha, who was able to teach the path to liberation more effectively than any other because of his telepathic knowledge of the capacities and interests of his disciples. It was not the case, then, that bodhisattvas were postponing their enlightenment as buddhas; instead, they would forego the lesser enlightenment of the arhat, which offered freedom from suffering for oneself alone, in favor of the greater enlightenment of a buddha, whereby others could also be liberated.

Formal ceremonies were designed for taking the vow to become a bodhisattva and then follow the long bodhisattva path to buddhahood in order to liberate others from saṃsāra. This included the promise to follow a specific code of conduct. At those ceremonies, the officiant, speaking as the Buddha, would declare that a particular disciple, at a point several eons in the future, would complete the long bodhisattva path and become a buddha of such and such a name, presiding over such and such a pure land. So, with the rise of the Mahāyāna we see the goal of enlightenment recede to a point beyond the horizon, but with the millions of intervening lives, beginning with this one, consecrated by the Buddha's prophecy that these present lives are a future buddha's former lives, part of a buddha's story and thus sacred history.

But the bodhisattva was not simply an object of emulation; the bodhisattva was also an object of devotion, for if the bodhisattva had vowed to liberate all beings in the universe from suffering, all beings were the object of the bodhisattva's compassionate deeds. The bodhisattvas mentioned in the Mahāyāna sūtras were worshiped for the varieties of mundane and supramundane succor they could bestow—bodhisattvas such as Mañjuśrī, the bodhisattva of wisdom; Kṣitigarbha, who as Jizō in Japan rescues children, both born and unborn; Maitreya, the bodhisattva who will become the next buddha; and most of all, Avalokiteśvara, the most widely worshiped bodhisattva, who takes a female form as Guanyin in China and Kannon in Japan, and who in Tibet takes human form in the succession of Dalai Lamas.

Yet another substitute for the absent Buddha is to be found in the Vajrayāna, in which rituals (called *sādhana,* literally, "means of achievement") are set forth in which the practitioner, through a practice of visualization, petitions a buddha or bodhisattva to come into the practitioner's presence. Much of the practice described in tantric sādhanas involves the enactment of a world—the fantastic jewel-encrusted world of the Mahāyāna sūtras or the horrific world of the charnel ground. In the sūtras, these worlds appear before the audience of the sūtra at the command of the Buddha, as in the *Lotus Sūtra,* or are described by him, as in the Pure Land sūtras. In the tantric sādhana, the practitioner manifests that world through visualization, through a process of invitation, descent, and identification, evoking the world that the sūtras declare to be immanent, yet only describe. The tantric sādhana is, in this sense, the making of the world of the Mahāyāna sūtras here and now. Tantric sādhanas usually take one of two forms. In the first, the buddha or bodhisattva is requested to appear before the meditator and is then worshiped in the hope of receiving blessings. In the other type of tantric sādhana, the meditator imagines himself or herself to be a fully enlightened buddha or bodhisattva now, to have the exalted body, speech, and mind of an enlightened being. Those who become particularly skillful at this practice, it is said, gain the ability to appear in this form to others.

Dharma

Before the Buddha passed away, it is said that he was asked who would succeed him as leader of the community. He answered that his teaching should be the teacher. That teaching is most commonly referred to with the name *dharma,* a word derived from the root *dhṛ,* "to hold," a term with a wide range of meanings. Indeed, ten meanings of *dharma,* including "path," "virtue," "quality," "vow," and "nirvāṇa" were enumerated by a fifth-century scholar. Nineteenth-century translators often rendered *dharma* as "the law." But two meanings predominate. The first is the teaching of the Buddha, creatively etymologized from *dhṛ* to mean "that which holds one back from falling into suffering." The second meaning of dharma, appearing particularly in philosophical contexts, is often rendered in English as "phenomenon" or "thing," as in "all dharmas lack self."

The ambiguities encountered in translating the term are emblematic of a wide range of practices that have been regarded as the teaching of the Buddha. And because the Buddha adapted his teachings to the situation and because (at least according to the Mahāyāna), the Buddha did not actually disappear into nirvāṇa but remains forever present, works that represented themselves as his teaching (which begin with the standard formula, "Thus did I hear") have continued to be composed throughout the history of Buddhism. The term "Buddhist apocrypha" has generally been used to describe those texts composed outside of India (in China, for example) which represent themselves as being of Indian origin. Yet strictly speaking all Buddhist texts, even those composed in Indian languages, are apocryphal because none can be identified with complete certainty as a record of the teaching of the historical Buddha. This has, on the one hand, led to a certain tolerance for accepting diverse doctrines and practices as Buddhist. Sometimes new texts were written as ways of summarizing what was most important from an unwieldy and overwhelming canon. In some cases, these new texts represented themselves as the words of the historical Buddha; in other cases, essays were composed in poetry and prose with the purpose of explicating for a newly converted society the most essential teachings from a bewildering scriptural tradition.

The absence of the Buddha did not merely occasion the creation of substitutes for him. Over the course of the history of Buddhism in Asia, it also portended crisis, notably in a variety of texts that responded to the notion of the decline of the dharma. Within a century or two after the Buddha's death, there were predictions of the eventual disappearance of the dharma from the world. Various reasons were given for its demise, ranging from a general deterioration in human virtue to the fact that the Buddha had agreed to admit women into the order. These texts, like most Buddhist sūtras, are set at the time of the Buddha, and the dire circumstances that signal the demise of the dharma are expressed in terms of prophecies by the Buddha of what will happen in the future. We can assume that the authors of the sūtras were in fact describing the events of their own day, usually including the corrupt and greedy behavior of monks, the persecution of Buddhism by the state, or the threat posed by foreign invaders. Some works of this genre not only prophesied decline of the dharma but offered prescriptions so that decline could be averted. One Chinese work criticizes the traditional practice of offering gifts to monks and monasteries, and advocates acts of charity directed instead toward the poor, the orphaned, the aged, the sick, and even animals and insects. An Indian work composed at the time of the first major incursion of Muslim armies into northern India foretells an apocalyptic war in which Buddhist forces will sweep out of the Himalayas to defeat the barbarians and establish a utopian Buddhist kingdom. In another Indian text, there is no such threat. Instead, the text may be addressed to a community whose very security and complacency would allow the eventual disappearance of the dharma.

When works such as these were composed to respond to a particular historical circumstance, it was sometimes necessary to account for the fact that there had been no previous record of such a text. It was explained that a certain text had been found locked inside an iron stūpa, having been placed there long ago to be discovered at the appropriate time. The fact that the version which eventually reached China seemed little more than an outline was the result of an unfortunate circumstance: the larger and more comprehensive version of the work had inadvertently been thrown overboard on the sea journey from India to China. Likewise, the Tibetan ritual text of the Great Bliss Queen is an example of a Tibetan genre of texts known as *gter ma* (treasures). It is believed that the Indian tantric master who visited Tibet in the late eighth century, Padmasambhava, and his followers buried texts all over Tibet, knowing that they would be uncovered at an appropriate time in the future.

As one might imagine, there were those who found such claims fantastic, and the Mahāyāna was challenged by the foundational schools for fabricating new sūtras and distorting the Buddhist teaching. A sixth-century Mahāyāna author, Bhāvaviveka, summarizes the Hīnayāna argument that the Mahāyāna is not the word of the Buddha: the Mahāyāna sūtras were not included in either the original or subsequent compilations of the word of the Buddha; by teaching that the Buddha is permanent, the Mahāyāna contradicts the dictum that all conditioned phenomena are impermanent; because the Mahāyāna teaches that the buddha nature is all-pervasive, it does not relinquish the belief in self; because the Mahāyāna teaches that the Buddha did not pass into nirvāṇa, it suggests that nirvāṇa is not the final state of peace; the Mahāyāna contains prophecies that the great early disciples will become buddhas; the Mahāyāna belittles the arhats; the Mahāyāna praises bodhisattvas above the Buddha; the Mahāyāna perverts the entire teaching by claiming that the historical Buddha was an emanation; the statement in the Mahāyāna sūtras that the Buddha was constantly in meditative absorption is unfeasible; by teaching that great sins can be completely absolved, the Mahāyāna teaches that actions have no effects, contradicting the law of karma. Therefore, the opponents of the Mahāyāna claim, the Buddha did not set forth the Mahāyāna; it was created by beings who were demonic in order to deceive the obtuse and those with evil minds.

Centuries earlier we find implied responses to these criticisms in the Mahāyāna sūtras themselves, side by side with the assertions that the Hīnayāna found so heretical. The most influential defense of new sūtras as authoritative teachings of the Buddha is found in the *Lotus Sūtra*, with its doctrine of skillful means (*upāya*). In that work the validity of the Mahāyāna and the Mahāyāna vision of buddhahood is defended by the use of parables. Because the *Lotus* is the most influential of Buddhist texts in all of East Asia, it is worthwhile to consider some of these.

The *Lotus Sūtra* must somehow account for the fact that the Mahāyāna has appeared late, after the Buddha had taught a path to nirvāṇa that had already been successfully followed to its terminus by his original disciples, the great arhats such as Śāriputra, Maudgalyāyana, and Kāśyapa. If the Mahāyāna is the superior teaching why had it not been evident earlier? Several of the parables place the fault with the disciples themselves. Thus, in the parable of the hidden jewel, a man falls asleep drunk in the house of a friend who, unbeknownst to him, sews a jewel into the hem of his garment. The man awakes and goes on his way, only to suffer great poverty and hardship. He encounters his friend, who reveals the jewel, showing him that he had been endowed with great wealth all the while. In the same way, the disciples of the Buddha have constant access to the path to supreme enlightenment but are unaware of it; they are bodhisattvas unaware of their true identity. Again, the Buddha compares his teaching to the rainfall that descends without discrimination on the earth. That this rain causes some seeds to grow into flowers and some into great trees implies no differentiation in the rain but rather is due to the capacities of the seeds that it nurtures. Thus, the teaching of the Buddha is of a single flavor but benefits beings in a variety of ways according to their capacity. The Buddha knows the abilities and dispositions of his disciples and causes them to hear his dharma in a way most suitable to them.

Other parables employ a more radical strategy of authorization, suggesting that the Hīnayāna nirvāṇa is but a fiction. The oft-cited parable of the burning house tells of a father distraught as his children blithely play, unaware that the house is ablaze. Knowing of their respective predilections for playthings, he lures them from the inferno with the promise that he has a cart for each waiting outside, a deer-drawn cart for one, a goat-drawn cart for another, and so on. When they emerge from the conflagration, they find only one cart, a magnificent conveyance drawn by a great white ox, something that they had never even dreamed of. The burning house is saṃsāra, the children are ignorant sentient beings, unaware of the dangers of their abode, the father is the Buddha, who lures them out of saṃsāra with the teaching of a variety of vehicles—the vehicle of the śrāvaka, the vehicle of the pratyekabuddha, the vehicle of the bodhisattva—knowing that in fact there is but one vehicle, the buddha vehicle whereby all beings will be conveyed to unsurpassed enlightenment. And the Buddha tells the parable of the conjured city, in which a skillful guide leads a group of travelers on a long journey in search of a cache of jewels. Along the way, the travelers become exhausted and discouraged and decide to turn back. The guide magically conjures a great city in the near distance, where the travelers can rest before continuing toward their ultimate goal. The travelers enter the city where they regain their strength, at which point the guide dissolves the city and announces that the jewel cache is near. The travelers are those sentient beings who are weak and cowardly, intimidated by the thought of traversing the long Mahāyāna path to buddhahood. For their benefit, the Buddha creates the Hīnayāna nirvāṇa, more easily attained, which they mistakenly believe to be their final goal. He then announces to them that they have not reached their ultimate destination and exhorts them on to buddhahood, revealing that the nirvāṇa they had attained was but an illusion.

Thus, the claim to legitimacy of the earlier tradition is usurped by the Mahāyāna through the explanation that what the Buddha had taught before was in fact a lie, that there is no such thing as the path of the arhat, no such thing as nirvāṇa. There is only the Mahāyāna (also called the *ekayāna,* the "one vehicle"), which the Buddha intentionally misrepresents out of his compassionate understanding that there are many among his disciples who are incapable of assimilating so far-reaching a vision. But what of those disciples of the Buddha who are reported in the early sūtras to have become arhats, to have passed into nirvāṇa—what of their attainment? In an ingenious device (found also in other Mahāyāna sūtras) the great heroes of the Hīnayāna are drafted into the Mahāyāna by the Buddha's prophecies that even they will surpass the trifling goal of nirvāṇa and go on to follow the Mahāyāna path to eventual buddhahood. The first such prophecy is for the monk Śāriputra, renowned in the works of the foundational tradition as the wisest of the Buddha's disciples, who is transformed into a stock character in the Mahāyāna sūtras as one who is oblivious of the higher teaching. When his ignorance is revealed to him, he desires to learn more, coming to denounce as parochial the wisdom that he had once deemed supreme. The champion of the Hīnayāna is shown to reject it and embrace that which many adherents of the foundational tradition judged to be spurious. Thus the early history of the movement, already highly mythologized into a sacred history, was fictionalized further in the Mahāyāna sūtras, and another sacred history was eventually created. To legitimate these newly appearing texts, their authors claimed the principal figures of the earlier tradition, indeed its very codifiers, as converts to the Buddha's true teaching and central characters in its drama. The early story of Gautama Buddha and his disciples, preserved in the Pāli canon and already accepted as an historical account by the "pre-Mahāyāna" traditions, is radically rewritten in the *Lotus* in such a way as to glorify the *Lotus* itself as the record of what really happened. Such rewriting recurs throughout the history of the Buddhist traditions in the perpetual attempt to recount "what the Buddha taught."

And who is this Buddha that the *Lotus Sūtra* represents? In the fifteenth chapter, billions of bodhisattvas well up out of the earth and make offerings to the Buddha. The Buddha declares that all of these bodhisattvas who have been practicing the path for innumerable eons are in fact his own disciples, that he had set each of them on the long path to buddhahood. The bodhisattva Maitreya, who has witnessed this fantastic scene, asks the obvious question. He reckons that it had only been some forty years since the Buddha had achieved enlightenment under the tree at Bodhgayā. He finds it incredible that in that short period of time the Buddha could have trained so many bodhisattvas who had progressed so far on the path. "It is as if there were a man, his natural color fair and his hair black, twenty-five years of age, who pointed to men a hundred years of age and said, 'These are my sons!' " Maitreya, representing the self-doubt of the early Mahāyāna and reflecting the Hīnayāna critique, is deeply troubled by this inconsistency, fearing that people who hear of this after the Buddha's passing will doubt the truth of the Buddha's words and attack his teaching.

It is at this point that the Buddha reveals another lie. He explains that even though he is widely believed to have left the palace of his father in search of freedom from suffering and to have found that freedom six years later under a tree near Gayā, in fact, that is not the case. He achieved enlightenment innumerable billions of eons ago and has been preaching the dharma in this world and simultaneously in myriad other worlds ever since. Yet he recognizes the meager intelligence of many beings, and out of his wish to benefit them resorts to the use of skillful methods (*upāya*), recounting how he renounced his princely life and attained unsurpassed enlightenment. And, further recognizing that his continued presence in the world might cause those of little virtue to become complacent and not ardently seek to put his teaching into practice, he declares that he is soon to pass into nirvāṇa. But this also is a lie, because his lifespan will not be exhausted for many innumerable billions of eons.

Thus, the prince's deep anxiety at being confronted with the facts of sickness, aging, and death, his difficult decision to abandon his wife and child and go forth into the forest in search of a state beyond sorrow, his ardent practice of meditation and asceticism for six years, his triumphant attainment of the liberation and his imminent passage into the extinction of nirvāṇa—all are a pretense. He was enlightened all the time, yet feigned these deeds to inspire the world.

But we should not conclude that once the *Lotus* and other Mahāyāna sūtras declared the superiority of the bodhisattva path, the supremacy and authority of the Mahāyāna was finally and unequivocally established. Defenses of the Mahāyāna as the word of the Buddha remained the preoccupation of Mahāyāna scholastics throughout the history of Buddhism in India. Nor should we assume that teachings were ranked only as Hīnayāna and Mahāyāna. Even sects that exalted the *Lotus Sūtra* above all others, for example, could disagree about whether there was more than one true practice, one true sūtra, one true buddha. In Japan, a dispute over the meaning of "original enlightenment" in what is called the Matsumoto Debate led to a bloody conflict in 1536 that involved thousands of troops on each side. In China, the promotion and control of sacred scripture was the prerogative of the highest imperial offices. A sect that came into conflict with this authority, the "Teaching of the Three Stages," had its texts declared heretical and banned from the official collection of Buddhist texts.

Thus, the significance of Buddhist texts does not lie simply in their doctrinal or philosophical content but in the uses to which they have been put. We find, for example, that the Abhidharma (literally, "higher dharma," sometimes rendered as "phenomenology"), a class of Buddhist scriptures concerned with minute analyses of mental states, is chanted at Thai funerals. Contained in virtually every Mahāyāna sūtra was a proclamation of the marvelous benefits that would accrue to those who piously handled, recited, worshiped, copied, or circulated the text itself—again, the teaching had become the teacher. Ritual enshrinement and devotion to the sūtra as a vital embodiment of the dharma and, in a certain sense, as a substitute for the Buddha himself was instrumental to the rise of the disparate collections of cults of the book that came to be known as the Mahāyāna. In China, no text was more venerated than the *Lotus,* and tales were told of the miracles that attended its worship.

The importance of texts in Buddhism derives in part from the fact that the tradition represents the Buddha as being eventually persuaded to teach others after his enlightenment. This suggests that the dharma is something that can be passed on, something that is transmittable, transferable. The Buddha is said to have spoken not in Sanskrit, the formal language of the priests of his day, but in the vernacular, and he is said to have forbidden monks from composing his teachings in formal verses for chanting. The implication was that the content was more important than the form. This led to the notion that the dharma could be translated from one language to another, and the act of translation (and the sponsorship of translation) has been regarded throughout Asia as one of the most pious and meritorious acts that could be performed. It was therefore common for Buddhist kings and emperors to sponsor the translation of texts from one language into another: from Sanskrit into Chinese, from Sanskrit into Tibetan, from Tibetan into Manchu, from Pāli into Burmese, and so on. Adding to this notion of translatability was the fact that the primary objects of Buddhist devotion—texts, relics, icons—were all portable; stories of the transportation and enshrinement of a particularly potent image of the Buddha figure in the histories of almost all Buddhist cultures. We should not conclude, however, as Buddhists sometimes do, that the dharma is something self-identical and transcendent, that showers over the cultures of Asia, transforming and pacifying them. In a Japanese text, for example, Buddhism is portrayed as a Korean possession that can be offered in tribute to the Japanese court as a means of protecting the state. It is this universalism of the Buddhist dharma with its plastic pantheon into which any local deity could easily be enlisted, its doctrine of the Buddha's skillful methods for accommodating conflicting views, and its claims about the pervasive nature of reality that have made it a sometimes useful ideology for rulership and empire.

Buddhism has indeed transformed Asia, but it has been transformed in the process. We may consider even whether there ever was some entity called "Buddhism" to be transformed in the first place. What cannot be disputed is that if Buddhism exists, it is impossible to understand it outside the lives of Buddhists, outside the saṅgha.

Saṅgha

The last of the three jewels is the saṅgha, "the community." Technically taken to mean the assembly of enlightened disciples of the Buddha, the term more commonly connotes the community of Buddhist monks and nuns. In the rules governing the ordination ceremony, the saṅgha is said to be present when four fully ordained monks are in attendance. However, in its broadest sense the saṅgha is the whole body of Buddhist faithful. The selections in this section fall under two broad categories. The first deals with monastic life or, more specifically, life organized by vows. The second deals with the lives of Buddhists.

As mentioned earlier, Buddhist practice was traditionally subsumed under three headings: ethics (*śīla*), meditation (*dhyāna*), and wisdom (*prajñā*). Ethics, which in this context refers to refraining from nonvirtue through the conscious control of body and speech, was regarded as the essential prerequisite for progress in meditation and wisdom. It was the element of the triad most widely practiced both by lay people and monks and nuns, and this practice generally took the form of the observance of vows. Since in Buddhist ethical theory karma, both good and bad, depended not on the deed but on the intention, if one could make a promise not to kill humans, for example, and maintain that promise, the good karma accumulated by such restraint would be far greater than had one simply not had the occasion to commit murder. From the early days of the tradition, therefore, elaborate systems of rules for living one's life, called *vinaya,* were established, along with ceremonies for their conferral and maintenance. Lay people could take vows not to kill humans, not to steal, not to commit sexual misconduct, not to lie about spiritual attainments (for example, not to claim to be telepathic when one actually was not), and not to use intoxicants. Novice monks and nuns took these five vows, plus vows not to eat after the noon meal (a rule widely transgressed in some Buddhist cultures through recourse to the evening "medicinal meal"), not to handle gold or silver, not to adorn their bodies, not to sleep in high beds, and not to attend musical performances. Fully ordained monks (*bhikṣu*) and nuns (*bhikṣuṇī*) took many more vows, which covered the entire range of personal and public decorum, and regulated physical movements, social intercourse, and property. Monks and nuns convened twice monthly to confess their transgressions of the rules in a ceremony and reaffirm their commitment to the code, with transgressions carrying punishments of various weights. The gravest misdeeds entailed expulsion from the order, whereas others could be expiated simply by confessing them aloud. In Buddhist traditions across Asia, ritual maintenance of these monastic codes has served as the mark of orthodoxy, much more than adherence to a particular belief or doctrine. Indeed, it is said that the teaching of the Buddha will endure only as long as the vinaya endures.

The Buddha and his followers were probably originally a group of wandering ascetics. However, they adopted the practice of other ascetic groups in India of remaining in one place during the rainy season. Wealthy patrons had shelters built for their use, and these shelters evolved into monasteries that were inhabited throughout the year. It seems that early in the tradition, the saṅgha became largely sedentary, although the tradition of the wandering monk continued. Still, the saṅgha was by no means a homogeneous community. The vinaya texts describe monks from a wide variety of social backgrounds. Mention is made of monks from all four of India's social castes. There were also a wide variety of monastic specialties. The vinaya texts describe monks who are skilled in speech, those who memorize and recite the sūtras, those who memorize and recite the vinaya, and those who memorize and recite lists of technical terms. There are monks who live in the forest, who wear robes of felt, who wear robes made from discarded rags, who live only on the alms they have begged for, who live at the foot of a tree, who live in a cemetery, who live in the open air, who sleep sitting up, and so on. There were also monks who specialized in meditation, monks who served as advisors to kings, and monks responsible for the administration of the monastery and its property. One of the tasks of this administrator was to insure that the wandering monks were not given mundane work, that meditating monks not be disturbed by noise, and that monks who begged for alms received good food. Whether they wandered without a fixed abode or lived in monasteries, monks and nuns that lived in a designated region, called a *sīmā,* were to gather twice a month to confess and affirm their vows communally, a ceremony that laypeople also attended.

Throughout the Buddhist world, monks and laypeople have lived in a symbiotic relationship: the laity provide material support for monks while monks provide a locus for the layperson's accumulation of merit (by supporting monks who maintained their vows). The rules and regulations in the vinaya texts were meant to govern the lives of Buddhist monks and to structure their relations with the laity. Monks in the vinaya literature are caught in a web of social and ritual obligations, are fully and elaborately housed and permanently settled, and are preoccupied not with nirvāṇa, but with bowls and robes, bathrooms and buckets, and proper behavior in public. The saṅgha was also a community where disputes arose and had to be settled. Because it is said that the Buddha only prescribed a rule in response to a specific misdeed, the vinaya texts often provide the story of that first offense and the Buddha's pronouncement of a rule against such behavior in the future.

There were also rules for nuns, although these receive much less attention in the vinaya literature. According to several traditions, the Buddha was approached early in his career by his aunt and step-mother, Mahāpajāpatī, also called Gotamī, at the head of a delegation of women who wished him to institute a Buddhist order of nuns. The Buddha initially declined to institute such an order. But when the Buddha's cousin and personal attendant, Ānanda, asked him whether women were able to attain the fruits of the practice of the dharma, the Buddha unhesitatingly answered in the affirmative and agreed to establish an order for women. However, the same text states that if the Buddha had not agreed to establish an order for nuns, his teaching would not disappear from the world so quickly. The rules for nuns are both more numerous and stricter than those for monks, and placed nuns in a position of clear subordination to monks. For example, seniority in the order of monks and nuns is measured by the length of time one has been ordained, such that someone who has been a monk for five years must pay respect to a monk of six years, even if the first monk is chronologically older. However, the rules for nuns state that a woman who has been a nun for one hundred years must pay respect to a man who was ordained as a monk for one day. The difficulties entailed in maintaining the strict nuns' vows and a lack of institutional support led to the decline and eventual disappearance of the order of nuns in India, Sri Lanka, and Southeast Asia, and to an order of novices alone (rather than fully ordained nuns) in Tibet. The tradition of full ordination for women was maintained only in China.

Throughout the development of the Mahāyāna and the Vajrayāna, the rules for monks and nuns seem to have remained fairly uniform and the adherents of the new vehicles seem to have seen no contradiction between the monastic life and the practices of the Mahāyāna and the Vajrayāna. But if we understand the vinaya not as that which restricts individuals and their actions but as that which creates them, we will not be surprised that additional vows were formulated for the bodhisattva and the tantric practitioner, and that rituals which mimicked the monastic confession ceremony were designed for their administration. The vows of a bodhisattva included not only the vow to liberate all beings in the universe from suffering but also to act compassionately by always accepting an apology, not to praise oneself and belittle others, to give gifts and teachings upon request, and so on. Those who took the bodhisattva vows also promised never to claim that the Mahāyāna sūtras were not the word of the Buddha.

Vajrayāna practice also entailed extensive sets of vows. As mentioned above, it was common for Buddhist monks, especially in late Indian Buddhism and in Tibet, to hold bodhisattva and tantric vows in addition to their monk's vows. In the case of the more advanced tantric initiations, which involved sexual union with a consort, this presented problems, for monks were bound by the rule of celibacy. Whether or not monks were permitted to participate in such initiations became a question of some gravity when Buddhism was being established in Tibet, and a famous Indian monk and tantric master, Atiśa, composed a text that dealt with this issue.

The second type of selection found in this section are stories of Buddhists from across Asia. Some of these accounts are ancient, like the life story of a "miraculous and strange" Chinese monk of the sixth century; some are modern, like the autobiographies of Japanese Buddhist women after the Second World War. Some are hagiographies of famous masters, and some tell of miraculous voyages; others recount the deathbed visions of devotees of Amitābha. Some of the biographies are highly stereotyped with often transparent agendas.

Because of the portability of relics, texts, and icons, sacred sites were established across the Buddhist world and pilgrimages to those sites was a popular form of Buddhist practice throughout Asia. Pilgrimage was sometimes to a stūpa associated with the life of the Buddha; Bodhgayā, the site of the Buddha's enlightenment, has drawn pilgrims from the outer reaches of the Buddhist world for centuries. Particularly powerful buddha images also attracted pilgrims; it was not uncommon for pilgrims from as far east as Manchuria and as far west as the Mongol regions of Russia to travel to Lhasa, the capital of Tibet, to visit the statue of the Buddha there. They would travel on foot or on horseback; the most pious would proceed by prostration—bowing and then stretching their bodies on the ground before rising, taking one step forward and prostrating again, along the entire route. In China, mountains believed to be the abodes of munificent bodhisattvas were (and are) popular destinations of communal pilgrimages. Women pilgrims in modern China reported a variety of reasons for making the pilgrimage: to insure a good harvest, to protect the silkworms, to promote the health of family members and domestic animals. But we should not assume that Buddhist travel was always directed from the periphery to the center. A renowned Buddhist scholar left one of the great monastic universities of India on a perilous sea voyage to Sumatra, where the preeminent teacher of the practice of compassion was said to reside. Nor was travel always so concerned with what or who was to be found at the end of the journey; the Japanese monk Ippen saw travel itself as essential to his practice of devotion to Amitābha.

Thus, the category of the three jewels is not without its own ambiguities. The reader is asked again to consider: Who is the Buddha? What is the dharma? And who belongs to the saṅgha?

Note

1. The historical survey that follows is drawn largely from Joseph M. Kitagawa and Mark D. Cummings, ed., *Buddhism and Asian History* (New York: Macmillan, 1989), a collection of the most recent scholarship on Buddhist history. Readers are referred there for more detailed histories and bibliographies of sources.

RELIGIONS OF CHINA IN PRACTICE

Stephen F. Teiser

Acknowledging the wisdom of Chinese proverbs, most anthologies of Chinese religion are organized by the logic of the three teachings (*sanjiao*) of Confucianism, Daoism, and Buddhism. Historical precedent and popular parlance attest to the importance of this threefold division for understanding Chinese culture. One of the earliest references to the trinitarian idea is attributed to Li Shiqian, a prominent scholar of the sixth century, who wrote that "Buddhism is the sun, Daoism the moon, and Confucianism the five planets."[1] Li likens the three traditions to significant heavenly bodies, suggesting that although they remain separate, they also coexist as equally indispensable phenomena of the natural world. Other opinions stress the essential unity of the three religious systems. One popular proverb opens by listing the symbols that distinguish the religions from each other, but closes with the assertion that they are fundamentally the same: "The three teachings—the gold and cinnabar of Daoism, the relics of Buddhist figures, as well as the Confucian virtues of humanity and righteousness—are basically one tradition."[2] Stating the point more bluntly, some phrases have been put to use by writers in the long, complicated history of what Western authors have called "syncretism." Such mottoes include "the three teachings are one teaching"; "the three teachings return to the one"; "the three teachings share one body"; and "the three teachings merge into one."[3]

What sense does it make to subsume several thousand years of religious experience under these three (or three-in-one) categories? To answer this question, we need first to understand what the three teachings are and how they came into existence.

There is a certain risk in beginning this introduction with an archaeology of the three teachings. The danger is that rather than fixing in the reader's mind the most significant forms of Chinese religion—the practices and ideas associated with ancestors, the measures taken to protect against ghosts, or the veneration of gods—emphasis will instead be placed on precisely those terms we seek to avoid. Or, as one friendly critic stated in a review of an earlier draft of this introduction, why must "the tired old category of the three teachings be inflicted on yet another generation of students?" Indeed, why does this introduction begin on a negative note, as it were, analyzing the problems with subsuming Chinese religion under the three teachings, and insert a positive appraisal of what constitutes Chinese religion only at the end? Why not begin with "popular religion," the gods of China, and kinship and bureaucracy and then, only after those categories are established, proceed to discuss the explicit categories by which Chinese people have ordered their religious world? The answer has to do with the fact that Chinese religion does not come to us purely, or without mediation. The three teachings are a powerful and inescapable part of Chinese religion. Whether they are eventually accepted, rejected, or reformulated, the terms of the past can only be understood by examining how they came to assume their current status. And because Chinese religion has for so long been dominated by the idea of the three teachings, it is essential to understand where those traditions come from, who constructed them and how, as well as what forms of religious life are omitted or denied by constructing such a picture in the first place.

Confucianism

The myth of origins told by proponents of Confucianism (and by plenty of modern historians) begins with Confucius, whose Chinese name was Kong Qiu and who lived from 551 to 479 B.C.E. Judging from the little direct evidence that still survives, however, it appears that Kong Qiu did not view himself as the founder of a school of thought, much less as the originator of anything. What does emerge from the earliest layers of the written record is that Kong Qiu sought a revival of the ideas and institutions of a past golden age. Employed in a minor government position as a specialist in the governmental and family rituals of his native state, Kong Qiu hoped to disseminate knowledge of the rites and inspire their universal performance. That kin of broad-scale transformation could take place, he thought, only with the active encouragement of responsible rulers. The ideal ruler, as exemplified by the legendary sage-kings Yao and Shun or the adviser to the Zhou rulers, the Duke of Zhou, exercises ethical suasion, the ability to influence others by the power of his moral example. To the virtues of the ruler correspond values that each individual is supposed to cultivate: benevolence toward others, a general sense of doing what is right, and loyalty and diligence in serving one's superiors. Universal moral ideals are necessary but not sufficient conditions for the restoration of civilization. Society also needs what Kong Qiu calls *li,* roughly translated as "ritual." Although people are supposed to develop propriety or the ability to act appropriately in any given social situation (another sense of the same word, li), still the specific rituals people are supposed to perform (also li) vary considerably, depending on age, social status, gender, and context. In family ritual, for instance, rites of mourning depend on one's kinship relation to the deceased. In international affairs, degrees of pomp, as measured by ornateness of dress and opulence of gifts, depend on the rank of the foreign emissary. Offerings to the gods are also highly regulated: the sacrifices of each social class are restricted to specific classes of deities, and a clear hierarchy prevails. The few explicit statements attributed to Kong Qiu about the problem of history or tradition all portray him as one who "transmits but does not create."[4] Such a claim can, of course, serve the ends of innovation or revolution. But in this case it is clear that Kong Qiu transmitted not only specific rituals and values but also a hierarchical social structure and the weight of the past.

The portrayal of Kong Qiu as originary and the coalescence of a self-conscious identity among people tracing their heritage back to him took place long after his death. Two important scholar-teachers, both of whom aspired to serve as close advisers to a ruler whom they could convince to institute a Confucian style of government, were Meng Ke (or Mengzi, ca. 371–289 B.C.E.) and Xun Qing (or Xunzi, d. 215 B.C.E.). Mengzi viewed himself as a follower of Kong Qiu's example. His doctrines offered a program for perfecting the individual. Sageliness could be achieved through a gentle process of cultivating the innate tendencies toward the good. Xunzi professed the same goal but argued that the means to achieve it required stronger measures. To be civilized, according to Xunzi, people need to restrain their base instincts and have their behavior modified by a system of ritual built into social institutions.

It was only with the founding of the Han dynasty (202 B.C.E.–220 C.E.), however, that Confucianism became Confucianism, that the ideas associated with Kong Qiu's name received state support and were disseminated generally throughout upper-class society. The creation of Confucianism was neither simple nor sudden, as three examples will make clear. In the year 136 B.C.E. the classical writings touted by Confucian scholars were made the foundation of the official system of education and scholarship, to the exclusion of titles supported by other philosophers. The five classics (or five scriptures, *wujing*) were the *Classic of Poetry* (*Shijing*), *Classic of History* (*Shujing*), *Classic of Changes* (*Yijing*), *Record of Rites* (*Liji*), and *Chronicles of the Spring and Autumn Period* (*Chunqiu*) with the *Zuo Commentary* (*Zuozhuan*), most of which had existed prior to the time of Kong Qiu. (The word *jing* denotes the warp threads in a piece of cloth. Once adopted as a generic term for the authoritative texts of Han-dynasty Confucianism, it was applied by other traditions to their sacred books. It is translated variously as book, classic, scripture, and sūtra.) Although Kong Qiu was commonly believed to have written or edited some of the five classics, his own statements (collected in the *Analects* [*Lunyu*]) and the writings of his closest followers were not yet admitted into the canon. Kong Qiu's name was implicated more directly in the second example of the Confucian system, the state-sponsored cult that erected temples in his honor throughout the empire and that provided monetary support for turning his ancestral home into a national shrine. Members of the literate elite visited such temples, paying formalized respect and enacting rituals in front of spirit tablets of the master and his disciples. The third example is the corpus of writing left by the scholar Dong Zhongshu (ca. 179–104 B.C.E.), who was instrumental in promoting Confucian ideas and books in official circles. Dong was recognized by the government as the leading spokesman for the scholarly elite. His theories provided an overarching cosmological framework for Kong Qiu's ideals, sometimes adding ideas unknown to Kong Qiu's time, sometimes making more explicit or providing a particular interpretation of what was already stated in Kong Qiu's work. Dong drew heavily on concepts of earlier thinkers—few of whom were self-avowed Confucians—to explain the workings of the cosmos. He used the concepts of yin and yang to explain how change followed a knowable pattern, and he elaborated on the role of the ruler as one who connected the realms of Heaven, Earth, and humans. The social hierarchy implicit in Kong Qiu's ideal world was coterminous, thought Dong, with a division of all natural relationships into a superior and inferior member. Dong's theories proved determinative for the political culture of Confucianism during the Han and later dynasties.

What in all of this, we need to ask, was Confucian? Or, more precisely, what kind of thing is the "Confucianism" in each of these examples? In the first, that of the five classics, "Confucianism" amounts to a set of books that were mostly written before Kong Qiu lived but that later tradition associates with his name. It is a curriculum instituted by the emperor for use in the most prestigious institutions of learning. In the second example, "Confucianism" is a complex ritual apparatus, an empire-wide network of shrines patronized by government authorities. It depends upon the ability of the government to maintain religious institutions throughout the empire and upon the willingness of state officials to engage regularly in worship. In the third example, the work of Dong Zhongshu, "Confucianism" is a conceptual scheme, a fluid synthesis of some of Kong Qiu's ideals and the various cosmologies popular well after Kong Qiu lived. Rather than being an updating of something universally acknowledged as Kong Qiu's philosophy, it is a conscious systematizing, under the symbol of Kong Qiu, of ideas current in the Han dynasty.

If even during the Han dynasty the term "Confucianism" covers so many different sorts of things—books, a ritual apparatus, a conceptual scheme—one might well wonder why we persist in using one single word to cover such a broad range of phenomena. Sorting out the pieces of that puzzle is now one of the most pressing tasks in the study of Chinese history, which is already beginning to replace the wooden division of the Chinese intellectual world into the three teachings—each in turn marked by phases called "proto-," "neo-," or "revival of"—with a more critical and nuanced understanding of how traditions are made and sustained. For our more limited purposes here, it is instructive to observe how the word "Confucianism" came to be applied to all of these things and more.[5] As a word, "Confucianism" is tied to the Latin name, "Confucius," which originated not with Chinese philosophers but with European missionaries in the sixteenth century. Committed to winning over the top echelons of Chinese society, Jesuits and other Catholic orders subscribed to the version of Chinese religious history supplied to them by the educated elite. The story they told was that their teaching began with Kong Qiu, who was referred to as Kongfuzi, rendered into Latin as "Confucius." It was elaborated by Mengzi (rendered as "Mencius") and Xunzi and was given official recognition—as if it had existed as the same entity, unmodified for several hundred years—under the Han dynasty. The teaching changed to the status of an unachieved metaphysical principle during the centuries that Buddhism was believed to have been dominant and was resuscitated—still basically unchanged—only with the teachings of Zhou Dunyi (1017–1073), Zhang Zai (1020), Cheng Hao (1032–1085), and Cheng Yi (1033–1107), and the commentaries authored by Zhu Xi (1130–1200). As a genealogy crucial to the self-definition of modern Confucianism, that myth of origins is both misleading and instructive. It lumps together heterogeneous ideas, books that predate Kong Qiu, and a state-supported cult under the same heading. It denies the diversity of names by which members of a supposedly unitary tradition chose to call themselves, including *ru* (the early meaning of which remains disputed, usually translated as "scholars" or "Confucians"), *daoxue* (study of the Way), *lixue* (study of principle), and *xinxue* (study of the mind). It ignores the long history of contention over interpreting Kong Qiu and overlooks the debt owed by later thinkers like Zhu Xi and Wang Yangming (1472–1529) to Buddhist notions of the mind and practices of meditation and to Daoist ideas of change. And it passes over in silence the role played by non-Chinese regimes in making Confucianism into an orthodoxy, as in the year 1315, when the Mongol government required that the writings of Kong Qiu and his early followers, redacted and interpreted through the commentaries of Zhu Xi, become the basis for the national civil service examination. At the same time, Confucianism's story about itself reveals much. It names the figures, books, and slogans of the past that recent Confucians have found most inspiring. As a string of ideals, it illuminates what its proponents wish it to be. As a lineage, it imagines a line of descent kept pure from the traditions of Daoism and Buddhism. The construction of the latter two teachings involves a similar process. Their histories, as will be seen below, do not simply move from the past to the present; they are also projected backward from specific presents to significant pasts.

Daoism

Most Daoists have argued that the meaningful past is the period that preceded, chronologically and metaphysically, the past in which the legendary sages of Confucianism lived. In the Daoist golden age the empire had not yet been reclaimed out of chaos. Society lacked distinctions based on class, and human beings lived happily in what resembled primitive, small-scale agricultural collectives. The lines between different nation-states, between different occupations, even between humans and animals were not clearly drawn. The world knew nothing of the Confucian state, which depended on the carving up of an undifferentiated whole into social ranks, the imposition of artificially ritualized modes of behavior, and a campaign for conservative values like loyalty, obeying one's parents, and moderation. Historically speaking, this Daoist vision was first articulated shortly after the time of Kong Qiu, and we should probably regard the Daoist nostalgia for a simpler, untrammeled time as roughly contemporary with the development of a Confucian view of origins. In Daoist mythology whenever a wise man encounters a representative of Confucianism, be it Kong Qiu himself or an envoy seeking advice for an emperor, the hermit escapes to a world untainted by civilization.

For Daoists the philosophical equivalent to the pre-imperial primordium is a state of chaotic wholeness, sometimes called *hundun,* roughly translated as "chaos." In that state, imagined as an uncarved block or as the beginning of life in the womb, nothing is lacking. Everything exists, everything is possible: before a stone is carved there is no limit to the designs that may be cut, and before the fetus develops the embryo can, in an organic worldview, develop into male or female. There is not yet any division into parts, any name to distinguish one thing from another. Prior to birth there is no distinction, from the Daoist standpoint, between life and death. Once birth happens—once the stone is cut—however, the world descends into a state of imperfection. Rather than a mythological sin on the part of the first human beings or an ontological separation of God from humanity, the Daoist version of the Fall involves division into parts, the assigning of names, and the leveling of judgments injurious to life. *The Classic on the Way and Its Power* (*Dao de jing*) describes how the original whole, the *dao* (here meaning the "Way" above all other ways), was broken up: "The Dao gave birth to the One, the One gave birth to the Two, the Two gave birth to the Three, and the Three gave birth to the Ten Thousand Things."[6] That decline-through-differentiation also offers the model for regaining wholeness. The spirit may be restored by reversing the process of aging, by reverting from multiplicity to the One. By understanding the road or path (the same word, dao, in another sense) that the great Dao followed in its decline, one can return to the root and endure forever.

Practitioners and scholars alike have often succumbed to the beauty and power of the language of Daoism and proclaimed another version of the Daoist myth of origins. Many people seem to move from a description of the Daoist faith-stance (the Dao embraces all things) to active Daoist proselytization masquerading as historical description (Daoism embraces all forms of Chinese religion). As with the term "Confucianism," it is important to consider not just what the term "Daoism" covers, but also where it comes from, who uses it, and what words Daoists have used over the years to refer to themselves.

The most prominent early writings associated with Daoism are two texts, *The Classic on the Way and Its Power,* attributed to a mythological figure named Lao Dan or Laozi who is presumed to have lived during the sixth century B.C.E., and the *Zhuangzi,* named for its putative author, Zhuang Zhou or Zhuangzi (ca. 370–301 B.C.E.). The books are quite different in language and style. *The Classic on the Way and Its Power* is composed largely of short bits of aphoristic verse, leaving its interpretation and application radically indeterminate. Perhaps because of that openness of meaning, the book has been translated into Western languages more often than any other Chinese text. It has been read as a utopian tract advocating a primitive society as well as a compendium of advice for a fierce, engaged ruler. Its author has been described as a relativist, skeptic, or poet by some, and by others as a committed rationalist who believes in the ability of words to name a reality that exists independently of them. The *Zhuangzi* is a much longer work composed of relatively discrete chapters written largely in prose, each of which brings sustained attention to a particular set of topics. Some portions have been compared to Wittgenstein's *Philosophical Investigations.* Others develop a story at some length or invoke mythological figures from the past. The *Zhuangzi* refers to Laozi by name and quotes some passages from the *Classic on the Way and Its Power,* but the text as we know it includes contributions written over a long span of time. Textual analysis reveals at least four layers, probably more, that may be attributed to different authors and different times, with interests as varied as logic, primitivism, syncretism, and egotism. The word "Daoism" in English (corresponding to Daojia, "the School [or Philosophy] of the Dao") is often used to refer to these and other books or to a free-floating outlook on life inspired by but in no way limited to them.

"Daoism" is also invoked as the name for religious movements that began to develop in the late second century C.E.; Chinese usage typically refers to their texts as Daojiao, "Teachings of the Dao" or "Religion of the Dao." One of those movements, called the Way of the Celestial Masters (Tianshi dao), possessed mythology and rituals and established a set of social institutions that would be maintained by all later Daoist groups. The Way of the Celestial Masters claims its origin in a revelation dispensed in the year 142 by the Most High Lord Lao (Taishang Laojun), a deified form of Laozi, to a man named Zhang Daoling. Laozi explained teachings to Zhang and bestowed on him the title of "Celestial Master" (Tianshi), indicating his exalted position in a system of ranking that placed those who had achieved immortality at the top and humans who were working their way toward that goal at the bottom. Zhang was active in the part of western China now corresponding to the province of Sichuan, and his descendants continued to build a local infrastructure. The movement divided itself into a number of parishes, to which each member-household was required to pay an annual tax of five pecks of rice—hence the other common name for the movement in its early years, the Way of the Five Pecks of Rice (Wudoumi dao). The administrative structure and some of the political functions of the organization are thought to have been modeled in part on secular government administration. After the Wei dynasty was founded in 220, the government extended recognition to the Way of the Celestial Masters, giving official approval to the form of local social administration it had developed and claiming at the same time that the new emperor's right to rule was guaranteed by the authority of the current Celestial Master.

Several continuing traits are apparent in the first few centuries of the Way of the Celestial Masters. The movement represented itself as having begun with divine-human contact: a god reveals a teaching and bestows a rank on a person. Later Daoist groups received revelations from successively more exalted deities. Even before receiving official recognition, the movement was never divorced from politics. Later Daoist groups too followed that general pattern, sometimes in the form of millenarian movements promising to replace the secular government, sometimes in the form of an established church providing services complementary to those of the state. The local communities of the Way of the Celestial Masters were formed around priests who possessed secret knowledge and held rank in the divine-human bureaucracy. Knowledge and position were interdependent: knowledge of the proper ritual forms and the authority to petition the gods and spirits were guaranteed by the priest's position in the hierarchy, while his rank was confirmed to his community by his expertise in a ritual repertoire. Nearly all types of rituals performed by Daoist masters through the ages are evident in the early years of the Way of the Celestial Masters. Surviving sources describe the curing of illness, often through confession; the exorcism of malevolent spirits; rites of passage in the life of the individual; and the holding of regular communal feasts.

While earlier generations (both Chinese bibliographers and scholars of Chinese religion) have emphasized the distinction between the allegedly pristine philosophy of the "School of the Dao" and the corrupt religion of the "Teachings of the Dao," recent scholarship instead emphasizes the complex continuities between them. Many selections in this anthology focus on the beginnings of organized Daoism and the liturgical and social history of Daoist movements through the fifth century. The history of Daoism can be read, in part, as a succession of revelations, each of which includes but remains superior to the earlier ones. In South China around the year 320 the author Ge Hong wrote *He Who Embraces Simplicity* (*Baopuzi*), which outlines different methods for achieving elevation to that realm of the immortals known as "Great Purity" (Taiqing). Most methods explain how, after the observance of moral codes and rules of abstinence, one needs to gather precious substances for use in complex chemical experiments. Followed properly, the experiments succeed in producing a sacred substance, "gold elixir" (*jindan*), the eating of which leads to immortality. In the second half of the fourth century new scriptures were revealed to a man named Yang Xi, who shared them with a family named Xu. Those texts give their possessors access to an even higher realm of Heaven, that of "Highest Clarity" (Shangqing). The scriptures contain legends about the level of gods residing in the Heaven of Highest Clarity. Imbued with a messianic spirit, the books foretell an apocalypse for which the wise should begin to prepare now. By gaining initiation into the textual tradition of Highest Clarity and following its program for cultivating immortality, adepts are assured of a high rank in the divine bureaucracy and can survive into the new age. The fifth century saw the canonization of a new set of texts, titled "Numinous Treasure" (Lingbao). Most of them are presented as sermons of a still higher level of deities, the Celestial Worthies (Tianzun) who are the most immediate personified manifestations of the Dao. The books instruct followers how to worship the gods supplicated in a wide variety of rituals. Called "retreats" (*zhai*, a word connoting both "fast" and "feast"), those rites are performed for the salvation of the dead, the bestowal of boons on the living, and the repentance of sins.

As noted in the discussion of the beginnings of the Way of the Celestial Masters,

Daoist and imperial interests often intersected. The founder of the Tang dynasty (618–907), Li Yuan (lived 566–635, reigned 618–626, known as Gaozu), for instance, claimed to be a descendant of Laozi's. At various points during the reign of the Li family during the Tang dynasty, prospective candidates for government service were tested for their knowledge of specific Daoist scriptures. Imperial authorities recognized and sometimes paid for ecclesiastical centers where Daoist priests were trained and ordained, and the surviving sources on Chinese history are filled with examples of state sponsorship of specific Daoist ceremonies and the activities of individual priests. Later governments continued to extend official support to the Daoist church, and vice-versa. Many accounts portray the twelfth century as a particularly innovative period: it saw the development of sects named "Supreme Unity" (Taiyi), "Perfect and Great Dao" (Zhenda dao), and "Complete Perfection" (Quanzhen). In the early part of the fifteenth century, the forty-third Celestial Master took charge of compiling and editing Daoist ritual texts, resulting in the promulgation of a Daoist canon that contemporary Daoists still consider authoritative.

Possessing a history of some two thousand years and appealing to people from all walks of life, Daoism appears to the modern student to be a complex and hardly unitary tradition. That diversity is important to keep in mind, especially in light of the claim made by different Daoist groups to maintain a form of the teaching that in its essence has remained the same over the millennia. The very notion of immortality is one way of grounding that claim. The greatest immortals, after all, are still alive. Having conquered death, they have achieved the original state of the uncarved block and are believed to reside in the heavens. The highest gods are personified forms of the Dao, the unchanging Way. They are concretized in the form of stars and other heavenly bodies and can manifest themselves to advanced Daoist practitioners following proper visualization exercises. The transcendents (*xianren,* often translated as "immortals") began life as humans and returned to the ideal embryonic condition through a variety of means. Some followed a regimen of gymnastics and observed a form of macrobiotic diet that simultaneously built up the pure elements and minimized the coarser ones. Others practiced the art of alchemy, assembling secret ingredients and using laboratory techniques to roll back time. Sometimes the elixir was prepared in real crucibles; sometimes the refining process was carried out eidetically by imagining the interior of the body to function like the test tubes and burners of the lab. Personalized rites of curing and communal feasts alike can be seen as small steps toward recovering the state of health and wholeness that obtains at the beginning (also the infinite ending) of time. Daoism has always stressed morality. Whether expressed through specific injunctions against stealing, lying, and taking life, through more abstract discussions of virtue, or through exemplary figures who transgress moral codes, ethics was an important element of Daoist practice. Nor should we forget the claim to continuity implied by the institution of priestly investiture. By possessing revealed texts and the secret registers listing the members of the divine hierarchy, the Daoist priest took his place in a structure that appeared to be unchanging.

Another way that Daoists have represented their tradition is by asserting that their activities are different from other religious practices. Daoism is constructed, in part, by projecting a non-Daoist tradition, picking out ideas and actions and assigning them a name that symbolizes "the other."[7] The most common others in the history of Daoism have been the rituals practiced by the less institutionalized, more poorly educated religious specialists at the local level and any phenomenon connected with China's other organized church, Buddhism. Whatever the very real congruences in belief and practice among Daoism, Buddhism, and popular practice, it has been essential to Daoists to assert a fundamental difference. In this perspective the Daoist gods differ in kind from the profane spirits of the popular tradition: the former partake of the pure and impersonal Dao, while the latter demand the sacrifice of meat and threaten their benighted worshippers with illness and other curses. With their hereditary office, complex rituals, and use of the classical Chinese language, modern Daoist masters view themselves as utterly distinct from exorcists and mediums, who utilize only the language of everyday speech and whose possession by spirits appears uncontrolled. Similarly, anti-Buddhist rhetoric (as well as anti-Daoist rhetoric from the Buddhist side) has been severe over the centuries, often resulting in the temporary suppression of books and statues and the purging of the priesthood. All of those attempts to enforce difference, however, must be viewed alongside the equally real overlap, sometimes identity, between Daoism and other traditions. Records compiled by the state detailing the official titles bestowed on gods prove that the gods of the popular tradition and the gods of Daoism often supported each other and coalesced or, at other times, competed in ways that the Daoist church could not control. Ethnographies about modern village life show how all the various religious personnel cooperate to allow for coexistence; in some celebrations they forge an arrangement that allows Daoist priests to officiate at the esoteric rituals performed in the interior of the temple, while mediums enter into trance among the crowds in the outer courtyard. In imperial times the highest echelons of the Daoist and Buddhist priesthoods were capable of viewing their roles as complementary to each other and as necessarily subservient to the state. The government mandated the establishment in each province of temples belonging to both religions; it exercised the right to accept or reject the definition of each religion's canon of sacred books; and it sponsored ceremonial debates between leading exponents of the two churches in which victory most often led to coexistence with, rather than the destruction of, the losing party.

Buddhism

The very name given to Buddhism offers important clues about the way that the tradition has come to be defined in China. Buddhism is often called Fojiao, literally meaning "the teaching (*jiao*) of the Buddha (Fo)." Buddhism thus appears to be a member of the same class as Confucianism and Daoism: the three teachings are Rujiao ("teaching of the scholars" or Confucianism), Daojiao ("teaching of the

Dao" or Daoism), and Fojiao ("teaching of the Buddha" or Buddhism). But there is an interesting difference here, one that requires close attention to language. As semantic units in Chinese, the words Ru and Dao work differently than does Fo. The word Ru refers to a group of people and the word Dao refers to a concept, but the word Fo does not make literal sense in Chinese. Instead it represents a sound, a word with no semantic value that in the ancient language was pronounced as "bud," like the beginning of the Sanskrit word "buddha."[8] The meaning of the Chinese term derives from the fact that it refers to a foreign sound. In Sanskrit the word "buddha" means "one who has achieved enlightenment," one who has "awakened" to the true nature of human existence. Rather than using any of the Chinese words that mean "enlightened one," Buddhists in China have chosen to use a foreign word to name their teaching, much as native speakers of English refer to the religion that began in India not as "the religion of the enlightened one," but rather as "Buddhism," often without knowing precisely what the word "Buddha" means. Referring to Buddhism in China as Fojiao involves the recognition that this teaching, unlike the other two, originated in a foreign land. Its strangeness, its non-native origin, its power are all bound up in its name.

Considered from another angle, the word buddha (*fo*) also accentuates the ways in which Buddhism in its Chinese context defines a distinctive attitude toward experience. Buddhas—enlightened ones—are unusual because they differ from other, unenlightened individuals and because of the truths to which they have awakened. Most people live in profound ignorance, which causes immense suffering. Buddhas, by contrast, see the true nature of reality. Such propositions, of course, were not advanced in a vacuum. They were articulated originally in the context of traditional Indian cosmology in the first several centuries B.C.E., and as Buddhism began to trickle haphazardly into China in the first centuries of the common era, Buddhist teachers were faced with a dilemma. To make their teachings about the Buddha understood to a non-Indian audience, they often began by explaining the understanding of human existence—the problem, as it were—to which Buddhism provided the answer. Those basic elements of the early Indian worldview are worth reviewing here. In that conception, all human beings are destined to be reborn in other forms, human and nonhuman, over vast stretches of space and time. While time in its most abstract sense does follow a pattern of decline, then renovation, followed by a new decline, and so on, still the process of reincarnation is without beginning or end. Life takes six forms: at the top are gods, demigods, and human beings, while animals, hungry ghosts, and hell beings occupy the lower rungs of the hierarchy. Like the gods of ancient Greece, the gods of Buddhism reside in the heavens and lead lives of immense worldly pleasure. Unlike their Greek counterparts, however, they are without exception mortal, and at the end of a very long life they are invariably reborn lower in the cosmic scale. Hungry ghosts wander in search of food and water yet are unable to eat or drink, and the denizens of the various hells suffer a battery of tortures, but they will all eventually die and be reborn again. The logic that determines where one will be reborn is the idea of *karma.* Strictly speaking the Sanskrit word karma means "deed" or "action." In its relevant sense here it means that every deed has a result: morally good acts lead to good consequences, and the commission of evil has a bad result. Applied to the life of the individual, the law of karma means that the circumstances an individual faces are the result of prior actions. Karma is the regulating idea of a wide range of good works and other Buddhist practices.

The wisdom to which buddhas awaken is to see that this cycle of existence (*saṃsāra* in Sanskrit, comprising birth, death, and rebirth) is marked by impermanence, unsatisfactoriness, and lack of a permanent self. It is impermanent because all things, whether physical objects, psychological states, or philosophical ideas, undergo change; they are brought into existence by preceding conditions at a particular point in time, and they eventually will become extinct. It is unsatisfactory in the sense that not only do sentient beings experience physical pain, they also face continual disappointment when the people and things they wish to maintain invariably change. The third characteristic of sentient existence, lack of a permanent self, has a long and complicated history of exegesis in Buddhism. In China the idea of "no-self" (Sanskrit: *anātman*) was often placed in creative tension with the concept of repeated rebirth. On the one hand, Buddhist teachers tried to convince their audience that human existence did not end simply with a funeral service or memorial to the ancestors, that humans were reborn in another bodily form and could thus be related not only to other human beings but to animals, ghosts, and other species among the six modes of rebirth. To support that argument for rebirth, it was helpful to draw on metaphors of continuity, like a flame passed from one candle to the next and a spirit that moves from one lifetime to the next. On the other hand, the truth of impermanence entailed the argument that no permanent ego could possibly underlie the process of rebirth. What migrated from one lifetime to the next were not eternal elements of personhood but rather temporary aspects of psychophysical life that might endure for a few lifetimes—or a few thousand—but would eventually cease to exist. The Buddha provided an analysis of the ills of human existence and a prescription for curing them. Those ills were caused by the tendency of sentient beings to grasp, to cling to evanescent things in the vain hope that they remain permanent. In this view, the very act of clinging contributes to the perpetuation of desires from one incarnation to the next. Grasping, then, is both a cause and a result of being committed to a permanent self.

The wisdom of buddhas is neither intellectual nor individualistic. It was always believed to be a soteriological knowledge that was expressed in the compassionate activity of teaching others how to achieve liberation from suffering. Traditional formulations of Buddhist practice describe a path to salvation that begins with the observance of morality. Lay followers pledged to abstain from the taking of life, stealing, lying, drinking intoxicating beverages, and engaging in sexual relations outside of marriage. Further injunctions applied to householders who could observe a more demanding life-style of purity, and the lives of monks and nuns were regulated in even greater detail. With morality as a basis, the ideal path also included the cultivation of pure states of mind through the practice of meditation and the achieving of wisdom rivaling that of a buddha.

The discussion so far has concerned the importance of the foreign component in the ideal of the buddha and the actual content to which buddhas are believed to awaken. It is also important to consider what kind of a religious figure a buddha is thought to be. We can distinguish two separate but related understandings of what a buddha is. In the first understanding the Buddha (represented in English with a capital B) was an unusual human born into a royal family in ancient India in the sixth or fifth century B.C.E. He renounced his birthright, followed established religious teachers, and then achieved enlightenment after striking out on his own. He gathered lay and monastic disciples around him and preached throughout the Indian subcontinent for almost fifty years, and he achieved final "extinction" (the root meaning of the Sanskrit word *nirvāṇa*) from the woes of existence. This unique being was called Gautama (family name) Siddhārtha (personal name) during his lifetime, and later tradition refers to him with a variety of names, including Śākyamuni (literally "Sage of the Śākya clan") and Tathāgata ("Thus-Come One"). Followers living after his death lack direct access to him because, as the word "extinction" implies, his release was permanent and complete. His influence can be felt, though, through his traces—through gods who encountered him and are still alive, through long-lived disciples, through the places he touched that can be visited by pilgrims, and through his physical remains and the shrines (*stūpa*) erected over them. In the second understanding a buddha (with a lowercase b) is a generic label for any enlightened being, of whom Śākyamuni was simply one among many. Other buddhas preceded Śākyamuni's appearance in the world, and others will follow him, notably Maitreya (Chinese: Mile), who is thought to reside now in a heavenly realm close to the surface of the Earth. Buddhas are also dispersed over space: they exist in all directions, and one in particular, Amitāyus (or Amitābha, Chinese: Amituo), presides over a land of happiness in the West. Related to this second genre of buddha is another kind of figure, a bodhisattva (literally "one who is intent on enlightenment," Chinese: *pusa*). Budhisattvas are found in most forms of Buddhism, but their role was particularly emphasized in the many traditions claiming the polemical title of Mahāyāna ("Greater Vehicle," in opposition to Hīnayāna, "Smaller Vehicle") that began to develop in the first century B.C.E. Technically speaking, bodhisattvas are not as advanced as buddhas on the path to enlightenment. Bodhisattvas particularly popular in China include Avalokiteśvara (Chinese: Guanyin, Guanshiyin, or Guanzizai), Bhaiṣajyaguru (Chinese: Yaoshiwang), Kṣitigarbha (Chinese: Dizang), Mañjuśrī (Wenshu), and Samantabhadra (Puxian). While buddhas appear to some followers as remote and all-powerful, bodhisattvas often serve as mediating figures whose compassionate involvement in the impurities of this world makes them more approachable. Like buddhas in the second sense of any enlightened being, they function both as models for followers to emulate and as saviors who intervene actively in the lives of their devotees.

In addition to the word "Buddhism" (Fojiao), Chinese Buddhists have represented the tradition by the formulation of the "three jewels" (Sanskrit: *triratna*, Chinese: *sanbao*). Coined in India, the three terms carried both a traditional sense as well as a more worldly reference that is clear in Chinese sources.[9] The first jewel is Buddha, the traditional meaning of which has been discussed above. In China the term refers not only to enlightened beings, but also to the materials through which buddhas are made present, including statues, the buildings that house statues, relics and their containers, and all the finances needed to build and sustain devotion to buddha images.

The second jewel is the dharma (Chinese: *fa*), meaning "truth" or "law." The dharma includes the doctrines taught by the Buddha and passed down in oral and written form, thought to be equivalent to the universal cosmic law. Many of the teachings are expressed in numerical form, like the three marks of existence (impermanence, unsatisfactoriness, and no-self, discussed above), the four noble truths (unsatisfactoriness, cause, cessation, path), and so on. As a literary tradition the dharma also comprises many different genres, the most important of which is called *sūtra* in Sanskrit. The Sanskrit word refers to the warp thread of a piece of cloth, the regulating or primary part of the doctrine (compare its Proto-Indo-European root, *syū, which appears in the English words suture, sew, and seam). The earliest Chinese translators of Buddhist Sanskrit texts chose a related loaded term to render the idea in Chinese: *jing*, which denotes the warp threads in the same manner as the Sanskrit, but which also has the virtue of being the generic name given to the classics of the Confucian and Taoist traditions. Sūtras usually begin with the words "Thus have I heard. Once, when the Buddha dwelled at. . . ." That phrase is attributed to the Buddha's closest disciple, Ānanda, who according to tradition was able to recite all of the Buddha's sermons from memory at the first convocation of monks held after the Buddha died. In its material sense the dharma referred to all media for the Buddha's law in China, including sermons and the platforms on which sermons were delivered, Buddhist rituals that included preaching, and the thousands of books—first handwritten scrolls, then booklets printed with wooden blocks—in which the truth was inscribed.

The third jewel is saṅgha (Chinese: *sengqie* or *zhong*), meaning "assembly." Some sources offer a broad interpretation of the term, which comprises the four sub-orders of monks, nuns, lay men, and lay women. Other sources use the term in a stricter sense to include only monks and nuns, that is, those who have left home, renounced family life, accepted vows of celibacy, and undertaken other austerities to devote themselves full-time to the practice of religion. The differences and interdependencies between householders and monastics were rarely absent in any Buddhist civilization. In China those differences found expression in both the spiritual powers popularly attributed to monks and nuns and the hostility sometimes voiced toward their way of life, which seemed to threaten the core values of the Chinese family system. The interdependent nature of the relationship between lay people and the professionally religious is seen in such phenomena as the use of kinship terminology—an attempt to re-create family—among monks and nuns and the collaboration between lay donors and monastic officiants in a wide range of rituals designed to bring comfort to the ancestors. "Saṅgha" in China also referred to all of the phenomena considered to belong to the Buddhist establishment. Everything and everyone needed to sustain monastic life, in a very concrete sense, was included: the living quarters of monks; the lands deeded to temples for occupancy and profit; the tenant families and slaves who worked on the farm land and served the saṅgha; and even the animals attached to the monastery farms.

Standard treatments of the history of Chinese Buddhism tend to emphasize the place of Buddhism in Chinese dynastic history, the translation of Buddhist texts, and the development of schools or sects within Buddhism. While these research agenda are important for our understanding of Chinese Buddhism, many of the contributors to this anthology have chosen to ask rather different questions, and it is worthwhile explaining why.

Many overviews of Chinese Buddhist history are organized by the template of Chinese dynasties. In this perspective, Buddhism began to enter China as a religion of non-Chinese merchants in the later years of the Han dynasty. It was during the following four centuries of disunion, including division between non-Chinese rulers in the north and native ("Han") governments in the south as well as warfare and social upheaval, that Buddhism allegedly took root in China. Magic and meditation ostensibly appealed to the "barbarian" rulers in the north, while the dominant style of religion pursued by the southerners was philosophical. During the period of disunion, the general consensus suggests, Buddhist translators wrestled with the problem of conveying Indian ideas in a language their Chinese audience could understand; after many false starts Chinese philosophers were finally able to comprehend common Buddhist terms as well as the complexities of the doctrine of emptiness. During the Tang dynasty Buddhism was finally "Sinicized" or made fully Chinese. Most textbooks treat the Tang dynasty as the apogee or mature period of Buddhism in China. The Tang saw unprecedented numbers of ordinations into the ranks of the Buddhist order; the flourishing of new, allegedly "Chinese" schools of thought; and lavish support from the state. After the Tang, it is thought, Buddhism entered into a thousand-year period of decline. Some monks were able to break free of tradition and write innovative commentaries on older texts or reshape received liturgies, some patrons managed to build significant temples or sponsor the printing of the Buddhist canon on a large scale, and the occasional highly placed monk found a way to purge debased monks and nuns from the ranks of the saṅgha and revive moral vigor, but on the whole the stretch of dynasties after the Tang is treated as a long slide into intellectual, ethical, and material poverty. Stated in this caricatured fashion, the shortcomings of this approach are not hard to discern. This approach accentuates those episodes in the history of Buddhism that intersect with important moments in a political chronology, the validity of which scholars in Chinese studies increasingly doubt. The problem is not so much that the older, dynastic-driven history of China is wrong as that it is limited and one-sided. While traditional history tends to have been written from the top down, more recent attempts argue from the bottom up. Historians in the past forty years have begun to discern otherwise unseen patterns in the development of Chinese economy, society, and political institutions. Their conclusions, which increasingly take Buddhism into account, suggest that cycles of rise and fall in population shifts, economy, family fortunes, and the like often have little to do with dynastic history—the implication being that the history of Buddhism and other Chinese traditions can no longer be pegged simply to a particular dynasty. Similarly, closer scrutiny of the documents and a greater appreciation of their biases and gaps have shown how little we know of what really transpired in the process of the control of Buddhism by the state. The Buddhist church was always, it seems, dependent on the support of the landowning classes in medieval China. And it appears that the condition of Buddhist institutions was tied closely to the occasional, decentralized support of the lower classes, which is even harder to document than support by the gentry. The very notion of rise and fall is a teleological, often theological, one, and it has often been linked to an obsession with one particular criterion—accurate translation of texts, or correct understanding of doctrine—to the exclusion of all others.

The translation of Buddhist texts from Sanskrit and other Indic and Central Asian languages into Chinese constitutes a large area of study. Although written largely in classical Chinese in the context of a premodern civilization in which relatively few people could read, Buddhist sūtras were known far and wide in China. The seemingly magical spell (Sanskrit; *dhāraṇī*) from the *Heart Sūtra* was known by many; stories from *Lotus Sūtra* were painted on the walls of popular temples; religious preachers, popular storytellers, and low-class dramatists alike drew on the rich trove of mythology provided by Buddhist narrative. Scholars of Buddhism have tended to focus on the chronology and accuracy of translation. Since so many texts were translated (one eighth-century count of the extant number of canonical works is 1,124),[10] and the languages of Sanskrit and literary Chinese are so distant, the results of that study are foundational to the field. To understand the history of Chinese Buddhism it is indispensable to know what texts were available when, how they were translated and by whom, how they were inscribed on paper and stone, approved or not approved, disseminated, and argued about. On the other hand, within Buddhist studies scholars have only recently begun to view the act of translation as a conflict-ridden process of negotiation, the results of which were Chinese texts whose meanings were never closed. Older studies, for instance, sometimes distinguish between three different translation styles. One emerged with the earliest known translators, a Parthian given the Chinese name An Shigao (fl. 148–170) and an Indoscythian named Lokakṣema (fl. 167–186), who themselves knew little classical Chinese but who worked with teams of Chinese assistants who peppered the resulting translations with words drawn from the spoken language. The second style was defined by the Kuchean translator Kumārajīva (350–409), who retained some elements of the vernacular in a basic framework of literary Chinese that was more polished, consistent, and acceptable to contemporary Chinese tastes. It is that style—which some have dubbed a "church" language of Buddhist Chinese, by analogy with the cultural history of medieval Latin—that proved most enduring and popular. The third style is exemplified in the work of Xuanzang (ca. 596–664), the seventh-century Chinese monk, philosopher, pilgrim, and translator. Xuanzang was one of the few translators who not only spoke Chinese and knew Sanskrit, but also knew the Chinese literary language well, and it is hardly accidental that Chinese Buddhists and modern scholars alike regard his translations as the most accurate and technically precise. At the same time, there is an irony in Xuanzang's situation that forces us to view the process of translation in a wider context. Xuanzang's is probably the most popular Buddhist image in Chinese folklore: he is the hero of the story *Journey to the West* (*Xiyou ji*), known to all classes as the most prolific translator in Chinese history and as an indefatigable, sometimes overly serious and literal, pilgrim who embarked on a sacred mission to recover original texts from India. Though the mythological character is well known, the surviving writings of the seventh-century translator are not. They are, in fact, rarely read, because their grammar and style smack more of Sanskrit than of literary Chinese. What mattered to Chinese audiences—both the larger audience for the novels and dramas about the pilgrim and the much smaller one capable of reaching his translations—was that the Chinese texts were based on a valid foreign original, made even more authentic by Xuanzang's personal experiences in the Buddhist homeland.

The projection of categories derived from European, American, and modern Japanese religious experience onto the quite different world of traditional Chinese religion is perhaps most apparent in the tendency of traditional scholarship to treat Chinese Buddhism primarily as a matter of distinct schools or sects. Monks and other literati did indeed make sense of their history by classifying the overwhelming number of texts and teachings they inherited under distinctive trends, and some members of the Buddhist elite claimed allegiance to certain ideals at the expense of others. But any clear-cut criterion of belief, like the Nicene Creed, or a declaration of faith like Martin Luther's, is lacking in the history of Chinese Buddhism. It may have been only in the fourteenth century that there developed any social reality even approximating Ernst Troeltsch's definition of a sect as a voluntary religious association that people consciously choose to join and that excludes participation in other religious activities—and even then, the type of sect that developed, the Teaching of the White Lotus (Bailian jiao), was only tenuously connected to the "schools" of Chinese Buddhist thought on which scholars usually focus. Trends of thought and clearly identified philosophical issues are part of Chinese Buddhist history from the early centuries, and in the sixth through eighth centuries some figures identified themselves as concerned with one particular scripture: authors in the Tiantai school (named after Mount Tiantai) focused on the *Lotus Sūtra,* and figures of the Huayan school emphasized the comprehensive nature of the *Huayan* ("Flower Garland") *Sūtra.* But the founders of these schools—identified as such only by later generations—and their followers never stopped reading broadly in a wide range of Buddhist texts. Certain emphases also developed in Chinese Buddhist practice and Buddhology, foremost among them the invocation of the name of Amitāyus Buddha (*nianfo,* "keeping the Buddha in mind"), whose powers to assist those who chanted his name and whose resplendent paradise are described at length in scriptures affiliated with the Pure Land (Jingtu) school. In China, however—in contrast to late medieval Japan—dedication to Amitāyus Buddha was rarely viewed as a substitute for other forms of practice. Esoteric forms of Buddhism, characterized by restricting the circulation of knowledge about rituals to a small circle of initiates who perform rituals for those who lack the expertise, were also a strong force in Chinese Buddhism. But here too, even as they performed rites on behalf of individuals or to benefit the state, the monks of the Zhenyan (Sanskrit: Mantra, "True Word") school participated in other forms of Buddhist thought and practice as well. Even the school of Chan ("Meditation"), known in Japanese as Zen, which claimed to be founded on an unbroken transmission from Sākyamuni through twenty-eight Indian disciples to the first Chinese disciple in the late fifth century, was far less exclusive than its rhetoric seems to allow. Claims about transmission, the naming of founders, and the identification of crucial figures in the drama of Chan history were always executed retroactively. The tradition, which claimed its own content to be a non-content, was not so much handed down from past to present as it was imagined in the present, a willful projection into the future, against the reality of a heterogeneous past. As a"school" in the sense of an establishment for teaching and learning with monastery buildings, daily schedule, and administrative structure, Chan came into existence only in the twelfth and thirteenth centuries, and even then the social institution identified as "Chan" was nearly identical to institutions affiliated with other schools.

The Problem of Popular Religion

The brief history of the three teachings offered above provides, it is hoped, a general idea of what they are and how their proponents have come to claim for them the status of a tradition. It is also important to consider what is not named in the formulation of the three teachings. To define Chinese religion primarily in terms of the three traditions is to exclude from serious consideration the ideas and practices that do not fit easily under any of the three labels. Such common rituals as offering incense to the ancestors, conducting funerals, exorcising ghosts, and consulting fortunetellers; belief in the patterned interaction between light and dark forces or in the ruler's influence on the natural world; the tendency to construe gods as government officials; the preference for balancing tranquility and movement—all belong as much to none of the three traditions as they do to one or three.

The focus on the three teachings is another way of privileging precisely the varieties of Chinese religious life that have been maintained largely through the support of literate and often powerful representatives. The debate over the unity of the three teachings, even when it is resolved in favor of toleration or harmony—a move toward the one rather than the three—drowns out voices that talk about Chinese religion as neither one nor three. Another problem with the model of the three teachings is that it equalizes what are in fact three radically incommensurable things. Confucianism often functioned as a political ideology and a system of values; Daoism has been compared, inconsistently, to both an outlook on life and a system of gods and magic; and Buddhism offered, according to some analysts, a proper soteriology, an array of techniques and deities enabling one to achieve salvation in the other world. Calling all three traditions by the same unproblematic term, "teaching," perpetuates confusion about how the realms of life that we tend to take for granted (like politics, ethics, ritual, religion) were in fact configured differently in traditional China.

Another way of studying Chinese religion is to focus on those aspects of religious life that are shared by most people, regardless of their affiliation, or lack of affiliation with the three teachings. Such forms of popular religion as those named above (offering incense, conducting funerals, and so on) are important to address, although the category of "popular religion" entails its own set of problems.

We can begin by distinguishing two senses of the term "popular religion." The first refers to the forms of religion practiced by almost all Chinese people, regardless of social and economic standing, level of literacy, region, or explicit religious identification. Popular religion in this first sense is the religion shared by people in general, across all social boundaries. Three examples, all of which can be dated as early as the first century of the common era, help us gain some understanding of what counts as popular religion in the first sense. The first example is a typical Chinese funeral and memorial service. Following the death of a family member and the unsuccessful attempt to reclaim his or her spirit, the corpse is prepared for burial. Family members are invited for the first stage of mourning, with higher-ranking families entitled to invite more distant relatives. Rituals of wailing and the wearing of coarse, undyed cloth are practiced in the home of the deceased. After some days the coffin is carried in a procession to the grave. After burial the attention of the living shifts toward caring for the spirit of the dead. In later segments of the funerary rites the spirit is spatially fixed—installed—in a rectangular wooden tablet, kept at first in the home and perhaps later in a clan hall. The family continues to come together as a corporate group on behalf of the deceased; they say prayers and send sustenance, in the form of food, mock money, and documents addressed to the gods who oversee the realm of the dead. The second example of popular or common religion is the New Year's festival, which marks a passage not just in the life of the individual and the family, but in the yearly cycle of the cosmos. As in most civilizations, most festivals in China follow a lunar calendar, which is divided into twelve numbered months of thirty days apiece, divided in half at the full moon (fifteenth night) and new moon (thirtieth night); every several years an additional (or intercalary) month is added to synchronize the passage of time in lunar and solar cycles. Families typically begin to celebrate the New Year's festival ten or so days before the end of the twelfth month. On the twenty-third day, family members dispatch the God of the Hearth (Zaojun), who watches over all that transpires in the home from his throne in the kitchen, to report to the highest god of Heaven, the Jade Emperor (Yuhuang dadi). For the last day or two before the end of the year, the doors to the house are sealed and people worship in front of the images of the various gods kept in the house and the ancestor tablets. After a lavish meal rife with the symbolism of wholeness, longevity, and good fortune, each junior member of the family prostrates himself and herself before the head of the family and his wife. The next day, the first day of the first month, the doors are opened and the family enjoys a vacation of resting and visiting with friends. The New Year season concludes on the fifteenth night (the full moon of the first month, typically marked by a lantern celebration.

The third example of popular religion is the ritual of consulting a spirit medium in the home or in a small temple. Clients request the help of mediums (sometimes called "shamans" in Western-language scholarship; in Chinese they are known by many different terms) to solve problems like sickness in the family, nightmares, possession by a ghost or errant spirit, or some other misfortune. During the séance the medium usually enters a trance and incarnates a tutelary deity. The divinity speaks through the medium, sometimes in an altered but comprehensible voice, sometimes in sounds, through movements, or by writing characters in sand that require deciphering by the medium's manager or interpreter. The deity often identifies the problem and prescribes one among a wide range of possible cures. For an illness a particular herbal medicine or offering to a particular spirit may be recommended, while for more serious cases the deity himself, as dramatized in the person of the medium, does battle with the demon causing the difficulty. The entire drama unfolds in front of an audience composed of family members and nearby residents of the community. Mediums themselves often come from marginal groups (unmarried older women, youths prone to sickness), yet the deities who speak through them are typically part of mainstream religion, and their message tends to affirm rather than question traditional morality.

Some sense of what is at stake in defining "popular religion" in this manner can be gained by considering when, where, and by whom these three different examples are performed. Funerals and memorial services are carried out by most families, even poor ones; they take place in homes, cemeteries, and halls belonging to kinship corporations; and they follow two schedules, one linked to the death date of particular members (every seven days after death, 100 days after death, etc.) and one linked to the passage of nonindividualized calendar time (once per year). From a sociological perspective, the institutions active in the rite are the family, a complex organization stretching back many generations to a common male ancestor, and secondarily the community, which is to some extent protected from the baleful influences of death. The family too is the primary group involved in the New Year's celebration, although there is some validity in attributing a trans-social dimension to the festival in that a cosmic passage is marked by the occasion. Other social spheres are evident in the consultation of a medium; although it is cured through a social drama, sickness is also individuating; and some mediumistic rituals involve the members of a cult dedicated to the particular deity, membership being determined by personal choice.

These answers are significant for the contrast they suggest between traditional Chinese popular religion and the forms of religion characteristic of modern or secularized societies, in which religion is identified largely with doctrine, belief about god, and a large, clearly discernible church. None of the examples of Chinese popular religion is defined primarily by beliefs that necessarily exclude others. People take part in funerals without any necessary commitment to the existence of particular spirits, and belief in the reality of any particular tutelary deity does not preclude worship of other gods. Nor are these forms of religion marked by rigidly drawn lines of affiliation; in brief, there are families, temples, and shrines, but no church. Even the "community" supporting the temple dedicated to a local god is shifting, depending on those who choose to offer incense or make other offerings there on a monthly basis. There are specialists involved in these examples of Chinese popular religion, but their sacerdotal jobs are usually not full-time and seldom involve the theorizing about a higher calling typical of organized religion. Rather, their forte is considered to be knowledge or abilities of a technical sort. Local temples are administered by a standing committee, but the chairmanship of the committee usually rotates among the heads of the dominant families in the particular locale.

Like other categories, "popular religion" in the sense of shared religion obscures as much as it clarifies. Chosen for its difference from the unspoken reality of the academic interpreter (religion in modern Europe and America), popular religion as a category functions more as a contrastive notion than as a constitutive one; it tells us what much of Chinese religion is not like, rather than spelling out a positive content. It is too broad a category to be of much help to detailed understanding—which indeed is why many scholars in the field avoid the term, preferring to deal with more discrete and meaningful units like family religion, mortuary ritual, seasonal festivals, divination, curing, and mythology. "Popular religion" in the sense of common religion also hides potentially significant variation: witness the number of times words like "typical," "standard," "traditional," "often," and "usually" recur in the preceding paragraphs, without specifying particular people, times, and places, or naming particular understandings of orthodoxy. In addition to being static and timeless, the category prejudices the case against seeing popular religion as a conflict-ridden attempt to impose one particular standard on contending groups. The presence of non-Han peoples in China suggests that we view China not as a unitary Han culture peppered with "minorities," but as a complex region in which a diversity of cultures are interacting. To place all of them under the heading of "popular religion" is to obscure a fascinating conflict of cultures.

We may expect a similar mix of insight and erasure in the second sense of "popular religion," which refers to the religion of the lower classes as opposed to that of the elite. The bifurcation of society into two tiers is hardly a new idea. It began with some of the earliest Chinese theorists of religion. Xunzi, for instance, discusses the emotional, social, and cosmic benefits of carrying out memorial rites. In his opinion, mortuary ritual allows people to balance sadness and longing and to express grief, and it restores the natural order to the world. Different social classes, writes Xunzi, interpret sacrifices differently: "Among gentlemen [*junzi*], they are taken as the way of humans; among common people [*baixing*], they are taken as matters involving ghosts."[11] For Xunzi, "gentlemen" are those who have achieved nobility because of their virtue, not their birth; they consciously dedicate themselves to following and thinking about a course of action explicitly identified as moral. The common people, by contrast, are not so much amoral or immoral as they are unreflective. Without making a conscious decision, they believe that in the rites addressed to gods or the spirits of the dead, the objects of the sacrifice—the spirits themselves—actually exist. The true member of the upper class, however, adopts something like the attitude of the secular social theorist: bracketing the existence of spirits, what is important about death ritual is the effect it has on society. Both classes engage in the same activity, but they have radically different interpretations of it.

Dividing what is clearly too broad a category (Chinese religion or ritual) into two discrete classes (elite and folk) is not without advantages. It is a helpful pedagogical tool for throwing into question some of the egalitarian presuppositions frequently encountered in introductory courses on religion: that, for instance, everyone's religious options are or should be the same, or that other people's religious life can be understood (or tried out) without reference to social status. Treating Chinese religion as fundamentally affected by social position also helps scholars to focus on differences in styles of religious practice and interpretation. One way to formulate this view is to say that while all inhabitants of a certain community might take part in a religious procession, their style–both their pattern of practice and their understanding of their actions—will differ according to social position. Well-educated elites tend to view gods in abstract, impersonal terms and to demonstrate restrained respect, but the uneducated tend to view gods as concrete, personal beings before whom fear is appropriate.

In the social sciences and humanities in general there has been a clear move in the past forty years away from studies of the elite, and scholarship in Chinese religion is beginning to catch up with that trend. More and more studies focus on the religion of the lower classes and on the problems involved in studying the culture of the illiterati in a complex civilization. Much recent scholarship reflects a concern not only with the "folk" as opposed to the "elite," but with how to integrate our knowledge of those two strata and how our understanding of Chinese religion, determined unreflectively for many years by accepting an elite viewpoint, has begun to change. In all of this, questions of social class (Who participates? Who believes?) and questions of audience (Who writes or performs? For what kind of people?) are paramount.

At the same time, treating "popular religion" as the religion of the folk can easily perpetuate confusion. Some modern Chinese intellectuals, for instance, are committed to an agenda of modernizing and reviving Chinese spiritual life in a way that both accords with Western secularism, and does not reject all of traditional Chinese religion. The prominent twentieth-century Confucian and interpreter of Chinese culture Wing-tsit Chan, for instance, distinguishes between "the level of the masses" and "the level of the enlightened." The masses worship idols, objects of nature, and nearly any deity, while the enlightened confine their worship to Heaven, ancestors, moral exemplars, and historical persons. The former believe in heavens and hells and indulge in astrology and dream interpretation, but the latter "are seldom contaminated by these diseases."[12] For authors like Chan, both those who lived during the upheavals of the last century in China and those in Chinese diaspora communities, Chinese intellectuals still bear the responsibility to lead their civilization away from superstition and toward enlightenment. In that worldview there is no doubt where the religion of the masses belongs. From that position it can be a short step—one frequently taken by scholars of Chinese religion—to treating Chinese popular religion in a dismissive spirit. Modern anthologies of Chinese tradition can still be found that describe Chinese popular religion as "grosser forms of superstition," capable only of "facile syncretism" and resulting in "a rather shapeless tradition."

Kinship and Bureaucracy

It is often said that Chinese civilization has been fundamentally shaped by two enduring structures, the Chinese family system and the Chinese form of bureaucracy. Given the embeddedness of religion in Chinese social life, it would indeed be surprising if Chinese religion were devoid of such regulating concepts. The discussion below is not confined to delineating what might be considered the "hard" social structures of the family and the state, the effects of which might be seen in the "softer" realms of religion and values. The reach of kinship and bureaucracy is too great, their reproduction and representation far richer than could be conveyed by treating them as simple, given realities. Instead we will explain them also as metaphors and strategies.

Early Christian missionaries to China were fascinated with the religious aspects of the Chinese kinship system, which they dubbed "ancestor worship." Recently anthropologists have changed the wording to "the cult of the dead" because the concept of worship implies a supernatural or transcendent object of veneration, which the ancestors clearly are not. The newer term, however, is not much better, because "the dead" are hardly lifeless. As one modern observer remarks, the ancestral cult "is not primarily a matter of belief. . . . The cult of ancestors is more nearly a matter of plain everyday behavior. . . . No question of belief ever arises. The ancestors . . . literally live among their descendants, not only biologically, but also socially and psychologically."[13] The significance of the ancestors is partly explained by the structure of the traditional Chinese family: in marriages women are sent to other surname groups (exogamy); newly married couples tend to live with the husband's family (virilocality); and descent—deciding to which family one ultimately belongs—is traced back in time through the husband's male ancestors (patrilineage). A family in the normative sense includes many generations, past, present, and future, all of whom trace their ancestry through their father (if male) or their husband's father (if female) to an originating male ancestor. For young men the ideal is to grow up "under the ancestors' shadow" (in Hsu's felicitous phrase), by bringing in a wife from another family, begetting sons and growing prosperous, showering honor on the ancestors through material success, cooperating with brothers in sharing family property, and receiving respect during life and veneration after death from succeeding generations. For young women the avowed goal is to marry into a prosperous family with a kind mother-in-law, give birth to sons who will perpetuate the family line, depend upon one's children for immediate emotional support, and reap the benefits of old age as the wife of the primary man of the household.

Early philosophers assigned a specific term to the value of upholding the ideal family: they call it *xiao,* usually translated as "filial piety" or "filiality." The written character is composed of the graph for "elder" placed above the graph for "son," an apt visual reminder of the interdependence of the generations and the subordination of sons. If the system works well, then the younger generations support the senior ones, and the ancestors bestow fortune, longevity, and the birth of sons upon the living. As each son fulfills his duty, he progresses up the family scale, eventually assuming his status as revered ancestor. The attitude toward the dead (or rather the significant and, it is hoped, benevolent dead—one's ancestors) is simply a continuation of one's attitude toward one's parents while they were living. In all cases, the theory goes, one treats them with respect and veneration by fulfilling their personal wishes and acting according to the dictates of ritual tradition.

Like any significant social category, kinship in China is not without tension and self-contradiction. One already alluded to is gender: personhood as a function of the family system is different for men and women. Sons are typically born into their lineage and hope to remain under the same roof from childhood into old age and ancestorhood. By contrast, daughters are brought up by a family that is not ultimately theirs; at marriage they move into a new home; as young brides without children they are not yet inalienable members of their husband's lineage; and even after they have children they may still have serious conflicts with the de facto head of the household, their husband's mother. Women may gain more security from their living children than from the prospect of being a venerated ancestor. In the afterlife, in fact, they are punished for having polluted the natural world with the blood of parturition; the same virtue that the kinship system requires of them as producers of sons it also defines as a sin. There is also in the ideal of filiality a thinly veiled pretense to universality and equal access that also serves to rationalize the *status inaequalis.* Lavish funerals and the withdrawal from employment by the chief mourner for three years following his parents' death are the ideal. In the Confucian tradition such examples of conspicuous expenditure are interpreted as expressions of the highest devotion, rather than as a waste of resources and blatant unproductivity in which only the leisure class is free to indulge. And the ideals of respect of younger generations for older ones and cooperation among brothers often conflict with reality.

Many aspects of Chinese religion are informed by the metaphor of kinship. The kinship system is significant not only for the path of security it defines but also because of the religious discomfort attributed to all those who fall short of the ideal. It can be argued that the vagaries of life in any period of Chinese history provide as many counterexamples as fulfillments of the process of becoming an ancestor. Babies and children die young, before becoming accepted members of any family; men remain unmarried, without sons to carry on their name or memory; women are not successfully matched with a mate, thus lacking any mooring in the afterlife; individuals die in unsettling ways or come back from the dead as ghosts carrying grudges deemed fatal to the living. There are plenty of people, in other words, who are not caught by the safety net of the Chinese kinship system. They may be more prone than others to possession by spirits, or their anomalous position may not be manifest until after they die. In either case they are religiously significant because they abrogate an ideal of proper kinship relations.

Patrilineage exercises its influence as a regulating concept even in religious organizations where normal kinship—men and women marrying, having children, and tracing their lineage through the husband's father—is impossible. The Buddhist monkhood is a prime example;[14] sororities of unmarried women, adoption of children, and the creation of other "fictive" kinship ties are others. One of the defining features of being a Buddhist monk in China is called "leaving the family" (*chujia,* a translation of the Sanskrit *pravrajya*). Being homeless means not only that the boy has left the family in which he grew up and has taken up domicile in a monastery, but also that he has vowed to abstain from any sexual relations. Monks commit themselves to having no children. The defining feature of monasticism in China is its denial, its interruption of the patrilineage. At the same time, monks create for themselves a home—or a family—away from home; the Buddhist order adopts some of the important characteristics of the Chinese kinship system. One part of the ordination ceremony is the adoption of a religious name, both a new family name and a new personal name, by which one will hence forth be known. The family name for all Chinese monks, at least since the beginning of the fifth century, is the same surname attributed to the historical Buddha (Shi in Chinese, which is a shortened transliteration of the first part of Śākyamuni). For personal names, monks are usually assigned a two-character name by their teacher. Many teachers follow a practice common in the bestowal of secular personal names: the first character for all monks in a particular generation is the same, and the second character is different, bestowing individuality. "Brothers" of the same generation can be picked out because one element of their name is the same, as far as their names are concerned, their relationship to each other is the same as that between secular brothers. Not only do monks construct names and sibling relations modeled on those of Chinese kinship, they also construe themselves as Buddhist sons and descendants of Buddhist fathers and ancestors. Monks of the past are not only called "ancestors," they are also treated as secular ancestors are treated. The portraits and statues of past members are installed, in order, in special ancestral halls where they receive offerings and obeisance from current generations.

Another domain of Chinese religion that bears the imprint of Chinese kinship is hagiography, written accounts of gods and saints. Biographies of secular figures have long been part of the Chinese written tradition. Scholarly opinion usually cites the biographies contained in the first-century B.C.E. *Records of the Historian* (*Shiji*) as the paradigm for later biographical writing. Such accounts typically begin not with the birth of the protagonist, but rather with his or her family background. They narrate the individual's precocious abilities, posts held in government, actions deemed particularly virtuous or vile, and posthumous fate, including titles awarded by the government and the disposition of the corpse or grave. They are written in polished classical prose, and, like the writing of Chinese history, they are designed to cast their subjects as either models for emulation or unfortunate examples to be avoided. Gods who are bureaucrats, goddesses, incarnations of bodhisattvas, even immortals like Laozi and deities of the stars are all conceived through the lens of the Chinese family.

The logic of Chinese kinship can also be seen in a wide range of rituals, many of which take place outside the family and bear no overt relationship to kinship. The basic premise of many such rites is a family banquet, a feast to which members of the oldest generation of the family (the highest ancestors) are invited as honored guests. Placement of individuals and the sequence of action often follow seniority, with older generations coming before younger ones. Such principles can be observed even in Buddhist rites and the community celebrations enacted by groups defined by locale rather than kinship.

What about the other organizing force in Chinese civilization, the bureaucratic form of government used to rule the empire? It too has exerted tremendous influence on Chinese religious life. Before discussing bureaucracy proper, it is helpful to introduce some of the other defining features of Chinese government.

Chinese political culture has, at least since the later years of the Shang dynasty (ca. 1600–1028 B.C.E.), been conceived of as a dynastic system. A dynasty is defined by a founder whose virtue makes clear to all—both common people and other factions vying for control—that he and his family are fit to take over from a previous, corrupt ruler. Shortly after assuming the position of emperor, the new ruler chooses a name for the dynasty: Shang, for instance, means to increase or prosper. Other cosmically significant actions follow. The new emperor installs his family's ancestral tablets in the imperial ancestral hall; he performs the sacrifices to Heaven and Earth that are the emperor's duty; he announces new names of offices and institutes a reorganization of government; and the office of history and astronomy in the government keeps careful watch over any unusual phenomena (the appearance of freakish animals, unusual flora, comets, eclipses, etc.) that might indicate the pleasure or displeasure of Heaven at the change in rule. All activities that take place leading up to and during the reign of the first emperor in a new dynasty appear to be based on the idea that the ruler is one whose power is justified because of his virtue and abilities. When the new emperor dies and one of his sons succeeds to the throne, however, another principle of sovereignty is invoked: the second emperor is deemed fit to rule because he is the highest-ranking son in the ruling family. First emperors legitimate their rule by virtue; second and later emperors validate their rule by family connections. The latter rationale is invoked until the end of the dynasty, when another family asserts that its moral rectitude justifies a change. Thus, the dynastic system makes use of two theories of legitimation, one based on virtue and one based on birth.

Another important principle of Chinese politics, at least since the early years of the Zhou dynasty, is summarized by the slogan "the mandate of Heaven" (Tianming). In this conception, the emperor and his family carry out the commands of Heaven, the latter conceived as a divine, semi-natural, semi-personal force. Heaven demonstrates its approval of an emperor by vouchsafing plentiful harvests, social order, and portents of nature that are interpreted positively. Heaven manifests its displeasure with an emperor and hints at a change in dynasty by sending down famine, drought, widespread sickness, political turmoil, or other portents. It is important to note that the notion of the mandate of Heaven can serve to justify revolution as well as continuity. Rebellions in Chinese history, both those that have failed and those that have succeeded, usually claim that Heaven has proclaimed its displeasure with the ruling house and is transferring its mandate to a new group. The judgment of whether the mandate has indeed shifted is in principle always open to debate. It furnishes a compelling rationale for all current regimes at the same time that it holds open the possibility of revolution on divine grounds.

The dynastic system and the mandate of Heaven were joined to a third basic idea, that of bureaucracy. A bureaucratic form of government is not, of course, unique to China. What is important for our purposes is the particular shape and function of the bureaucracy and its reach into nearly all spheres of Chinese life, including religion.

Max Weber's listing of the characteristics of bureaucracy offers a helpful starting point for discussing the Chinese case. According to Weber, bureaucracy includes: (1) the principle of official jurisdictional areas, so that the duties and powers of each office are clearly stipulated; (2) the principle of hierarchy, which makes clear who ranks above and who ranks below, with all subordinates following their superiors; (3) the keeping of written records or files and a class of scribes whose duty is to make copies; (4) training of officials for their specific tasks; (5) full-time employment of the highest officials; and (6) the following of general rules.[15] Virtually all of these principles can be found in one form or another in the Chinese bureaucracy, the root of which some scholars trace to the religion of the second millennium B.C.E. The only consistent qualification that needs to be made (as Weber himself points out[16]) concerns the fourth point. Aspirants to government service were admitted to the job, in theory at least, only after passing a series of examinations, but the examination system rewarded a general course of learning in arts and letters rather than the technical skills demanded in some posts like engineering, forensic medicine, and so on.

The central government was also local; the chief government official responsible for a county was a magistrate, selected from a central pool on the basis of his performance in the examinations and assigned to a specific county where he had no prior family connections. He was responsible for employing lower-level functionaries in the county like scribes, clerks, sheriffs, and jailers; for collecting taxes; for keeping the peace; and, looking upward in the hierarchy, for reporting to his superiors and following their instructions. He performed a number of overtly religious functions. He made offerings at a variety of officially recognized temples, like those dedicated to the God of Walls and Moats (the so-called "City God," Chenghuang shen) and to local deified heroes; he gave lectures to the local residents about morality; and he kept close watch over all religious activities, especially those involving voluntary organizations of people outside of family and locality groups, whose actions might threaten the sovereignty and religious prerogative of the state. He was promoted on the basis of seniority and past performance, hoping to be named to higher posts with larger areas of jurisdiction or to a position in the central administration resident in the capital city. In his official capacity his interactions with others were highly formalized and impersonal.

One of the most obvious areas influenced by the bureaucratic metaphor is the Chinese pantheon. For many years it has been a truism that the Chinese conception of gods is based on the Chinese bureaucracy, that the social organization of the human government is the essential model that Chinese people use when imagining the gods. At the apex of the divine bureaucracy stands the Jade Emperor (Yuhuang dadi) in Heaven, corresponding to the human Son of Heaven (Tianzi, another name for emperor) who rules over Earth. The Jade Emperor is in charge of an administration divided into bureaus. Each bureaucrat-god takes responsibility for a clearly defined domain or discrete function. The local officials of the celestial administration are the Gods of Walls and Moats, and below them are the Gods of the Hearth, one per family, who generate a never-ending flow of reports on the people under their jurisdiction. They are assisted in turn by gods believed to dwell inside each person's body, who accompany people through life and into death, carrying with them the records of good and evil deeds committed by their charges. The very lowest officers are those who administer punishment to deceased spirits passing through the purgatorial chambers of the underworld. They too have reports to fill out, citizens to keep track of, and jails to manage. Recent scholarship has begun to criticize the generalization that most Chinese gods are bureaucratic, raising questions about the way in which the relation between the human realm and the divine realm should be conceptualized. Should the two realms be viewed as two essentially different orders, with one taking priority over the other? Should the two bureaucracies be seen as an expression in two spheres of a more unitary conceptualization of power? Is the attempt to separate a presumably concrete social system from an allegedly idealized project wrong in the first place? Other studies (and the discussion in the next section) suggest that some of the more significant deities of Chinese religion are not approached in bureaucratic terms at all.

An important characteristic of any developed bureaucratic system, earthly or celestial, is that it is wrapped in an aura of permanence and freedom from blame.

Office-holders are distinct from the office they fill. Individual magistrates and gods come and go, but the functions they serve and the system that assigns them their duties do not change. Government officials always seem capable of corruption, and specific individuals may be blameworthy, but in a sprawling and principled bureaucracy, the blame attaches only to the individuals currently occupying the office, and wholesale questioning of the structure as a whole is easily deferred. Graft may be everywhere—local magistrates and the jailers of the other world are equally susceptible to bribes—but the injustice of the bureaucracy in general is seldom broached. When revolutionary groups have succeeded or threatened to succeed in overthrowing the government, their alternative visions are, as often as not, couched not in utopian or apolitical terms, but as a new version of the old kingdom, the bureaucracy of which is staffed only by the pure.

Bureaucratic logic is also a striking part of Chinese iconography, temple archictecture, and ritual structure. For peasants who could not read in traditional times, the bureaucratic nature of the gods was an apodictic matter of appearance: gods were dressed as government officials. Their temples are laid out like imperial palaces, which include audience halls where one approaches the god with the proper deportment. Many rituals involving the gods follow bureaucratic procedures. Just as one communicates with a government official through his staff, utilizing proper written forms, so too common people depend on literate scribes to write out their prayers, in the correct literary form, which are often communicated to the other world by fire.

The Spirits of Chinese Religion

Up to this point the discussion has touched frequently on the subject of gods without explaining what gods are and how they are believed to be related to other kinds of beings. To understand Chinese theology (literally "discourse about gods"), we need to explore theories about human existence, and before that we need to review some of the basic concepts of Chinese cosmology.

What is the Chinese conception of the cosmos? Any simple answer to that question, of course, merely confirms the biases assumed but not articulated by the question—that there is only one such authentically Chinese view, and that the cosmos as such, present unproblematically to all people, was a coherent topic of discussion in traditional China. Nevertheless, the answer to that question offered by one scholar of China, Joseph Needham, provides a helpful starting point for the analysis. In Needham's opinion, the dominant strand of ancient Chinese thought is remarkable for the way it contrasts with European ideas. While the latter approach the world religiously as created by a transcendent deity or as a battleground between spirit and matter, or scientifically as a mechanism consisting of objects and their attributes, ancient Chinese thinkers viewed the world as a complete and complex "organism." "Things behaved in particular ways," writes Needham, "not necessarily because of prior actions or impulsions of other things, but because their position in the ever-moving cyclical universe was such that they were endowed with intrinsic natures which made that behaviour inevitable for them."[17] Rather than being created out of nothing, the world evolved into its current condition of complexity out of a prior state of simplicity and undifferentiation. The cosmos continues to change, but there is a consistent pattern to that change discernible to human beings. Observation of the seasons and celestial realms, and methods like plastromancy and scapulimancy (divination using tortoise shells and shoulder blades), dream divination, and manipulating the hexagrams of the *Classic of Changes* allow people to understand the pattern of the universe as a whole by focusing on the changes taking place in one of its meaningful parts.

The basic stuff out of which all things are made is called *qi*. Everything that ever existed, at all times, is made of qi, including inanimate matter, humans and animals, the sky, ideas and emotions, demons and ghosts, the undifferentiated state of wholeness, and the world when it is teeming with different beings. As an axiomatic concept with a wide range of meaning, the word qi has over the years been translated in numerous ways. Because it involves phenomena we would consider both psychological—connected to human thoughts and feelings—and physical, it can be translated as "psychophysical stuff." The translation "pneuma" draws on one early etymology of the word as vapor, steam, or breath. "Vital energy" accentuates the potential for life inherent to the more ethereal forms of qi. These meanings of qi hold for most schools of thought in early Chinese religion; it is only with the renaissance of Confucian traditions undertaken by Zhu Xi and others that qi is interpreted not as a single thing, part-matter and part-energy, pervading everything, but as one of two basic metaphysical building blocks. According to Zhu Xi, all things partake of both qi and *li* (homophonous to but different from the *li* meaning "ritual" or "propriety"), the latter understood as the reason a thing is what it is and its underlying "principle" or "reason."

While traditional cosmology remained monistic, in the sense that qi as the most basic constituent of the universe was a single thing rather than a duality or plurality of things, still qi was thought to move or to operate according to a pattern that did conform to two basic modes. The Chinese words for those two modalities are *yin* and *yang;* I shall attempt to explain them here but shall leave them untranslated. Yin and yang are best understood in terms of symbolism. When the sun shines on a mountain at some time other than midday, the mountain has one shady side and one sunny side. Yin is the emblem for the shady side and its characteristics; yang is the emblem for the sunny side and its qualities. Since the sun has not yet warmed the yin side, it is dark, cool, and moist; plants are contracted and dormant; and water in the form of dew moves downward. The yang side of the mountain is the opposite. It is bright, warm, and dry; plants open up and extend their stalks to catch the sun; and water in the form of fog moves upward as it evaporates. This basic symbolism was extended to include a host of other oppositions. Yin is female, yang is male. Yin occupies the lower position, yang the higher. Any situation in the human or natural world can be analyzed within this framework; yin and yang can be used to understand the modulations of qi on a mountainside as well as the relationships within the family. The social hierarchies of gender and age, for instance—the duty of the wife to honor her husband, and of younger generations to obey older ones—were interpreted as the natural subordination of yin to yang. The same reasoning can be applied to any two members of a pair. Yin-yang symbolism simultaneously places them on an equal footing and ranks them hierarchically. On the one hand, all processes are marked by change, making it inevitable that yin and yang alternate and imperative that humans seek a harmonious balance between the two. On the other hand, the system as a whole attaches greater value to the ascendant member of the pair, the yang. Such are the philosophical possibilities of the conceptual scheme. Some interpreters of yin and yang choose to emphasize the nondualistic, harmonious nature of the relationship, while others emphasize the imbalance, hierarchy, and conflict built into the idea.

How is human life analyzed in terms of the yin and yang modes of "material energy" (yet another rendering of qi)? Health for the individual consists in the harmonious balancing of yin and yang. When the two modes depart from their natural course, sickness and death result. Sleep, which is dark and therefore yin, needs to be balanced by wakefulness, which is yang. Salty tastes (yin) should be matched by bitter ones (yang); inactivity should alternate with movement and so on. Normally the material energy that constitutes a person, though constantly shifting, is unitary enough to sustain a healthy life. When the material energy is blocked, follows improper patterns, or is invaded by pathogens, then the imbalance between yin and yang threatens to pull the person apart, the coarser forms of material energy (which are yin) remaining attached to the body or near the corpse, the more ethereal forms of material energy (which are yang) tending to float up and away. Dream-states and minor sicknesses are simply gentler forms of the personal dissociation—the radical conflict between yin and yang—that comes with spirit-possession, serious illness, and death. At death the material force composing the person dissipates, and even that dissipation follows a pattern analyzable in terms of yin and yang. The yin parts of the person—collectively called "earthly souls" (*po*)—move downward, constituting the flesh of the corpse, perhaps also returning as a ghost to haunt the living. Since they are more like energy than matter, the yang parts of the person—collectively called "heavenly souls" (*hun*)—float upward. They—notice that there is more than one of each kind of "soul," making a unique soul or even a dualism of the spirit impossible in principle—are thought to be reborn in Heaven or as another being, to be resident in the ancestral tablets, to be associated more amorphously with the ancestors stretching back seven generations, or to be in all three places at once.

Above I claimed that a knowledge of Chinese cosmology and an anthropology was essential to understanding what place gods occupy in the Chinese conceptual world. That is because the complicated term "god," in the sense either of a being believed to be perfect in power, wisdom, and goodness or a superhuman figure worthy of worship, does not correspond straightforwardly to a single Chinese term with a similar range of meanings. Instead, there are general areas of overlap, as well as concepts that have no correspondence, between the things we would consider "gods" and specific Chinese terms. Rather than pursuing this question from the side of modern English usage, however, we will begin with the important Chinese terms and explain their range of meanings.

One of the terms crucial to understanding Chinese religion is *shen,* which in this introduction I translate with different versions of the English word "spirit." Below these three words are analyzed separately as consisting of three distinct spheres of meaning, but one should keep in mind that the three senses are all rooted in a single Chinese word. They differ only in degree or realm of application, not in kind.

The first meaning of shen is confined to the domain of the individual human being; it may be translated as "spirit" in the sense of "human spirit" or "psyche." It is the basic power or agency within humans that accounts for life. To extend life to full potential the spirit must be cultivated, resulting in ever clearer, more luminous states of being. In physiological terms "spirit" is a general term for the "heavenly souls," in contrast to the yin elements of the person.

The second meaning of shen may be rendered in English as "spirits" or "gods," the latter written in lowercase because Chinese spirits and gods need not be seen as all-powerful, transcendent, or creators of the world. They are intimately involved in the affairs of the world, generally lacking a perch or time frame completely beyond the human realm. An early Chinese dictionary explains: "Shen are the spirits of Heaven. They draw out the ten thousand things."[18] As the spirits associated with objects like stars, mountains, and streams, they exercise a direct influence on things in this world, making phenomena appear and causing things to extend themselves. In this sense of "spirits," shen are yang and opposed to the yin class of things known in Chinese as *gui,* "ghosts" or "demons." The two words put together, as in the combined form *guishen* ("ghosts and spirits"), cover all manner of spiritual beings in the largest sense, those benevolent and malevolent, lucky and unlucky. In this view, spirits are manifestations of the yang material force, and ghosts are manifestations of the yin material force. The nineteenth-century Dutch scholar Jan J. M. de Groot emphasized this aspect of the Chinese worldview, claiming that "animism" was an apt characterization of Chinese religion because all parts of the universe—rocks, trees, planets, animals, humans—could be animated by spirits, good or bad. As support for that thesis he quotes a disciple of Zhu Xi's: "Between Heaven and Earth there is no thing that does not consist of yin and yang, and there is no place where yin and yang are not found. Therefore there is no place where gods and spirits do not exist."[19]

Shen in its third meaning can be translated as "spiritual." An entity is "spiritual" in the sense of inspiring awe or wonder because it combines categories usually kept separate, or it cannot be comprehended through normal concepts. The *Classic of Changes* states, " 'Spiritual' means not measured by yin and yang."[20] Things that are numinous cross categories. They cannot be fathomed as either yin or yang, and they possess the power to disrupt the entire system of yin and yang. A related synonym, one that emphasizes the power of such spiritual things, is *ling*, meaning "numinous" or possessing unusual spiritual characteristics. Examples that are considered shen in the sense of "spiritual" include albino members of a species; beings that are part-animal, part-human; women who die before marriage and turn into ghosts receiving no care; people who die in unusual ways like suicide or on battlefields far from home; and people whose bodies fail to decompose or emit strange signs after death.

The fact that these three fields of meaning ("spirit," "spirits," and "spiritual") can be traced to a single word has important implications for analyzing Chinese religion. Perhaps most importantly, it indicates that there is no unbridgeable gap separating humans from gods or, for that matter, separating good spirits from demons. All are composed of the same basic stuff, qi, and there is no ontological distinction between them. Humans are born with the capacity to transform their spirit into one of the gods of the Chinese pantheon. Hagiographies offer details about how some people succeed in becoming gods and how godlike exemplars and saints inspire people to follow their example.

The broad range of meaning for the word shen is related to the coexistence, sometimes harmonious, sometimes not, of a number of different idioms for talking about Chinese gods. An earlier section quoted Xunzi's comment that distinguishes between a naive fear of gods on the part of the uneducated and a pragmatic, agonistic attitude on the part of the literati. Although they share common practices and might use the same words to talk about them, those words mean different things. Similarly, Zhu Xi uses homonyms and etymology to abstract—to disembody—the usual meaning of spirits and ghosts. Spirits (*shen*), he says, are nothing but the "extension" (*shen*, pronounced the same but in fact a different word) of material energy, and ghosts (*gui*) amount to the "returning" (*gui*, also homophonous but a different word) of material energy.

Chinese gods have been understood—experienced, spoken to, dreamed about, written down, carved, painted—according to a number of different models. The bureaucratic model (viewing gods as office-holders, not individuals, with all the duties and rights appropriate to the specific rank) is probably the most common but by no means the only one. Spirits are also addressed as stern fathers or compassionate mothers. Some are thought to be more pure than others, because they are manifestations of astral bodies or because they willingly dirty themselves with birth and death in order to bring people salvation. Others are held up as paragons of the common values thought to define social life, like obedience to parents, loyalty to superiors, sincerity, or trustworthiness. Still others possess power, and sometimes entertainment value, because they flaunt standard mores and conventional distinctions.

Books on Chinese religion can still be found that attempt to portray the spirit—understood in the singular, in the theoretical sense of essential principle—of Chinese tradition. That kind of book treats the subject of gods, if it raises the question at all, as an interesting but ultimately illogical concern of the superstitious. We might instead attempt to move from a monolithic or abstract conception of the Chinese spirit to a picture, or an occasionally contentious series of pictures, of the many spirits of Chinese religion.

Notes

I am grateful to several kind spirits who offered helpful comments on early drafts of this essay. They include the anonymous readers of the book manuscript, Donald S. Lopez, Jr., Yang Lu, Susan Naquin, Daniel L. Overmyer, and Robert H. Sharf.

1. Li's formulation is quoted in *Beishi,* Li Yanshou (seventh century), Bona ed. (Beijing: Zhonghua shuju, 1974), p. 1234. Unless otherwise noted, all translations from Chinese are mine.

2. The proverb, originally appearing in the sixteenth-century novel *Investiture of the Gods* (*Fengshen yanyi*), is quoted in Clifford H. Plopper, *Chinese Religion Seen through the Proverb* (Shanghai: The China Press, 1926), p. 16.

3. The first three are quoted in Plopper, *Chinese Religion,* p. 15. The last is quoted in Judith Berling, *The Syncretic Religion of Lin Chao-en* (New York: Columbia University Press, 1980), p. 8. See also Timothy Brook, "Rethinking Syncretism: The Unity of the Three Teachings and Their Joint Worship in Late-Imperial China," *Journal of Chinese Religions* 21 (Fall 1993): 13–44.

4. The phrase is *shu er bu zuo,* quoted from the *Analects, Lunyu zhengi,* annot. Liu Baonan (1791–1855), in *Zhuzi jicheng* (Shanghai: Shijie shuju, 1936), 2:134.

5. For further details, see Lionel M. Jensen, "The Invention of 'Confucius' and His Chinese Other, 'Kong Fuzi,'" *Positions: East Asia Cultures Critique* 1.2 (Fall 1993): 414–59; and Thomas A. Wilson, *Geneaology of the Way: The Construction and Uses of the Confucian Tradition in Late Imperial China* (Stanford: Stanford University Press, 1995).

6. *Laozi dao de jing,* ch. 42, *Zhuzi jicheng* (Shanghai: Shijie shuju, 1936), 3:26.

7. For three views on the subject, see Kristofer Schipper, "Purity and Strangers: Shifting Boundaries in Medieval Taoism," *T'oung Pao* 80 (1994): 61–81; Rolf A. Stein, "Religious Taoism and Popular Religion from the Second to Seventh Centuries," in *Facets of Taoism,* ed. Holmes Welch and Anna Siedel (New Haven: Yale University Press, 1979), pp. 53–81; and Michel Strickmann, "History, Anthropology, and Chinese Religion," *Harvard Journal of Asiatic Studies* 40.1 (June 1980): 201–48.

8. In fact the linguistic situation is more complex. Some scholars suggest that Fo is a transliteration not from Sanskrit but from Tocharian; see, for instance, Ji Xianlin, "Futu yu Fo," *Guoli zhongyang yanjiuyuan Lishi yuyan yanjisuo jikan* 20.1 (1948): 93–105.

9. On the extended meaning of the three jewels in Chinese sources, see Jacques Gernet, *Buddhism in Chinese Society: An Economic History from the Fifth to the Tenth Centuries,* trans. Franciscus Verellen (New York: Columbia University Press, 1995), p. 67.

10. *Kaiyuan shijiao lu,* Zhisheng (669–740), T 2154, 55:572b.

11. *Xunzi jijie,* ed. Wang Xianqian, in *Zhuzi jicheng* (Shanghai: Shijie shuju, 1935), 2:250.

12. Wing-tsit Chan, *Religious Trends in Modern China* (New York: Columbia University Press, 1953), pp. 141, 142.

13. Francis L. K. Hsu, *Under the Ancestors' Shadow: Kinship, Personality, and Social Mobility in China,* 2d ed. (Stanford: Stanford University Press, 1971), p. 246.

14. See John Jorgensen, "The 'Imperial' Lineage of Ch'an Buddhism: The Role of Confucian Ritual and Ancestor Worship in Ch'an's Search for Legitimation in the Mid-T'ang Dynasty," *Papers on Far Eastern History* 35 (March 1987): 89–134.

15. Max Weber, *Economy and Society: An Outline of Interpretive Sociology,* ed. Guenther Roth and Claus Wittich, trans. Ephraim Fischoff et al., 2 vols. (Berkeley: University of California Press, 1978), pp. 956–68.

16. Ibid., p. 1049.

17. Joseph Needham, with the research assistance of Wang Ling, *Science and Civilisation in China,* vol. 2: *History of Scientific Thought* (Cambridge: Cambridge University Press, 1956), p. 281.

18. *Shuowen jiezi,* Xu Shen (d. 120), in *Shuowen jiezi gulin zhengbu hebian,* ed. Duan Yucai (1735–1815) and Ding Fubao, 12 vols. (Taibei: Dingwen shuju, 1977), 2:86a.

19. Jan J. M. de Groot, *The Religious System of China: Its Ancient Forms, Evolution, History and Present Aspect, Manners, Customs and Social Institutions Connected Therewith,* 6 vols. (Leiden: E.J. Brill, 1892–1910), 4:51. My translation differs slightly from de Groots.

20. *Zhouyi yinde,* Harvard-Yenching Institute Sinological Index Series, Supplement no. 10 (reprint ed., Taibei: Ch'eng-wen Publishing Co., 1966), p. 41a.

RELIGIONS OF TIBET IN PRACTICE

Donald S. Lopez, Jr.

The religions of Tibet have long been objects of Western fascination and fantasy. From the time that Venetian travelers and Catholic missionaries encountered Tibetan monks at the Mongol court, tales of the mysteries of their mountain homeland and the magic of their strange religions have held a peculiar hold over the European and American imagination. Over the past two centuries, the valuation of Tibetan society and, particularly, its religion has fluctuated wildly. Tibetan Buddhism has been portrayed sometimes as the most corrupt deviation from the Buddha's true dharma, sometimes as its most direct descendant. These fluctuations have occurred over the course of this century, as Tibet resisted the colonial ambitions of a European power at its beginning and succumbed to the colonial ambitions of an Asian power at its end.

Until some thirty years ago, knowledge of the religions of Tibet in the West had largely been derived from the reports of travelers and adventurers, who often found the religions both strange and strangely familiar, noting similarities between Tibetan Buddhism and Roman Catholicism, calling the Dalai Lama the Tibetan pope, for example. It is only since the Tibetan diaspora that took place beginning in 1959, after the Chinese invasion and occupation of Tibet, that the texts of the religions of Tibet have begun to be widely translated.

The history of Tibet prior to the seventh century C.E. is difficult to determine. According to a number of chronicles discovered at Dunhuang dating from the seventh through the tenth centuries, Tibet was ruled by a lineage of kings, the first seven of whom descended from the heavens by means of a cord or ladder. Each king ruled until his first son was old enough to ride a horse, at which point the king returned to heaven via the rope. (Buddhist historians say that the first king in the lineage was an Indian prince who arrived by crossing the Himalayas; when the Tibetans asked where he had come from he pointed up, and the credulous Tibetans assumed he had descended from the sky.) These kings founded a system of law that reflected the cosmic order of heaven. As a literal descendant of heaven, the king was the embodiment and protector of the cosmic order and the welfare of the state. The king's stable presence on the throne thus ensured harmony in the realm.

It was only when the eighth king lost his protective warrior god in battle that the sky rope was severed and the king was slain, leaving his corpse behind. To deal with this crisis, according to later sources, priests were invited from an area called Shangshung (Zhang zhung, the precise location and extent of which is unknown but is assumed to include much of western Tibet) to perform death rituals and bury the king. The story reflects the popular notion of Tibet as an untamed and uncivilized realm, with civilization arriving only from the outside. Recent scholarship thus does not assume from this account that foreign priests were actually summoned, seeing it instead as a creation myth meant to explain the origin of the elaborate royal mortuary cult. A class of priests called "reciters" (*bon*) performed a range of sacerdotal functions in service of the divine king, such as officiating at coronation ceremonies and in rites of allegiance to the king. There was also another class of priests, called *shen* (*gshen*), who seem to have performed divinations.

The cult of the divine king included the belief that he was endowed with both magical power and a special magnificence. There was a trinity of the king, the head priest, and the chief minister, with the active power of government in the hands of the head priest and the minister who represented the priestly hierarchy and the clan nobility. The king represented the continually reborn essence of the divine ancestor, who was reincarnated in each king at the age of maturity and remained incarnated in him until his son reached the same age of maturity and ascended the throne as the consecutive link of the ancestral reincarnation. This procedure applied also to both the priest and the minister, so a new trinity was instituted at the accession of each king. The king also had a special guardian called the "body spirit" (*sku bla*) who protected the king's power, encompassing everything from his body to his political authority to the order of the universe. One of the primary responsibilities of the royal priests and ministers, then, seems to have been the maintenance of the king's health, for if the king became ill or if the body spirit was determined otherwise to be displeased, the safety of the kingdom and even of the universe was in jeopardy. Epidemics and droughts were interpreted as signs of this displeasure.

The notion of *la* (*bla*), generally translated as "soul," "spirit," or "life," dates from the ancient period and remains an important component in the religions of Tibet. The *la* is an individual's life force, often associated with the breath. It is seen as the essential support of the physical and mental constitution of the person but is mobile and can leave the body and wander, going into trees, rocks, or animals, to the detriment of the person it animates, who will become either ill or mentally unbalanced. The *la* is especially susceptible during dreams and can be carried off by demons, who particularly covet the life forces of children. There are thus rites designed to bring the *la* back into the body, known as "calling the *la*" (*bla 'bod*).

Even when the *la* is properly restored to its place in the body, it may simultaneously reside in certain external abodes, most often in a particular lake, tree, mountain, or animal. The person in whom the *la* resides stands in a sympathetic relationship with these phenomena, such that if the *la* mountain is dug into, the person will fall sick. The Tibetan epic hero Gesar, in his attempt to conquer a certain demoness, cuts down her *la* tree and empties her *la* lake; he fails because he does not kill her *la* sheep. The identity of these external *la* are thus often kept secret, and portable abodes of the *la*, usually a precious object of some kind (often a turquoise), are kept in special receptacles and hidden by the person who shares the *la*.

There were thus regular offerings made to the king's body spirit at the site of the king's sacred mountain, the physical locus of his power. Of particular importance to the royal cult, however, were the funeral ceremonies. A king was still expected to abdicate upon the majority of his son and retire to his tomb with a large company of retainers, although whether this entailed the execution of the king and his retinue or simply their exile into a tomb complex remains unknown. The royal funerals were apparently elaborate affairs, with food and other necessities provided for the perilous journey to the next world, a bucolic heaven called the "land of joy" (*bde ba can*). Animals, especially yaks, sheep, and horses, were also offered in sacrifice. Chinese sources suggest that humans were also sacrificed, perhaps to serve as servants to the departed king, perhaps to be offered as gifts or "ransoms" (*glud*) to various spirits who otherwise would block the king's route. This concern with death and the fate of the dead has continued throughout the history of Tibetan religions.

Although Buddhism was flourishing all around Tibet in the first centuries of the common era, there is no mention of Buddhist elements in the chronicles apart from the account of a small stūpa and an illegible Buddhist sūtra falling from the sky into the palace of one of the prehistoric kings. The formal introduction of Buddhism to the Tibetan court seems to have occurred during the reign of King Songtsen Gampo (Srong btsan sgam po, ruled c. 614–650), at a time when Tibet was the dominant military power of Inner Asia. According to later chronicles, as a result of treaties with the courts of China and Nepal, the king received two princesses as wives. Each was a Buddhist, and each brought a precious statue of the Buddha with her to Lhasa, the capital. They are credited with converting their new husband to the dharma, although what this meant in practice is difficult to say. The king dispatched an emissary to India to learn Sanskrit and then return to design a written language for Tibet. Among the many purposes to which such a script could be put, it is said that the king's pious motivation was the translation of Buddhist texts from Sanskrit into Tibetan.

The script invented was modeled on one current in northern India at the time. Tibetan is, like Sanskrit, an inflected language, with case endings used to mark grammatical functions. Words are made up of combinations of independent syllables, each of which is constructed by grouping letters in various combinations. The simplest syllable can be made up of a single letter while the most complex can have as many as six, with a prefix, a superscription, a root letter, a subscription, a suffix, and an additional suffix, not to mention a vowel marker. Historical linguists speculate that originally all of these letters were pronounced, but over the centuries the auxiliary letters became silent, such that there is a vast difference today between the way a word is written and the way it is pronounced. To render the spelling of a Tibetan word in English requires that all of the letters be represented. The result, however, appears to be utterly unpronounceable to someone who does not already know Tibetan. For that reason, phonetic renderings (for which there is no widely accepted convention) must be provided. For example, the name of the current Dalai Lama in transliteration is Bstan 'dzin rgya mtsho, but it is commonly written in English as Tenzin Gyatso. Although the same script is employed throughout the Tibetan cultural domain, dozens of regional dialects have developed, many of which are mutually incomprehensible.

The conversion of Tibet to Buddhism is traditionally presented as a process of forceful but ultimately compassionate subjugation (rather than destruction) of native Tibetan deities by the more powerful imported deities of Buddhism, often invoked by Indian yogins. The profoundly chthonic nature of Tibetan religion is evident even from the traditional chronicles, which represent the conversion of Tibet to the true dharma not so much as a matter of bringing new teachings to the populace but of transforming the landscape by bringing the myriad deities of place—of valleys, mountains, hills, passes, rivers, lakes, and plains—under control. Thus Songtsen Gampo was said to have ordered the construction of Buddhist temples at key points throughout his realm, each temple functioning as a great nail impaling a giant demoness (*srin mo*) lying supine over the expanse of Tibet, immobilizing her from impeding the progress of the dharma, the symmetry of a Buddhist maṇḍala superimposed over the unruly landscape of Tibet.

But all this derives from chronicles composed centuries after the fact by authors concerned to promote Buddhism and link the introduction of the dharma to Tibet's greatest king, the king who unified Tibet and led its armies in victory against Chinese, Indians, Nepalese, Turks, and Arabs. The few records surviving from the period make no mention of Buddhism, nor even of the Nepalese princess. The historicity of the emissary to India is questionable. Songtsen Gampo seems to have remained committed to and even to have developed further the cult of divine kingship, a cult that involved both animal and human sacrifice (an anathema to Buddhists), while continuing to worship local deities and supporting his own ministers and priests of the royal mortuary cult. At the same time, it seems unlikely that the Tibetan kingdom, surrounded as it was for centuries by Buddhist societies, should have remained untouched by Buddhist influence until the seventh century, as the traditional histories claim.

The first king to make a choice between Buddhism and the native religion of the Tibetan court was Tri Songdetsen (Khri srong lde btsan, ruled 754–797). Both later Buddhist and Bönpo chronicles report that he promoted Buddhism and suppressed the practices of priests of the native cult; his support of Buddhism may have been motivated by the desire to escape the restricting bonds of the feudal clan nobility who supported the priests. Contemporary inscriptions, however, also indicate that he continued to have rituals performed that involved animal sacrifice. During these ceremonies, the old oaths of loyalty between king and servant were sworn. Before taking the oath, it was the custom for the participants to smear their lips with the blood of the sacrificial animal, a practice from which the Buddhist monks who were present apparently demurred.

Tri Songdetsen invited to Tibet the prominent Indian Buddhist abbot Śāntarakṣita, whose presence angered the local spirits sufficiently for the Indian abbot to request the king to invite a tantric master to aid in the further subjugation of the local spirits. The great master Padmasambhava was invited and proved equal to the task, after which it was possible to establish the first Buddhist monastery at Samye (Bsam yas) circa 779. The further activities of Padmasambhava and the duration of his stay are unknown, but he remains a figure of mythic significance in the history of Tibet, often referred to simply as Guru Rimpoche, the precious guru. The stories of Padmasambhava's defeat and conversion of the local spirits and demons of Tibet are pervasive and popular, and they figure prominently in the descriptions of specific sites found in pilgrimage narratives.

Buddhism is famous for its ability to accommodate local deities into its pantheon. In the case of Tibet, most of the local deities became regarded as "mundane gods" (*'jigs rten pa'i lha*), that is, deities who are subject to the law of karma and cycle of rebirth, who, after a lifetime as a particular god, will take rebirth in some other form. The vast pantheon of deities imported from India included such gods, as well as "supramundane gods" (*'jigs rten las 'das pa'i lha*), that is, deities who—although they appear in horrifying forms, such as the protector of the Dalai Lama, the goddess Belden Lhamo (Dpal ldan lha mo, the "Glorious Goddess")—are in fact enlightened beings already liberated from the cycle of birth and death. Still, the process of the Buddhist conversion of Tibet should not be understood to mean that Buddhism was not also converted in that process; indeed, many deities cannot be identified as simply Indian or Tibetan.

The deities that Padmasambhava subdued and converted were often identified with mountains, rock formations, and other prominent elements of the topography of Tibet. The Tibetan plateau stands at 12,000 feet, with the surrounding mountains rising yet another mile above the plateau. The northern region is a vast uninhabited plane, but there are also dense forests and fertile valleys that are cultivated to produce barley, the staple crop. It is thus misleading to characterize Tibet as a desolate place, or to suggest (as Western travelers have) that the bleak landscape and vast sky (with its thin air) have turned men's minds toward the contemplation of a rarefied world of gods and demons, their unconscious releasing vivid hallucinations that appear in sharp relief against the distant horizon.

Yet it is difficult to overestimate the importance of the land in Tibetan religion. From early times Tibetans have held a belief in numerous local spirits, demons, and gods, who lived in lakes, rivers, creeks, wells, trees, fields, rocks, and mountains. Deities inhabited unusually shaped mounds; rocks shaped like animals; hills shaped liked sleeping oxen; burial mounds; juniper, birch, and spruce trees; and any anomalous geologic formation. Various types of demons roamed mountains and valleys and chose abodes in rocks, forests, ditches, and overhanging rocks, all places that could be disturbed by humans, to whom they sent both physical affliction (such as leprosy and smallpox) and social affliction (such as gossip). The atmosphere was the domain of another class of spirits, demons who appeared in the form of warriors who would attack travelers. Beneath the surface of the earth and in rivers and lakes lived a class of demons named *lu* (*klu*), who would become enraged if the earth was disturbed by digging, plowing, or laying the foundation for a house. Unless they were properly appeased, they also would inflict disease on humans and livestock. There are also *tsen (btsan)*, "rock spirits"; *sa dak* (*sa bdag*), "lords of the earth"; *ma mo*, "demonesses"; and *dre* (*'dre*), *drip* (*sgrib*), *dön* (*gdon*), and *gek* (*bgegs*). The Tibetan pantheon (although the term pantheon suggests a clearer system than in fact exists) of both benevolent and, especially, malevolent spirits is large and complex, and English lacks sufficient terms to render their names, beyond things like "demon" and "ogress." Even the terms "benevolent" and "malevolent" can be misleading, since many horrifying deities, despite an awful demeanor and testy disposition, can provide protection and aid if they are not offended or disturbed, but properly propitiated.

As mentioned above, Buddhist chronicles describe the Tibetan landscape as itself a giant demoness who must be subdued. There are gods of the plain and gods of the mountains; an entire mountain range is a god. This animated topography is itself further populated by all manner of spirits who must be honored to avoid their wrath. But the landscape is not only a domain of danger, it is also an abode of opportunity, blessing, and power. (There is a legend in which one of these spirits mates with a human, and the two serve as progenitors of a fierce Tibetan tribe.) Thus, pilgrimage is an essential element of Tibetan religious life, with pilgrims seeking to derive power and purification by visiting those places believed to embody a particular potency, either naturally—as when the place is the abode of a god or the god itself—or historically—as when the place is the site of the inspired deeds of a great yogin such as Padmasambhava or Milarepa. The topography even contains hidden countries (*sbas yul*), ideal sites for the practice of tantra, the most famous being the kingdom of Shambala; there are guidebooks with directions to such destinations. It is also the land that yields the treasures (*gter ma*), the texts left behind, hidden in rocks, caves, and pillars by Padmasambhava himself, left safely within the earth until the time is right for them to be discovered and their contents made known to the world. Thus, the landscape is not simply an animated realm of fearful demons and ogresses, but above all the abode of power for those who know where to seek what lies within.

During the reign of Tri Songdetsen, not long after the founding of the Samye monastery, a politically charged doctrinal controversy erupted in Tibet. In addition to the Indian party of Śāntarakṣita, there was also an influential Chinese Buddhist contingent who found favor with the Tibetan nobility. These were monks of the Chan (Zen) school, led by one Mohoyen. According to traditional accounts, Śāntarakṣita foretold of dangers from the Chinese position and left instructions in his will that his student Kamalaśīla be called from India to counter the Chinese view. A conflict seems to have developed between the Indian and Chinese partisans (and their allies in the Tibetan court) over the question of the nature of enlightenment, with the Indians holding that enlightenment takes place as the culmination of a gradual process of purification, the result of combining virtuous action, meditative serenity, and philosophical insight. The Chinese spoke against this view, holding that enlightenment was the intrinsic nature of the mind rather than the goal of a protracted path, such that one need simply to recognize the presence of this innate nature of enlightenment by entering a state of awareness beyond distinctions; all other practices were superfluous. According to both Chinese and Tibetan records, a debate was held between Kamalaśīla and Mohoyen at Samye circa 797, with King Tri Songdetsen himself serving as judge. According to Tibetan accounts (contradicted by the Chinese accounts), Kamalaśīla was declared the winner and Mohoyen and his party were banished from Tibet, with the king proclaiming that thereafter the Middle Way (Madhyamaka) school of Indian Buddhist philosophy (to which Śāntarakṣita and Kamalaśīla belonged) would be followed in Tibet. Recent scholarship has suggested that although a controversy between the Indian and Chinese Buddhists (and their Tibetan partisans) occurred, it is unlikely that a face-to-face debate took place or that the outcome of the controversy was so unequivocal. Furthermore, it is probably important to recall that, regardless of the merits of the Indian and Chinese philosophical positions, China was Tibet's chief military rival at the time, whereas India posed no such threat. Nonetheless, it is significant that from this point Tibet largely sought its Buddhism from India; no school of Chinese Buddhism had any further influence in Tibet. Mohoyen himself was transformed into something of a trickster figure, popular in Tibetan art and drama.

The king Ralpajen (Ral pa can, ruled c. 815–835) seems to have been an even more enthusiastic patron of Buddhism, supporting numerous Indian-Tibetan translation teams who continued the formidable task of rendering a vast corpus of Sanskrit literature into Tibetan. Translation academies were established and standard glossaries of technical terms were developed during the ninth century. The relatively late date of the introduction of Buddhism to Tibet compared with China (first century C.E.) and Japan (fifth century) had important ramifications for the development of the Tibetan Buddhist tradition, the foremost being that the Tibetans had access to large bodies of Indian Buddhist literature that either never were translated into Chinese (and thus never transmitted to Japan) or had little influence in East Asia. This literature fell into two categories: tantras and śāstras.

The origins of tantric Buddhism in India remain nebulous, with some scholars dating the early texts from the fourth century C.E. Its literature, including all manner of ritual texts and meditation manuals, continued to be composed in India for the next six centuries. This literature offered a speedy path to enlightenment, radically truncating the eons-long path set forth in the earlier discourses attributed to the Buddha, called sūtras. To this end, the tantric literature set forth a wide range of techniques for the attainment of goals both mundane and supramundane, techniques for bringing the fantastic worlds described in the sūtras into actuality. Tantric practices were considered so potent that they were often conducted in secret, and aspirants required initiation. The practices themselves involved elaborate and meticulous visualizations, in which the practitioner mentally transformed himself or herself into a fully enlightened buddha, with a resplendent body seated on a throne in the center of a marvelous palace (called a maṇḍala), with speech that intoned sacred syllables (called mantras), and with a mind that saw the ultimate reality directly.

A second body of literature, more important for Buddhist philosophy per se, were the śāstras (treatises). Buddhist literature is sometimes divided into sūtras—those texts traditionally held to be either the word of the Buddha or spoken with his sanction—and śāstras—treatises composed by Indian commentators. In the case of Mahāyāna literature, sūtras often contain fantastic visions of worlds populated by enlightened beings, with entrance to such a world gained through devotion to the sūtra itself. When points of doctrine are presented, it is often in the form of narrative, allegory, or the repetition of stock phrases. The śāstras are closer to what might be called systematic philosophy or theology, with positions presented with reasoned argumentation supported by relevant passages from the sūtras and tantras. East Asian Buddhism was predominantly a sūtra-based tradition, with schools forming around single texts, such as the *Lotus Sūtra* and the *Avataṃsaka Sūtra*. Although many important śāstras were translated into Chinese, the major project of translating Indian texts into Chinese virtually ended with the work of Xuanzang (596–664), by whose time the major East Asian schools were well formed. Consequently, works by such figures as the Middle Way philosophers Candrakīrti (c. 600–650) and Śāntideva (early eighth century) and the logician Dharmakīrti (seventh century), who flourished when the Chinese Buddhist schools had already developed, never gained wide currency in East Asia but were highly influential in Tibet. The works by these and other authors became the basis of the scholastic tradition in Tibet, which from the early period was a śāstra-based Buddhism. Sūtras were venerated but rarely read independently; the śāstras were studied and commented upon at great length.

To undertake the task of translation of the sūtras, tantras, and śāstras, a whole new vocabulary had to be created. To render an often technical Sanskrit vocabulary, hundreds of neologisms were invented. In some cases, these were relatively straightforward translations of folk etymologies; in other cases, rather unwieldy terms were fabricated to capture multiple denotations of a Sanskrit term. When these eighth-century exegetes came to decide upon a Tibetan equivalent for the Sanskrit term for teacher, *guru*, a term classically etymologized in India as "one who is heavy (with virtue)," the translators departed from their storied penchant for approximating the meaning of the Sanskrit and opted instead for the word lama (*bla ma*). Here they combined the term *la* ("soul") with *ma*, which has as least three meanings: as a negative particle, as a substantive indicator, and as the word for "mother." Subsequent Buddhist etymologies, drawing on the meaning of *la* as "high" rather than its pre-Buddhist usage as "soul," were then construed, which explained *la ma* as meaning either "highest" (literally, "above-not," that is, "none above") or as "exalted mother." Although the original intention of the translators remains obscure, lama came to be the standard term for one's religious teacher, a person of such significance as to be appended to the threefold refuge formula: Tibetans say, "I go for refuge to the lama, I go for refuge to the Buddha, I go for refuge to the dharma, I go for refuge to the saṅgha."

It would be impossible to summarize the contents of the myriad sūtras, tantras, and śāstras translated into Tibetan, but it might be appropriate at this juncture to review some of the basic elements of Indian Buddhism that were important in Tibet. Tibetans, both Bönpo and Buddhist, conceive of a beginningless cycle of birth and death, called *korwa* (*'khor ba*, a translation of the Sanskrit *saṃsāra*, "wandering"), in six realms of rebirth: gods, demigods, humans, animals, ghosts, and hell beings. The realms of animals, ghosts, and hell beings are regarded as places of great suffering, whereas the godly realms are abodes of great bliss. Human rebirth falls in between, bringing as it does both pleasure and pain. The engine of saṃsāra is driven by karma, the cause and effect of actions. Like other Buddhists, Tibetans believe that every intentional act, whether it be physical, verbal, or mental, leaves a residue in its agent. That residue, like a seed, will eventually produce an effect at some future point in this life or another life, an effect in the form of pleasure or pain for the person who performed the act. Thus Tibetans imagine a moral universe in which virtuous deeds create experiences of pleasure and nonvirtuous deeds create experiences of pain. These latter are often delineated in a list of ten nonvirtuous deeds: killing, stealing, sexual misconduct, lying, divisive speech, harsh speech, senseless speech, covetousness, harmful intent, and wrong view (notably belief that actions do not have effects). The ten virtues are the opposites of this list: sustaining life, giving gifts, maintaining sexual decorum, and so on. Much of Tibetan religious practice is concerned with accumulating virtuous deeds and preventing, through a variety of ritual means, the fruition of negative deeds already committed. These deeds determine not only the quality of a given life but also the place of the rebirth after death. Depending on the gravity of a negative deed (killing being more serious than senseless speech, and killing a human more serious than killing an insect, for example), one may be reborn as an animal, as a ghost, or in one of the hot or cold hells, where the life span is particularly lengthy.

As in India, karma is not concerned simply with what might be termed in the West moral and immoral deeds. There is, in conjunction with the belief that virtue brings happiness and nonvirtue sorrow, a powerful system of purity and pollution, generally concerned with one's behavior not toward humans but nonhumans, the various gods and spirits that inhabit the world. In determining the cause of some affliction, there is often an attempt by the afflicted or his or her ritual agent to determine both the karmic cause (some nonvirtuous deed in the past) and polluting acts (such as associating with a blacksmith, building a fire on a mountain, or accepting food from a widow) that contributed to that past evil deed coming to fruition in the form of a particular misfortune.

Rebirth as a god or human in the realm of desire is the result of a virtuous deed and is considered very rare. Rarer still is rebirth as a human who has access to the teachings of the Buddha. In a famous analogy, a single blind tortoise is said to swim in a vast ocean, surfacing for air only once every century. On the surface of the ocean floats a single golden yoke. It is rarer, said the Buddha, to be reborn as a human with the opportunity to practice the dharma than it is for the tortoise to surface for its centennial breath with its head through the hole in the golden yoke. One is said to be reborn as a god in the realm of desire as a result of an act of charity: giving gifts results in future wealth. Rebirth as a human is said to result from consciously refraining from a nonvirtuous deed, as when one takes a vow not to kill humans.

Although the various sects of Tibetan Buddhism derive their monastic regulations from the Indian schools known pejoratively as the Hīnayāna ("low vehicle"), all sects of Tibetan Buddhism identify themselves as proponents of the Mahāyāna, both in their practice and in their philosophy. Mahāyāna, a Sanskrit word that means "great vehicle," is the term used to distinguish a rather disparate group of cults of the book that arose in India some four hundred years after the death of the Buddha and continued in India into the twelfth century. During these centuries, the followers of the Mahāyāna produced a vast literature of sūtras that purport to be the word of the historical Buddha, as well as commentaries upon them. Among the factors characteristic of the Mahāyāna are the view of the Buddha as an eternal presence, associated physically with reliquaries (stūpas) and with texts that embody his words, a belief in the existence of myriad buddhas working in multiple universes for the benefit of all beings, and an attendant emphasis on the universal possibility of enlightenment for all, monks and laypeople alike. It is from this last tenet that the term "Great Vehicle" is derived: the proponents of the Mahāyāna believed that their path was capable of bringing all beings in the universe to buddhahood, whereas the earlier teachings were capable only of delivering the individual disciple to a state of solitary peace.

Perhaps the most famous feature of the Mahāyāna is its emphasis on the bodhisattva, a person who makes the compassionate vow to become a buddha in order to lead all beings in the universe out of suffering and to the bliss of enlightenment. The Sanskrit term *bodhisattva* was rendered into Tibetan as *jang chup sem ba (byang chub sems dpa')*, "one who is heroic in his or her aspiration to enlightenment." The path of the bodhisattva is portrayed as one of extraordinary length, encompassing billions of lifetimes devoted to cultivating such virtues as generosity, ethics, patience, effort, concentration, and wisdom, the so-called six perfections, all of these deeds motivated by the wish to liberate all beings from the beginningless cycle of rebirth.

A common tenet of Buddhism is that all suffering is ultimately the result of ignorance. This ignorance is defined as a belief in self. Mahāyāna philosophy expands upon earlier teachings to see ignorance not simply as a misconception concerning the nature of the person, but as a misunderstanding of all things. According to the Middle Way school, the fundamental error is to conceive of things as existing in and of themselves—independently, autonomously, possessed of some intrinsic nature, some inherent existence. Wisdom, the sixth of the perfections to be cultivated by the bodhisattva, is the understanding that all things, including persons, are utterly devoid of such a nature and are, in fact, empty of an independent status, although they exist conventionally. To say that things exist conventionally means, for example, that cause and effect remain viable and that things perform functions; one can sit on a chair and drink tea from a cup. Emptiness, then, does not mean that things do not exist at all, but rather that they do not exist as they appear to the unenlightened.

To become enlightened, then, the bodhisattva must develop not only this wisdom but infinite compassion as well, that is, must dedicate himself or herself to work forever for the welfare of others while simultaneously understanding that all beings, including oneself, do not exist ultimately, that they do not exist as they appear.

The practice of the Mahāyāna generally may be said to take two forms, both focused on the bodhisattva. The most influential of the Mahāyāna sūtras, such as the *Lotus Sūtra*, proclaim that all beings will eventually become buddhas, and that, consequently, all beings will traverse the bodhisattva path. Thus, one form of Mahāyāna belief emphasizes practices for becoming a bodhisattva and performing the bodhisattva's deeds. As bodhisattvas advance along the path, they become increasingly adept at allaying the sufferings of sentient beings who call upon them for aid, often through miraculous intercession. Consequently, the other major form of Mahāyāna practice is concerned with devotions intended to procure the aid of these compassionate beings. The bodhisattva who is said to be the physical manifestation of all the compassion of all the buddhas in the universe, Avalokiteśvara, is the particular object of such reverence in Tibet, as discussed below. Avalokiteśvara is invoked by the famous mantra *oṃ maṇi padme hūṃ*, which might be rendered as, "O you who hold the jeweled [rosary] and the lotus [have mercy on us]." (It certainly does not mean "the jewel in the lotus.") Avalokiteśvara is depicted in a wide variety of forms in Tibetan art, two of the most frequent being with one head and four arms (two of which hold a rosary and a lotus evoked in the mantra) or with eleven heads and a thousand arms. The multiple arms are said to represent the bodhisattva's extraordinary ability to come to the aid of suffering sentient beings. Paintings of the thousand-armed Avalokiteśvara often show an eye in the palm of each of the hands. The bodhisattva thus serves as both role model and object of devotion in Mahāyāna Buddhism, functions that are by no means deemed mutually exclusive; it is quite common for persons who consider themselves to have embarked on the bodhisattva path to seek the assistance of more advanced bodhisattvas in their long quest for enlightenment.

In the realm of Buddhist practice, the Tibetans were able to witness and assimilate the most important development of late Indian Buddhism, Buddhist tantra. Tantra, known also as the *vajrayāna*, the "Diamond Vehicle," and the *mantrayāna*, the "Mantra Vehicle," was considered an esoteric approach to the Mahāyāna path whereby the length of time required to achieve buddhahood could be abbreviated from the standard length of three periods of countless aeons (reckoned by some as 384×10^{58} years) to as little as three years and three months. One of the chief techniques for effecting such an extraordinary reduction in the length of the path was an elaborate system of ritual, visualization, and meditation, sometimes called deity yoga, in which the practitioner imagined himself or herself to be already fully enlightened with the marvelous body, speech, mind, and abode of a buddha. In addition to the ultimate attainment of buddhahood, tantric practice was said to bestow a wide range of lesser magical powers, such as the power to increase wealth and life span, to pacify the inauspicious, and to destroy enemies, both human and nonhuman. Yogins who developed these powers were known as *mahāsiddhas*, "great adepts"; they are popular subjects of Tibetan Buddhist literature.

Among the elements of tantric Buddhism most commonly identified in the West are its erotic and wrathful motifs, where male and female are depicted in sexual union and bull-headed deities, adorned with garlands of human heads, brandish cleavers and skullcups. In Mahāyāna Buddhism, as already mentioned, wisdom and compassion (also referred to as method, that is, the compassionate means whereby bodhisattvas become buddhas) are the essential components of the bodhisattva's path to buddhahood. Wisdom, especially the perfection of wisdom, is identified with the female. In tantra, the symbolism is rendered in more explicitly sexual terms, with wisdom as female and method male, their union being essential to the achievement of enlightenment. Buddhist tantra is said to be the "Diamond Vehicle" because wisdom and method are joined in an adamantine and indivisible union, bestowing buddhahood quickly. This is the chief symbolic meaning of depiction of sexual union. However, part of the unique nature of the tantric path is its capacity to employ deeds that are ordinarily prohibited in practices that speed progress on the path to enlightenment, hence the great emphasis on antinomian behavior, such as the consumption of meat and alcohol, in the hagiographies of the *mahāsiddhas*. One such deed is sexual intercourse, and many tantric texts, especially of the Unexcelled Yoga (*anuttarayoga*) variety, prescribe ritual union as a means of unifying the mind of the clear light and the immutable bliss. Whether this intercourse is to be performed only in imagination or in fact, and at what point on the path it is to take place, has been a point of considerable discussion in Tibetan tantric exegesis.

Wrathful deities also populate the tantric pantheon. Despite claims by nineteenth-century scholars that continue to be repeated, the most important of these deities are not of Tibetan shamanic origin, added to Indian Buddhism after its arrival in Tibet. It is clear from Indian tantric texts that these deities derive directly from India. Some are buddhas and bodhisattvas in their wrathful aspects, the most famous of these being Yamantaka, the wrathful manifestation of the bodhisattva of wisdom, Mañjuśrī. His terrifying form is said to be intended to frighten away the egotism and selfishness that are the cause of all suffering. Other wrathful deities have the task of protecting the dharma; others are worldly deities with specific powers that may be propitiated. Despite such explanations, Western scholars of Tibet have yet to engage adequately the issue of the apparent presence of the demonic in the divine that confronts the observer so richly in Tibetan religious iconography.

Tantric Buddhism places especial emphasis on the role of the teacher. The teacher-student relationship was always of great importance in Buddhism, providing the means by which the dharma was passed from one generation to the next. In tantra, however, the teacher or guru took on an even more important role. The practice of the Vajrayāna, the rapid path to enlightenment, was regarded as a secret teaching, not suitable for everyone. For that reason, the teacher was both the repository of secret knowledge and the person who was to judge the qualifications of the student as a receptacle for that knowledge. Once the student was deemed ready, the teacher provided the student with an initiation, serving as the surrogate of the Buddha, and one of the basic practices of Buddhist tantra is thus to regard one's own teacher as the Buddha. In fact, Tibetans are fond of saying that the teacher is actually kinder than the Buddha, because the Buddha did not remain in the world to teach us benighted beings of this degenerate age. This great emphasis on the importance of the teacher was inherited from India, as the accounts of Tibetans' sojourns to India make clear. Because of this importance of the teacher, or lama, during the nineteenth century Tibetan Buddhism was dubbed "Lamaism," a term that continues to appear today. Tibetan Buddhists regard this as a pejorative term, because it suggests that whereas there is Chinese Buddhism, Japanese Buddhism, Thai Buddhism, and so forth, the Buddhism of Tibet is so different that it does not warrant the name "Tibetan Buddhism" but should be called "Lamaism."

In the Vajrayāna, rituals called *sādhanas* (literally, "means of achievement") are set forth in which the practitioner, through a practice of visualization, petitions a buddha or bodhisattva to come into his or her presence. Much of the practice described in tantric sādhanas involves the enactment of a world—the fantastic jewel-encrusted world of the Mahāyāna sūtras or the horrific world of the charnel ground. In the tantric sādhana, the practitioner manifests that world through visualization, through a process of invitation, descent, and identification. Tantric sādhanas generally take one of two forms. In the first, the buddha or bodhisattva is requested to appear before the meditator and is then worshipped in the expectation of receiving blessings. In the other type of tantric sādhana, the meditator imagines himself or herself to be a fully enlightened buddha or bodhisattva now, to have the exalted body, speech, and mind of an enlightened being. In either case, the central deity in the visualization is called a *yi dam*, a word difficult to translate into English. It is sometimes rendered as "tutelary deity," but the *yi dam* offers much more than protection. The *yi dam* is the tantric buddha with which the meditator identifies in daily meditation and whom he or she propitiates in daily rituals. Some *yi dams* take peaceful forms, adorned with the silks and jewels of an Indian monarch. Others appear in wrathful forms, brandishing weapons and wreathed in flames.

Tantric sādhanas tend to follow a fairly set sequence, whether they are simple and brief or more detailed and prolix. More elaborate sādhanas may include the recitation of a lineage of gurus; the creation of a protection wheel guarded by wrathful deities to subjugate enemies; the creation of a body maṇḍala, in which a pantheon of deities take residence at various parts of the meditator's body; etc.

In many sādhanas, the meditator is instructed to imagine light radiating from the body, inviting buddhas and bodhisattvas from throughout the universe. Visualizing them arrayed in the space before him or her, the meditator then performs a series of standard preliminary practices called the sevenfold service, a standard component of sādhanas and prayers that developed from an Indian Mahāyāna three-part liturgy (the *triskandhaka*). Prior to the actual sevenfold service, the assembled deities are offered (again, in visualization) a bath and new clothing and are treated just as an honored guest would be in India. The sevenfold service is then performed. The first of the seven elements is obeisance, an expression of homage to the assembled deities. Next comes offering, usually the longest section of the seven parts. Here fantastic gifts are imagined to be arrayed before the buddhas and bodhisattvas to please each of their five senses: beautiful forms for the eye, music for the ears, fragrances for the nose, delicacies for the tongue, and sensuous silks for the body. The offering often concludes with a gift of the entire physical universe with all its marvels. The third step is confession of misdeeds. Despite the apparent inexorability of the law of karma, it is nonetheless believed that by sincerely confessing a sin to the buddhas and bodhisattvas, promising not to commit it again in the future, and performing some kind of purificatory penance (usually the recitation of mantra) as an antidote to the sin, the eventual negative effect of the negative deed can be avoided. The fourth step, admiration, also relates to the law of karma. It is believed that acknowledging, praising, and otherwise taking pleasure in the virtuous deeds of others causes the taker of such pleasure to accumulate the same merit as that accrued by the person who actually performed the good deed.

The fifth step is an entreaty to the buddhas not to pass into nirvāna. A buddha is said to have the ability to live for aeons but will do so only if he is asked; otherwise, he will disappear from the world, pretending to die and pass into nirvāṇa. Indian sūtras recount the Buddha scolding his attendant for not making such a request. In Tibet this entreaty to the buddhas to remain in the world developed from a standard component of daily prayers to a separate genre of literature, called *shap den* (*zhabs brtan*); the term literally means "steadfast feet," suggesting that the buddhas remain with their feet firmly planted in this world. However, in Tibet these prayers were composed and recited for the surrogate of the absent Buddha, the lama. Prayers for "steadfast feet" or long-life prayers are hence composed for one's teacher. The sixth of the seven branches follows naturally from the entreaty to remain in the world; it is a supplication of the buddhas and bodhisattvas to teach the dharma. The final step is the dedication of the merit of performing the preceding toward the enlightenment of all beings.

The meditator then goes for refuge to the three jewels, creates the aspiration to enlightenment, the promise to achieve buddhahood in order to liberate all beings in the universe from suffering, and dedicates the merit from the foregoing and subsequent practices toward that end. The meditator next cultivates the four attitudes of love, compassion, joy, and equanimity, before meditating on emptiness and reciting the purificatory mantra, *oṃ svabhāvaśuddhāḥ sarvadharmāḥ svabhāvaśuddho 'haṃ*, "Oṃ, naturally pure are all phenomena, naturally pure am I," understanding that emptiness is the primordial nature of everything, the unmoving world and the beings who move upon it. Out of this emptiness, the meditator next creates the maṇḍala.

The meditator here creates an imaginary universe out of emptiness. The foundation is provided by the four elements wind, fire, water, and earth (represented by Sanskrit syllables). On top of these, the meditator visualizes the maṇḍala. The Sanskrit term *maṇḍala* simply means circle, but in this context within a tantric sādhana, a maṇḍala is the residence of a buddha, an extraordinary palace inhabited by buddhas and their consorts, by bodhisattvas, and protectors. A maṇḍala may be quite spare, an undescribed palace with only five deities, one deity in the center and one in each of the cardinal directions. But usually maṇḍalas are much more elaborate. The Guhyasamāja maṇḍala, for example, is articulated in great detail, with five layers of walls of white, yellow, red, green, and blue. It has a jeweled molding, archways, and a quadruple colonnade. It is festooned with jewels and pendants and is populated by thirty-two deities, each on its own throne, arrayed on two levels. The maṇḍala is the perfected world that the meditator seeks to manifest and then inhabit, either by identifying with the central deity or by making offerings to him or her. It was said to be essential that the visualization be carried out in precise detail, with each item of silk clothing and gold ornament appearing clearly. It was also necessary for the meditator to imagine the fantastic palace of the buddha, the maṇḍala, which he or she inhabited, noting the particular bodhisattvas, protectors, gods, and goddesses located throughout the multistoried dwelling. Part of this visualization was accomplished through the description of the details in the tantric text itself. However, meditators were typically advised to study a visual image of the particular buddha and maṇḍala, and this was one of the uses to which paintings and statues were put by those involved in meditation practice. Paintings and statues were not considered to be functional in any context, even as the object of simple devotion, until they were consecrated in a special ceremony in which the dharmakāya was caused to descend into and animate the icon.

The next step in the sādhana is for the meditator to animate the residents of the maṇḍala by causing the actual buddhas and bodhisattvas, referred to as "wisdom beings" (*ye shes sems dpa', jñānasattva*), to descend and merge with their imagined doubles, the "pledge beings" (*dam tshig sems dpa', samayasattva*). Light radiates from meditator's heart, drawing the wisdom beings to the maṇḍala where, through offerings and the recitation of the mantra *jaḥ hūṃ baṃ hoḥ* ("Be summoned, enter, become fused with, be pleased"), they are caused to enter the residents of the maṇḍala. The residents are then often blessed with three syllables: a white *oṃ* at the crown of the head, a red *āḥ* at the throat, and a blue *hūṃ* at the heart.

With the preliminary visualization now complete, the stage is set for the central meditation of the sādhana, and this varies depending upon the purpose of the sādhana. Generally, offerings and prayers are made to a sequence of deities and boons are requested from them, each time accompanied by the recitation of appropriate mantra. At the end of the session, the meditator makes mental offerings to the assembly before inviting them to leave, at which point the entire visualization, the palace and its residents, dissolves into emptiness. The sādhana ends with a dedication of the merit accrued from the session to the welfare of all beings.

From this brief survey of Buddhist doctrine and practice, several distinctive elements of Tibetan Buddhism become apparent. First, Tibetan Buddhism is the last of the major national Buddhisms to develop, having access to a larger corpus of Indian Buddhist literature than reached China or Japan, for example. As discussed above, this literature included the śāstras and the tantras, such that Tibetan Buddhism can generally be characterized as śāstra-based in its doctrine and tantra-based in its practice. It is important to note, however, that certain central elements of practice, such as monastic regulations and the techniques for creating the bodhisattva's compassionate aspiration to buddhahood, are delineated in śāstras. Furthermore, all sects of Tibetan Buddhism developed sophisticated scholastic traditions of tantric exegesis.

Second, the Tibetans had sustained contact with major figures of the late Indian Buddhist tradition for over a century, and the legacies of these figures, such as Atiśa and Niguma, remain powerful elements of the tradition. Third, Tibet was perhaps the least culturally evolved of the major Buddhist nations at the time of the introduction of Buddhism, when culture is measured in terms of written language, literature, and structures of state. The introduction of Buddhism encountered resistance, as noted above, but with the demise of the royal line in 842, the way was left open for Buddhism to provide the dominant ideology for the entire Inner Asian cultural area. Finally, Tibetan Buddhism is the only major form of Buddhism to continue in a fairly traditional form into the second half of this century.

The evidence of the early records indicates that, despite their patronage of Buddhism, Ralpajen and his two predecessor kings gave numerous public testimonies to their attachment to principles irreconcilable with Buddhism, principles pertaining to the highly structured politico-religious system of divine kingship (called *gtsug lag*), while at the same time propagating the new religion. The translation of Indian Buddhist literature, the sūtras, tantras, and śāstras, from Sanskrit into Tibetan was interrupted by the suppression of Buddhist monastic institutions in 838 by the king Langdarma (Glang dar ma, ruled c. 836–842). Although Langdarma is represented as the embodiment of evil in Buddhist accounts, persecuting monks and nuns and closing monasteries, recent scholarship indicates that his persecution, if it took place at all, amounted to a withdrawal of state patronage to the growing monastic institutions.

Nevertheless, his reign, which according to later Buddhist accounts ended with his assassination in 842 by a Buddhist monk (an event some scholars question), is traditionally seen as the end of what is called the early dissemination of Buddhism in Tibet and the beginning of a dark period of disorder, at least in central Tibet. It marked the beginning of the end of the royal line and the eventual disintegration of the Tibetan empire. Although it is the case that the status of

Buddhist thought and practice during the next century and a half remains only vaguely understood by modern scholars, its representation in traditional Buddhist histories as a time of degradation and chaos may be something of an exaggeration, motivated to provide a striking contrast with the glorious renaissance that was to follow. Nevertheless, little of "pre-Buddhist" religion of Tibet survived intact after this period. This religion, which Tibetans call "the religion of humans" (*mi chos*), as opposed to the "religion of the gods" (*lha chos*, identified with Buddhism and Bön) is all but impossible to identify, with much of its content assimilated by Buddhism and Bön after the eleventh century, leaving only a few legends, aphorisms, and folk songs.

After the so-called dark period a Buddhist revival began in western Tibet in the eleventh century, a period of active translation of numerous philosophical texts and the retranslation of texts, especially tantras, first translated during the period of the earlier dissemination. The eleventh century was also a time of active travel of Tibetan translators to India, where they studied with Indian Buddhist masters in Bihar, Bengal, and Kashmir. Many of the sects of Tibetan Buddhism trace their lineages back to these encounters.

The most famous Indian scholar to visit Tibet during what came to be called the second dissemination was the Bengali master Atiśa (982–1054). A Tibetan named Dromdön ('Brom ston pa) was Atiśa's first and closest Tibetan disciple. He urged Atiśa to visit central Tibet and organized his tour of the area, where Atiśa taught and translated until his death in 1054. Dromdön devoted the rest of his life to preserving Atiśa's teachings, establishing the monastery of Rva sgreng in 1056 and founding the first Tibetan Buddhist monastic order, the Kadampa (Bka' gdams pa, which is traditionally etymologized as "those who take all of the Buddha's words as instructions"). Although Drom was a respected scholar and translator, he is best remembered for the rigor and austerity of his Buddhist practice. He seems to have been wary of the potential for abuse in tantrism and imposed on his followers a strict discipline and devotion to practice for which they became famous. They abstained from marriage, intoxicants, travel, and the possession of money. Although later Tibetan orders were not as strict, the Kadampa provided the model for all later Tibetan monasticism.

The monastery was an institution of fundamental importance for all sects of Tibetan Buddhism. The first monastery was constructed around 779 under the direction of the Indian paṇḍita Śāntarakṣita and the tantric master Padmasambhava. From the outset, Tibetan monasteries were modeled on the great monastic centers of late Indian Buddhism, where the monastic code was maintained in conjunction with scholastic education and tantric practice. With the growth in lay and state patronage, some monasteries grew from small retreat centers to vast monastic complexes. The largest of these, such as Drepung (which, with some 13,000 monks in 1959, was the largest Buddhist monastery in the world), functioned as self-sufficient cities, with their own economy (with farms worked by sharecroppers), government, and police force. Tibetan monks were not fully supported by the monasteries, receiving only a small ration of tea and roasted barley for their subsistence; they had to rely on their families or their own earnings (from trade or performing rituals) for anything more. Monks did not go on begging rounds, like their counterparts in Southeast Asia, but engaged in a wide range of occupations. It is therefore inaccurate to imagine that all Tibetan monks spent their days in meditation or in debating sophisticated points of doctrine; only a small percentage were thus occupied. Furthermore, the majority of the occupants of Tibetan monasteries remained as novices throughout their lives, not going on to take the vows of a fully ordained monk (*dge slong*, *bhikṣu*).

To be a monk was to hold a respected social status in the Tibetan world, and monkhood provided one of the few routes to social advancement. Monks who distinguished themselves as scholars, teachers, or meditators commanded great respect and attracted substantial patronage, especially those considered to be effective in performance of rituals and divinations. Such monks could rise through the monastic ranks to positions of great authority as abbots or (among the Geluk) as government officials.

Each of the sects, both Buddhist and Bönpo, had large monasteries that drew monks from all over the Tibetan cultural sphere, which extended from as far west as the Kalmyk region between the Caspian Sea and the Black Sea, from as far east as Sichuan, from as far north as the Buryiat region near Lake Baikal, and from as far south as Nepal. Some came for an education and then returned to their home regions, while others remained for life. However, the majority of monasteries in Tibet were isolated places (as the Tibetan term for monastery, *dgon pa*, suggests), populated by a few dozen local monks who performed rituals for the local community and were supported by their families. Monastic life, whether in a major center or a remote hermitage, was not so much a matter of doctrine or belief, but of behavior, a behavior that creates the identity of the monk. That behavior was governed by a monastic code inherited from India but adapted for each monastery in its constitution called a *ja yik* (*bca' yig*).

Although a substantial segment of the male population of Tibetan was monks (estimated between 10 and 15 percent), the community of nuns (*a ni*) was much smaller (perhaps 3 percent). They lived in some six hundred nunneries, the largest of which, a Kagyu institution called Gechak Thekchen Ling (Dge chag theg chen gling), housed approximately one thousand nuns. Whereas Tibetan monks could eventually receive the full ordination of the gelong (*dge slong*), the order of full nuns was never established in Tibet, such that nuns could advance no higher than the rank of novice. (There have been efforts in recent years, led largely by Western women who have become Tibetan nuns, to receive full ordination from Chinese nuns in Taiwan and Singapore). Being a nun carried little of the status held by a monk; there is a Tibetan proverb that if you want to be a servant, make your son a monk; if you want a servant, make your daughter a nun. Unmarried daughters often became nuns (sometimes remaining at home). Other women became nuns to escape a bad marriage, to avoid pregnancy, or after the death of a spouse. The educational opportunities and chances for social advancement open to monks were generally absent for nuns, whose chief activities involved the memorization and recitation of prayer and the performance of ritual.

The role of women in Tibetan religions was not, however, limited simply to the order of nuns. There are many important females divinities, both peaceful and wrathful, benevolent and malevolent. The goddess Tārā stands with Avalokiteśvara as the most commonly invoked of Buddhist deities. The wrathful tantric goddess Belden Lhamo is the special protectoress of the Tibetan state. Among the many malevolent female forms, one finds the "gossip girl," who sows discord in the community. Women have also played significant roles in various meditation and ritual lineages, such as the Indian yoginī Niguma, the wife of king Tri Songdetsen and consort of Padmasambhava, Yeshe Tsogyal (Ye shes mtsho rgyal), and the tantric master Majik Lapdön (Ma gcig lab sgron). There are lines of female incarnations, the most famous of whom is Dorje Pamo (Rdo rje phag mo, the "Diamond Sow"). Beyond these famous figures, Tibetan women have played important roles as mediums for deities or as messengers for bodhisattvas. The majority of those who return from the dead to bring messages from the deceased and exhortations to observe the laws of karma are women. Despite the disproportionate investment of religious power and authority in the males of Tibetan society, women enjoyed a greater economic and sexual autonomy in Tibet than generally was the case elsewhere in Asia. Many of the rituals and practices described in this volume would have been practiced by women as well as men.

With the decline of the monarchy, both political and religious authority (although the strict distinction between the two should not be immediately assumed in the case of Tibet) shifted gradually to Buddhist teachers. Since many of these were Buddhist monks who had taken vows of celibacy, the problem of succession eventually arose. In some cases, authority was passed from a monk to his nephew. However, by the fourteenth century (and perhaps even earlier) a form of succession developed in Tibet that, although supported by standard Buddhist doctrine, seems unique in the Buddhist world. This was the institution of the incarnate lama or *tulku* (*sprul sku*).

In Mahāyāna literature there is a doctrine of the three bodies of the Buddha. The first is the *dharmakāya*. Prior to the rise of the Mahāyāna, this term meant the "body of [uncontaminated] qualities," those qualities of the Buddha, such as his wisdom, patience, and fearlessness, that were not subject to suffering and decay. It was this body that was deemed the true object of the practice of refuge. Thus, the term "body" came to shift its meaning from the physical form of the Buddha to a collection of timeless abstract virtues. In Mahāyāna literature, the dharmakāya is often represented as almost a cosmic principle, an ultimate reality in which all buddhas partake through their omniscient minds. For this reason, some scholars translate dharmakāya as "Truth Body." After the dharmakāya comes the enjoyment body (*saṃbhogakāya*), a fantastic form of a buddha that resides only in the highest pure land, adorned with thirty-two major and eighty minor physical marks, eternally teaching the Mahāyāna to highly advanced bodhisattvas; the enjoyment body does not appear to ordinary beings. Many tantric deities are depicted in the enjoyment body form. The third body is the emanation body (*nirmāṇakāya*). It is this body that appears in the world to teach the dharma. The emanation bodies are not limited to the form of the Buddha with which we are familiar; a buddha is able to appear in whatever form, animate or inanimate, that is appropriate to benefit suffering sentient beings.

Tibetans chose the term for the third body of a buddha to name their notion of incarnation. That is, the next incarnation of a former great teacher is called a tulku (*sprul sku*), the Tibetan translation of nirmāṇakāya, "emanation body." The implication is that there is a profound difference in the processes whereby ordinary beings and incarnate lamas take birth in the world. For the former, rebirth is harrowing process, a frightful journey into the unknown, a process over which one has no control. One is blown by the winds of karma into an intermediate state (*bar do*) and then into a new lifetime. There is a strong possibility that new life will be in the lower realms as an animal, hungry ghost, or hell being; Tibetans say that the number of beings in these three lower realms is as large as the number of stars seen on a clear night and the number of beings in the realms of gods and humans is as large as the number stars seen on a clear day. The fate of the denizens of hell is particularly horrific, and Tibetans recount the journeys of those who are able to visit the lower realms of rebirth and return to tell the tale. The process of powerless rebirth is a beginningless cycle and can only be brought to an end by the individual achievement of liberation and enlightenment through the practice of the path.

The rebirth of an incarnate lama is a very different matter. As "emanation bodies," incarnate lamas are technically buddhas, free from the bonds of karma. Their rebirth is thus entirely voluntary. They need not be reborn at all, yet they decide to return to the world out of their compassion for others. Furthermore, they exercise full control over their rebirth. For ordinary beings, rebirth must take place within forty-nine days from the time of death. Incarnate lamas are under no such constraints. For ordinary beings, the circumstances of the rebirth—the place, the parents, the form of the body, and the capacity of the mind—are all determined by karma. For the incarnate lama, all of these are a matter of choice and are said to have been decided in advance, so that a dying incarnation will often leave instructions for his disciples as to where to find his next rebirth.

Since the fourteenth century, all sects of Tibetan Buddhism have adopted the practice of identifying the successive rebirths of a great teacher, the most famous instance of which being of course the Dalai Lamas. But there some three thousand other lines of incarnation in Tibet (only several of whom are female). The institution of the incarnate lama has proved to be a central component of Tibetan society, providing the means by which authority and charisma, in all of their symbolic and material forms, are passed from one generation to another. Indeed, the spread of Tibetan Buddhism can usefully be traced by the increasingly large geographical areas in which incarnate lamas are discovered, extending today to Europe and North America.

A common use of the term "lama" is as the designation of incarnations. In ordinary Tibetan parlance, such persons are called "lamas" whether or not they have distinguished themselves as scholars, adepts, or teachers in their present lives. The ambiguity in usage between "lama" as a religious preceptor and "lama" as an incarnation has led the current Dalai Lama in his sermons to admonish his followers that a lama (as one's religious teacher) need not be an incarnation and that an incarnation is not necessarily a lama (in the sense of a fully qualified religious teacher).

The period of the thirteenth through fifteenth centuries was among the most consequential for the history of Tibetan Buddhism, with the development of distinct sects that evolved from the various lineages of teaching that had been initiated during the previous periods. These sects are traditionally divided under two major headings: those who base their tantric practice on texts translated during the period of the first dissemination and those who base their tantric practice on texts translated or retranslated during the period of the second dissemination. These two groups are referred to simply as the old (*rnying ma*) and the new (*gsar ma*), with the old obviously including the Nyingmapa (Rnying ma pa) sect and the new including the Kagyu, Sakya, and Geluk. The Nyingmapa sect traces its origins back to the first dissemination and the teachings of Padmasambhava, who visited Tibet during the eighth century. "Treasures," called *terma* (*gter ma*), believed to have been hidden by him, began to be discovered in the eleventh century and continue to be discovered even into the twentieth century; the fourteenth century was an especially active period for text discoverers (*gter ston*). According to their claim, these texts were sometimes discovered in physical form, often within stone, or mentally, within the mind of the discoverer. Often ignored in the old-new categorization are the Bönpos, who seem to have appeared as a self-conscious "sect" in the eleventh century, along with new sects, but who represent themselves as even older than the old (Nyingma), predating the introduction of Buddhism into Tibet.

The various institutional entities of Tibetan Buddhism are referred to in Tibetan as *chos lugs*, literally, "dharma systems." This term is generally rendered into English with one of three terms: order, school, or sect. Each of these translations is misleading. "Order" implies a monastic unit with its own code of conduct, whereas in Tibet all Buddhist monks followed the same Indian monastic code. Furthermore, many adherents of the Tibetan groups are not monks or nuns. "School" implies a group distinguished on the basis of philosophical tenets, and although there are differences among the Tibetan Buddhist groups, there is much more that they share. "Sect" carries the negative connotation of a group dissenting from a majority that perceives it as somehow heretical. If that connotation can be ignored, however, "sect" provides a serviceable translation and is used here. What is perhaps more important than the translation used is to understand that central to each of these groups is the notion of lineage. Like other Buddhist traditions, the Tibetans based claims to authority largely on lineage, and in their case, they claimed that the Buddhism taught in Tibet and by Tibetan lamas abroad could be traced backward in an unbroken line to the eleventh century, when the founders of the major Tibetan sects made the perilous journey to India to receive the dharma from the great masters of Bengal, Bihar, and Kashmir, who were themselves direct recipients of teachings that could be traced back to the Buddha himself. Moreover, this lineage was represented as essentially oral, with instructions being passed down from master to disciple as an unwritten commentary on a sacred text. Even those sects that could not so easily list a successive line of teachers stretching back through the past, such as the Nyingmapas and Bönpos, were able to maintain the power of their lineage through the device of the hidden and rediscovered text, the *terma*, designed to leapfrog over centuries, bringing the authentic teaching directly into the present. These texts thus provided the present with the sanction of the past by ascribing to their ancient and absent author (usually Padmasambhava) the gift of prophecy.

Nyingma (Rnying ma)

The Nyingma sect traces its origins back to the teachings of the mysterious figure Padmasambhava, who visited Tibet during the eight century. The Nyingmapas include in their canonical corpus a collection of tantras (the *Rnying ma rgyud 'bum*) as well as these discovered texts, all works that the other sects generally regard as apocryphal, that is, not of Indian origin.

The Nyingma sect produced many famous scholars and visionaries, such as Longchenpa (Klong chen rab 'byams, 1308–1363), Jigme Lingpa ('Jigs med gling pa, 1729–1798), and Mipham ('Ju Mi pham rnam rgyal, 1846–1912). Nyingma identifies nine vehicles among the corpus of Buddhist teachings, the highest of which is known as Atiyoga or, more commonly, the Great Perfection (*rdzogs chen*). These teachings, found also in Bön, describe the mind as the primordial basis, characterized by qualities such as presence, spontaneity, luminosity, original purity, unobstructed freedom, expanse, clarity, self-liberation, openness, effortlessness, and intrinsic awareness. It is not accessible through conceptual elaboration or logical analysis. Rather, the primordial basis is an eternally pure state free from dualism of subject and object, infinite and perfect from the beginning, ever complete. The Great Perfection tradition shares with certain Indian Buddhist schools the view that the mind creates the appearances of the world, the arena of human suffering. All of these appearances are said to be illusory, however. The ignorant mind believes that its own creations are real, forgetting its true nature of original purity. For the mind willfully to seek to liberate itself is both inappropriate and futile because it is already self-liberated. The technique for the discovery of the ubiquitous original purity and self-liberation is to engage in a variety of practices designed to eliminate karmic obstacles, at which point the mind eliminates all thought and experiences itself, thereby recognizing its true nature. The Great Perfection doctrine does not seem to be directly derived from any of the Indian philosophical schools; its precise connections to the Indian Buddhist tradition have yet to be established. Some scholars have claimed a historical link and doctrinal affinity between the Great Perfection and the Chan tradition of Chinese Buddhism, but the precise relationship between the two remains to be fully investigated. It is noteworthy that certain of the earliest extant Great Perfection texts specifically contrast their own tradition with that of Chan.

Unlike the Geluks, Kagyu, and Sakya, the Nyingma (along with the Bönpo, with whom they share much in common) remained largely uninvolved in politics, both within Tibet and in foreign relations. They also lacked the kind of hierarchies found in the other sects. Although they developed great monasteries such as Mindroling (Smin grol gling), they also maintained a strong local presence as lay tantric practioners (*sngags pa*) who performed a range of ritual functions for the community.

Kagyu (Bka' brgyud)

The Kagyu sect derives its lineage from the visits by Marpa the Translator (1012–1099) to India, where he studied under several of the famous tantric masters of the day, including Nāropa (the disciple of Tilopa) and Maitrīpa. Marpa's disciple Milarepa (Mi la ras pa, "Cotton-clad Mila") is said to have achieved buddhahood in one lifetime (an achievement usually considered to require aeons of practice) through his diligent meditation practice in the caves of southern Tibet, despite having committed murder as a youth through the practice of black magic. His moving biography and didactic songs are among the most famous works of Tibetan literature. Milarepa's most illustrious disciple was the scholar and physician Gampopa (Sgam po pa, 1079–1153), who gave a strong monastic foundation to the sect. His own disciples, in turn, are regarded as the founders of the four major schools and the eight minor schools of the Kagyu. The most important of these is the Karma Kagyu, led by a succession of incarnate lamas called the Karmapas, headquartered at Tshurpu (Mtshur pu) monastery. Among the prominent philosophers of the Kagyu sect are the eighth Karmapa, Migyö Dorje (Mi bskyod rdo rje, 1507–1554), Pema Garpo (Padma dkar po, 1527–1592), and Kongtrül (Kong sprul yon tan rgya mtsho, 1813–1899).

The defining doctrine of the Kagyu sect is the Great Seal (*phyag rgya chen mo, mahāmudrā*), which Kagyus regard as the crowning experience of Buddhist practice. The Great Seal is a state of enlightened awareness in which phenomenal appearance and noumenal emptiness are unified. Like the Great Perfection of the Nyingmapas, it is considered to be primordially present, that is, not something that is newly created. Rather than emphasizing the attainment of an extraordinary level of consciousness, the Great Seal literature exalts the ordinary state of mind as both the natural and ultimate state, characterized by lucidity and simplicity. In Kagyu literature, this ordinary mind is contrasted with the worldly mind. The former, compared to a mirror, reflects reality exactly as it is, simply and purely, whereas the worldly mind is distorted by its mistaken perception of subject and object as real. Rather than seeking to destroy this worldly mind as other systems do, however, in the Great Seal the worldly mind is valued for its ultimate identity with the ordinary mind; every deluded thought contains within it the lucidity and simplicity of the ordinary mind. This identity merely needs to be recognized to bring about the dawning of wisdom, the realization that a natural purity pervades all existence, including the deluded mind.

Sakya (Sa skya)

The Sakya sect looks back to another translator, Drokmi Shakya Yeshe ('Brog mi Shākya ye shes, 993–1050), who studied in India under disciples of the tantric master Virūpa. Khon Gonchok Gyalpo ('Khon dkon mchog rgyal po), a disciple of Drokmi, founded a monastery at Sakya ("gray earth") in 1073. This monastery became the seat of the sect, hence its name. The most influential scholars of the Sakya sect in the twelfth and thirteenth centuries were members of the 'Khon family, the most notable of whom was Gunga Gyaltsen (Kun dga' rgyal mtshan, 1181–1251), better known as Sakya Paṇḍita. He studied under one of the last generations of Indian Buddhist scholars to visit Tibet, notably Śākyaśrībhadra. Sakya Paṇḍita claims two important achievements in the history of Tibetan philosophy. First, he defeated a Hindu paṇḍita in formal philosophical debate. Second, his master work on logic, the *Treasury of Reasoning* (*Rigs gter*), was so highly regarded that it is said to have been translated from Tibetan into Sanskrit and circulated in northern India. In his other writings, Sakya Paṇḍita insisted on rational consistency and fidelity to Indian sources in all branches of Buddhist theory and practice. This conviction resulted in often polemical evaluations of the doctrines of other sects, particularly the Kagyu.

In 1244 Sakya Paṇḍita was selected to respond to the summons to the court of the Mongol prince Godan, who had sent raiding parties into Tibet 1239. He impressed the Mongols with his magical powers as much as with his learning and offered submission to Godan on behalf of Tibet in return for freedom from military attack and occupation. He remained at Godan's court as regent, sending orders to officials in Tibet. For roughly the next century, the head lamas of the Sakya sect exercised political control over Tibet with Mongol support. Sakya Paṇḍita's nephew, Pakpa ('Phags pa blo gros rgyal mtshan, 1235–1280?), became the religious teacher of Qubilai Khan.

The early Sakya tradition was concerned primarily with tantric practice, especially the "path and fruition" (*lam 'bras*) tradition associated with the *Hevajra Tantra*, but there was very soon a move to balance and harmonize tantric studies with the study of scholastic philosophy (*mtshan nyid*). Sakya scholars wrote extensively on Mādhyamika philosophy but are particularly famous for their work in logic and epistemology (*tshad ma, pramāṇa*). It was the Sakya scholar Budön (Bu ston, 1290–1364) who systematized the various collections of Indian Buddhist texts circulating in Tibet into the well-known Kanjur (*bka' 'gyur*, literally, "translation of the word [of the Buddha]") and the Tanjur (*bstan 'gyur*, literally "translation of the śāstras").

Geluk (Dge lugs)

Unlike the other major sects of Tibetan Buddhism, the Gelukpas do not identify a specific Indian master as the source of their tradition, although they see themselves as inheriting the tradition of Atiśa, the Bengali scholar who arrived in Tibet in 1042. The preeminent figure for the sect (who may only retrospectively be identified as the "founder") is Tsong kha pa (1357–1419). While known in the West primarily as a reformer, apparently because of his commitment to monasticism, Tsong kha pa was also a creative and controversial interpreter of Buddhist philosophy, especially of Mādhyamika. His stature, which seems to have been considerable during his lifetime, was only enhanced by the subsequent political ascendancy of his followers through the institution of the Dalai Lama, the first of whom (identified as such retrospectively) was Tsong kha pa's disciple Gendundrup (Dge 'dun grub, 1391–1474). Tsong kha pa founded the monastery of Ganden (Dga' ldan, named after the Buddhist heaven Tuṣita) outside Lhasa in 1409, and his followers were originally known as the Gandenpas (Dga' ldan pa). This eventually evolved to Gelukpa, the "system of virtue." The Gelukpas established large monastic universities throughout Tibet, one of which, Drepung ('Bras spung), was the largest Buddhist monastery in the world, with over 13,000 monks in 1959. The third of the "three seats" of the Geluk, in addition to Drepung and Ganden, is Sera monastery, just outside Lhasa.

Bön

Some scholars regard Bön as a heterodox sect of Tibetan Buddhism that began (or a least developed a self-conscious identity), like the other sects (with the exception of Nyingma), in the eleventh century. This is a characterization that both Buddhists and Bönpos would reject. There has been a long antagonism between the two, with Buddhists regarding Bönpos as the descendants of benighted performers of animal sacrifice who plagued Tibet prior to the introduction of the true dharma. For Bönpos, Buddhists are adherents of a heretical alien religion whose interference deprived Tibet of its past glory. The Buddhists look back to India as the source of their religion, portraying Tibet prior to the introduction of Buddhism as an amoral and even demonic realm. The Bönpos look back to Tibet and to Shangshung as their source, seeking to establish a link with the religious tradition(s) of Tibet prior to the seventh century, a link that most scholars regard as tenuous. Both Buddhist and Bönpo chronicles suggest that there was strong opposition to Buddhism among certain factions of the Tibetan court during the seventh and eighth centuries, especially among the priests who were called *bon*. But with the eventual triumph of the Buddhism, those priests seem to have completely disappeared. Little more than the name remained, to be taken up in the eleventh century by those who claimed to represent the continuation of that lost tradition. However, the pre-Buddhist practices centered around a royal funerary cult dedicated to assuring the arrival of the king in a pastoral heaven. The practices of post-eleventh-century Bönpos represent a fully elaborated path to enlightenment ending in liberation from rebirth and buddhahood.

Both Buddhists and Bönpos regard a buddha as their founder. For the Buddhists, he is the Indian Śākyamuni; for the Bönpos, he is the great teacher Shenrap

(Ston pa Gshen rab), from the land of Tazig (Stag gzig, identified by some scholars with Persia and Tajikistan) to the west of the kingdom of Shangshung. When Shenrap arrived in Tibet, he subdued the local demons and converted them to the true religion, much like Padmasambhava did. (Indeed, recent scholarship has shown that some of the accounts of Padmasambhava's conquests are based on Bönpo accounts of Shenrap.) Bönpos themselves regard their religion as having been imported by the teacher Shenrap, the true Buddha, long before the arrival of Indian Buddhists. Unlike the Indian Buddha, Śākyamuni, Shenrap was enlightened from birth and lived the life of a layman (eventually becoming a monk late in life). Thus, his extensive biography is not simply a version of the life of the Indian Buddha (although he also is said to have performed twelve major deeds) but tells a very different story. In an attempt at reconciliation and appropriation, later Bönpo texts state that Śākyamuni was actually an emanation of Shenrap.

Buddhists and Bönpos have different names for their traditions; Buddhists call theirs *chö* (*chos*) while Bönpos call their *bon*. The terms are equally untranslatable and multivalent, ranging from "law" to "truth," but their use is perfectly parallel in the two traditions. Each has its own canon, containing similar genres of texts, each believes in karma and rebirth, each has a bodhisattva path, and so forth. Like the Nyingmas, Bonpos have continued to rediscover treasure texts since at least the eleventh century. (However, rather than being texts left by Padmasambhava to be revealed at an appropriate moment in the future, the texts the Bönpos discover are said to be as those hidden to escape destruction during the persecutions of Bön by Tri Songdetsen.) Like Nyingma, the highest teaching is the Great Perfection (and the lines of influence are uncertain). Like the Geluks, Bönpo monks engage in formal debates on points of doctrine.

Because Bönpos do things in an opposite direction to Buddhists (they circumambulate and turn their prayer wheels counter-clockwise, for example), Bön has been long regarded as simply a "backwards Buddhism" that plagiarized everything from Buddhism, only substituting the word *bon* wherever the term *chö* occurred. Recent scholarship has demonstrated that this is inaccurate, that despite the protestations of both parties there has been significant mutual influence between the two, such that it is often very difficult to regard any Tibetan ritual as purely Buddhist or purely Bönpo. It is also not the case, as was once assumed, that all non-Buddhist Tibetan religion is by default Bönpo. Both Buddhists and Bönpos regard their lineages as self-conscious traditions with specific histories. And again, despite their protestations, both partake fully of rituals, beliefs, and pantheons that predate either of them. However, whereas Buddhists insist on the Indian origins of those practices, Bönpos appropriated pre-Buddhist Tibetan cosmologies, deities, and terminology, all of which were employed to establish the historical priority of Bön in Tibet and thus to demarcate their traditions from those of the Buddhists. Thus Bön is not the pre-Buddhist religion of Tibet, not Tibetan "folk religion," and not a primitive animism. It is perhaps best described as a heretical sect of Tibetan Buddhism, with its own creation myths, cosmology, and pantheon (sometimes with obvious Buddhist correlates, sometimes without), which does not accept the teachings of Śākyamuni Buddha and his tradition as the true dharma. It must be noted, however, that such a characterization could be taken to imply both a devaluation of Bönpo innovation and a capitulation to the anti-Bön polemics of Tibetan Buddhists. It may be, as some scholars have postulated, that Bön is a form of Buddhism that entered Tibet from Central Asia rather than from India. Regardless, the Bön tradition that exists today is difficult to trace back beyond the formation of the other sects of Tibetan Buddhism in the eleventh century.

As is clear from the foregoing description of the major sects, Tibetans (usually Buddhist or Bönpo monks or lamas) have produced a large corpus of what might be termed philosophical literature. What is clear from their works is that the Buddhist or Bönpo philosopher was also a Buddhist or Bönpo and thus a participant in rituals and institutions that provided the setting for his writing. Thus, what we might term "philosophy" was but one concern of these authors; a perusal of the titles in the collected works of any of Tibet's most revered scholars reveals that among the commentaries on Indian logical treatises and expositions of emptiness are works devoted to tantric initiations and consecrations, propitiations of deities, biographies of Indian and Tibetan masters, and instructions for drawing maṇḍalas, making rain, stopping smallpox, and manufacturing magical pills.

As mentioned above, during the Mongol Yuan dynasty (1260–1368), Tibetan Buddhism played an important role at the court of Qubilai Khan, where the emperor's Buddhist preceptor was the famous monk Pakpa ('Phags pa, died 1280) of the Sakya sect. When Pakpa's uncle, Sakya Paṇḍita, was summoned to the court of the Mongol prince Godan in 1244, he took his young nephew with him. As a result of Sakya Paṇḍita's influence, the head lamas of the Sakya sect were given political rule over Tibet with Mongol patronage. With the founding of the Yuan dynasty, the new emperor of China, Qubilai Khan, wished to keep an important member of the Sakya hierarchy at his court to ensure Tibet's continued submission to Mongol rule. Pakpa thus went to the Chinese court as a hostage. He soon so impressed the emperor with his learning and magical powers that he was asked to bestow tantric initiation on the emperor and his consort and later converted the members of the court to Tibetan Buddhism. Their interest seems to be have been based less on an appreciation of Buddhist doctrine than on the fact that Tibetan medicine and magic proved more efficacious than that of the court shamans. Qubilai Khan appointed Pakpa as teacher to the emperor (*dishi*) and teacher to the state (*guoshi*), making him in the process the vassal-ruler (in absentia) of Tibet. Their relationship provided the model for the subsequent relationship between Tibet and China, at least as perceived by the Tibetans. In this relationship, known as "patron and priest" (*yon mchod*), the leading lama of Tibet (in subsequent centuries, the Dalai Lama) was seen as spiritual adviser and chief priest to the emperor, who acted as patron and protector of the lama and, by extension, of Tibet.

With the decline of Mongol rule, there occurred a new sense of Tibetan national identity, especially under the rule of Jangchup Gyaltsen (Byang chub rgyal mtshan, 1302–1364). A nostalgia for the ancient Tibetan empire and its military dominance of Inner Asia was manifested in festivals in which officials dressed in the garb of the ancient kings. Native Tibetan deities, even those tamed by Buddhism, such as the *dapla* (*dgra lha*), are depicted as fierce warriors clad in armor and riding battle steeds. During Jangchup Gyaltsen's reign, many terma texts were unearthed that told of the glory of the imperial age.

Jangchup Gyaltsen and his descendants ruled Tibet for over a century. After that, rule came into the hands of the princes of Rinpung (Rin spung) and then the kings of the western province of Tsang (Gtsang), both groups being patrons of the Karmapas. Meanwhile, in China, the Ming (1368–1644) emperors continued to confer gifts and titles on lamas of the Kagyu, Sakya, and Geluk sects. The Gelukpas received important patronage from the Tümed Mongols when the third Dalai Lama, Sonam Gyatso (Bsod nams rgya mtsho), was summoned to the Altan Khan in 1578. It was actually the Altan Khan who bestowed the appellation "Dalai Lama" on the third incarnation of Tsong kha pa's disciple by translating part of his name, Gyatso ("ocean"), into Mongolian; Dalai Lama means "Ocean Lama." The Mongols converted to Tibetan Buddhism and proved powerful patrons of the Geluk, especially when, after Sonam Gyatso's death, a grandson of the Altan Khan was identified as the fourth Dalai Lama. Another Mongol leader, Gushri Khan of the Qoshot, supported the fifth Dalai Lama against his Kagyu rivals, eventually establishing him as the ruler of Tibet in 1642. This consolidation of religious and secular power in a single figure was an important moment in Tibetan history, a consolidation that received strong ideological support through the promotion of the cult of Avalokiteśvara.

In a treasure text discovered in the twelfth century (but with significant additions apparently made in the fourteenth century) called the *Hundred Thousand Words of Maṇi* (*Maṇi bka' 'bum*), Avalokiteśvara, the bodhisattva of compassion, was retrojected into Tibet's past as both Tibet's protector and the central agent in Tibetan history. Thus, in the prehistoric past, the bodhisattva was said to have taken the form of a monkey and mated with a ogress; their offspring were the first Tibetans. The illegible text that fell into the king's palace was none other than the *Kāraṇḍavyūha,* which tells many tales of Avalokiteśvara. And the three great "dharma kings" (*chos rgyal*) who oversaw the introduction of Buddhism into Tibet were none other than incarnations of Avalokiteśvara. The great epic hero Gesar of Ling is an emanation of Avalokiteśvara. Finally, the fifth Dalai Lama identified himself not only as the fifth incarnation of Tsong kha pa's disciple but as the present incarnation of Avalokiteśvara. From that point on, the bodhisattva protector of Tibet was believed to take human form as the Dalai Lama, thus establishing an unbroken link with Tibet's prehistoric past and exalting the religious lineage of one of many lines of incarnation to the level of kingship through identification with Avalokiteśvara; the Dalai Lama was both Tsong kha pa's historical successor and the human embodiment of the transhistorical bodhisattva of compassion. The fifth Dalai Lama also declared his own teacher to be an incarnation of Amitābha, the Buddha of Infinite Light, and Avalokiteśvara's teacher, bestowing upon him the title of Panchen Lama, establishing a new line of incarnation, which was to have its seat at Tashilhunpo (Bkra shis lhun po) monastery in Tsang province, the former center of his opponent's power. The Dalai Lama moved the capital back to Lhasa, the seat of the ancient kings, and built his palace there, a massive edifice called the Potala, taking its name from Potalaka, the name of Avalokiteśvara's palace. Thus, the power and authority that had once descended in the form of the ancient kings, which had then devolved to local incarnate lamas, was now arrogated (at least in part) back to a single divine figure, the Dalai Lama.

During the eighteenth and nineteenth centuries, the Gelukpas maintained their political control over central Tibet, with the occasional aid of the Manchu rulers of China's Qing dynasty. Especially from the time of the Kangxi emperor (ruled 1661–1722), imperial favor was directed especially toward the Gelukpas. Under the Qianlong emperor (ruled 1736–1795), for example, the entire Tibetan Kanjur was translated into Manchu under the direction of the Geluk hierarch Janggya (Lcang skya rol pa'i rdo rje, 1717–1786).

With the fall of the Qing, Chinese influence in Tibet dwindled through the Second World War (during which Tibet remained neutral). In 1950 Tibet was invaded and occupied by troops of the People's Liberation Army. The situation deteriorated over the next decade. A popular uprising against the Chinese began on March 17, 1959. When it became clear that the Chinese intended to arrest the Dalai Lama, he escaped to India, eventually to be followed by some 250,000 of his people, one-fourth of whom arrived safely in India and Nepal. Today there are over 100,000 Tibetans living in exile, while Tibet, much of its territory divided among Chinese provinces, remains a Chinese colony.

Since 1959 the practice of Tibetan religion has taken place in two very different domains. In Tibet, Tibetan religion has been severely proscribed, as have all forms of traditional Tibetan culture. The violent suppression reached its peak during the Cultural Revolution when all but a handful of the thousands of monasteries and temples that existed in Tibet in 1959 were destroyed. From 1959 to 1979 it has been estimated that one million of the six million ethnic Tibetans died as a result of Chinese policies. Since 1979 there has been some relaxation of the strictest constraints, and a number of monasteries and temples have been rebuilt, although whatever Chinese funds have been provided for this purpose seem directed ultimately toward the promotion of Western tourism. The monastic population has been reduced drastically, as has the program of monastic education.

The other domain of Tibetan religious practice is in exile, with most refugees living in India and Nepal. Of the approximately 70,000 Tibetans who successfully followed the Dalai Lama into exile in 1959 and 1960, an estimated 5,000–7,000 were monks, a tiny fraction of the monastic population of Tibet. But a disproportionate number of the monks who escaped (and remained monks in exile) were from the ranks of incarnate lamas and the scholarly elite, and they worked to reestablish their monastic institutions (of all sects) in exile. Their presence and accessibility has attracted the attention of a large number of Western scholars and enthusiasts, and the last three decades have seen an explosion in interest in Tibetan Buddhism, with a wide variety of translations of Tibetan Buddhist texts.

Indeed, a certain reversal in the perception of Tibetan religion has taken place since 1959. During the Victorian period and lasting well into this century, representations of Tibetan religions generally fell into one of two categories. By some it was portrayed as the most depraved deviation from the Buddha's true teaching, an abomination born from mixing superstition and animism (identified with Bön) with the decrepit remnants of original Buddhism, the remnants named Mahāyāna and tantra. By others, Tibet was seen as the abode of Atlantean masters who held the secrets of the universe; Tibet was a land of "magic and mystery," a Shangri-La.

The Victorian representation of Tibetan Buddhism as the most corrupt and therefore least truly Buddhist of the Asian traditions reached its inevitable antipodes. In the 1960s and 1970s, the earlier Buddhological valuation of Tibetan Buddhism was reversed, as a generation of young scholars came to exalt Tibet, just at the moment of its invasion and annexation by China, as a pristine preserve of authentic Buddhist doctrine and practice. Unlike the Buddhisms of China, Japan, and Southeast Asia, Tibetan Buddhism was perceived as uncorrupted because it had been untainted by Western domination. The value of Tibet to scholars of Buddhism was no longer simply as an archive of the scriptures of Indian Buddhism. The Tibetan diaspora after the Dalai Lama's flight to India in 1959 made widely available to the universities of Europe and North America (largely through the efforts of the Library of Congress office in New Delhi) a great flood of autochthonous Tibetan Buddhism literature, heretofore unstudied. This literature, scorned by scholars at the end of the last century as "contemptible mummery," was now hailed as a repository of ancient wisdom whose lineage could be traced back to the Buddha himself. Much of the scholarship and more popular translations produced since the Tibetan diaspora have, as if, sought to counter the prior negative valuation of Tibetan religion as polluted by representing it as pristine, reflecting largely the normative Buddhism of the scholarly elite, such that the essential ritual practices of Tibetan religions have been ignored to a great degree. In Bönpo studies, Bön has moved from being dismissed as a primitive animism to being hailed as the authentic and original source of Tibetan culture. Works on meditation, compassion, and the stages of the path to enlightenment are certainly famous in Tibet and hold an important place in the histories of the traditions. But without placing such works within their larger ritual context, the religions of Tibet can be misconstrued as merely a sophisticated philosophy divorced from the concerns of the everyday. This attitude is sometimes found among modern Buddhist clerics who see Tibetan Buddhism as entirely of Indian origin, free from any pollution by the pre-Buddhist past. It is important, therefore, to provide the materials for the foundation of a middle ground between these two extreme views of Tibetan religion by presenting a wide range of Tibetan religious literature, derived from many different centuries, regions, and sects, with no attempt to occlude those elements that some might construe as "magical," while attempting to demonstrate how those elements are designed most often to address the most quotidian of human concerns.

Further Reading

For general surveys of Tibetan religion and culture, see David Snellgrove and Hugh Richardson, *A Cultural History of Tibet* (Boston: Shambala, 1968); Giuseppe Tucci, *The Religions of Tibet* (Berkeley: University of California Press, 1980); R. A. Stein, *Tibetan Civilization* (Stanford: Stanford University Press, 1972); Geoffrey Samuel, *Civilized Shamans: Buddhism in Tibetan Societies* (Washington, D.C.: Smithsonian Institution Press, 1993); and the articles "The Religions of Tibet" by Per Kvaerne and "The Schools of Tibetan Buddhism" in *The Encyclopedia of Religion*, ed. Mircea Eliade (New York: Macmillan, 1987). For an encyclopedic survey of Tibetan literature, see José Ignacio Cabezón and Roger R. Jackson, eds., *Tibetan Literature: Studies in Genre* (Ithaca, N.Y.: Snow Lion Publications, 1995).

RELIGIONS OF JAPAN IN PRACTICE

George J. Tanabe, Jr.

Ninomiya Sontoku (1787–1856), affectionately called the Peasant Sage of Japan, likened his teaching to a pill consisting of "one spoon of Shintō, and a half-spoon each of Confucianism and Buddhism." When someone drew a circle, marking one half of it Shintō and the remaining two-quarters Confucianism and Buddhism, Ninomiya rejected this schematic diagram of his teaching and said, "You won't find medicine like that anywhere. In a real pill all the ingredients are thoroughly blended so as to be indistinguishable. Otherwise it would taste bad in the mouth and feel bad in the stomach."[1] Like Ninomiya, some scholars find the usual scheme of dividing Japanese religions into Shintō, Buddhist, Confucian, and other segments bad tasting for not being an accurate reflection of religious realities in Japan, and have pointed out the ways in which the different parts blend into each other.[2] This syncretic view is particularly valuable in the attempt to understand the practice of Japanese religions in their complex interrelationships rather than as neatly ordered, discrete systems of thought. For many Japanese there is little, if any, difference to be experienced in praying to a Shintō god (*kami*) or to a Buddhist deity.

This appreciation of the interwoven character of Japanese religions is also a reflection of recent methodological approaches that call into question essentialist readings of texts and highlight the manner in which their meanings are not only influenced by how they are placed in context but also by how researchers, according to their predilections, read them. Our knowledge has been enriched by recent studies that look into these complex relationships and offer insights about the invention of traditions, the history of changing interpretations, the uses of religious ideas and practices to legitimate power, and the impact of ideology on scholarship itself.[3]

This introduction was inspired and produced with an awareness of the inadequacies of the old categories of chronology (Nara, Heian, Kamakura, etc.), religious traditions (Shintō, Buddhism, Confucianism, etc.), and sects (Tendai, Shingon, Zen, etc.) as organizing principles for a reader about Japanese religions. Yet a solution is not to be found in the destabilization of an old order faulted for its assumption that distinctions exist in time, traditions, and sects. Neither is a solution to be found by making light of written texts, all of which are fixed in specific historical contexts, often with clearly discernible sectarian identities or agendas. While it is true that texts are malleable and can be elusive in meaning, they still bend only within a certain range, the boundaries of which define an integrity that can be discerned. Time periods and religious traditions are significant; unlike Ninomiya's pill, which would blend religions so perfectly as to be indistinguishable, texts, in the broadest sense of the term, can be discerned clearly in their historical contexts and with their sectarian identities, even when, for example, Shintō and Buddhist practices are combined together.

Taken as a whole, religious practices can be thought of as the holdings within a vast storehouse of diverse traditions, dozens of sects, large and small institutions, and a host of creative individuals. There is much more in the storehouse than can ever be treated in a single book. Only a portion of this storehouse can be aired, and some practices will lie forever in dusty storage bins. Etymologically related, the words practice and practicality overlap in meaning, but practicality, in the sense of usefulness, allows us to select those practices that are significant for their utilitarian value. Not all practices are useful, not all are practical, but all of the practices contained in the storeroom of this essay have been selected for the practical value they have in helping people make moral decisions, deal with death, realize meanings, ask for divine blessings, and give life to institutions.

In choosing to emphasize practice and practicality, I do not assume that they are always antagonistic to or can be freed from abstract theory. While theory can be distinguished from practice and sometimes has nothing to do with it, a strict dichotomy between the two is mostly false. Thinking, after all, is a practical activity, and, as the Buddhist cleric Eison (1201–1290) notes, scholarship and study are forms of practice for rectifying the mind and prescribing behavior. What I hope to gain in this focus on practice is not liberation from theory but a greater understanding of the different ways in which theory and practice work on each other toward practical ends. I wish to call attention to interrelationships: as the meaning of a text can be shaped by readers, so too can readers be shaped by texts, or at least that is the hope of writers.

The mutual relationship between writers and readers, texts and contexts, and theory and practice can be described as an association between hard rocks and shifting tides. The rocks—writers, texts, and theory—are fairly fixed as definite persons, set documents, and (for the most part) clear ideas. The shifting tides—the flow of different readers, changing contexts, and diverse practices—wash over the rocks and even change their shape, though they remain recognizable for a long time. This interaction of rocks and tides takes place in discernible patterns that are not entirely chaotic because the rocks are fixed points, and even the tides have rhythms of ebb and flow. The unique circumstances of each writer and reader, text and context, and theory and practice are important to this discernment within a structure of thematic patterns.

In organizing this essay under the categories of Ethical Practices, Ritual Practices, and Institutional Practices, I propose a typology that approximates as best we can the actual orientation of real people who engage in religious practices without giving much thought to whether or not they are Shintoists or Buddhists or Confucians, and certainly without having much of an awareness of their being of the Nara or Heian or Kamakura periods. It does not matter to the pilgrims visiting Kannon that they recite the "wrong" chant, the *nembutsu*, which is dedicated to Amida rather than Kannon, or that non-Shingon members go on a pilgrimage to worship Kōbō Daishi, the founder of Shingon. While some texts express an uncompromising sectarianism, others speak of a willingness and desirability to cross sectarian and religious boundaries, and the categories I have chosen fortunately allow for both exclusive and inclusive viewpoints to be expressed with a coherence that would be difficult to maintain in a structure organized according to religious or sectarian traditions.

Ethical Practices

The theme of ethical practices is very broad, covering matters ranging from individual behavior to national values. By further dividing this broad theme into subsections on social values, clerical precepts, and lay precepts, we see the levels at which formal rules and informal advice define preferred or mandatory action for different groups and communities. At the broadest level, ethical advice is given to society as a whole with the expectation that such values apply to all, or at least to all lay citizens. Being mostly without a professional clergy in Japan, Confucian writers did not have to concern themselves with defining clerical as opposed to lay behavior, and therefore could address social values as a whole. This is not to say that the other religions had little to contribute to the discussion, and indeed there are texts such as the *Selected Anecdotes to Illustrate Ten Maxims* (Jikkinshō), which mixes Confucian, Shintō, Buddhist, and even Daoist elements to retell and create short anecdotes illustrating maxims to aid in the formation of moral character in young people. An easy connection is made between the Buddhist idea of karma, in which one reaps what one sows, and Confucian imperatives for right action, such as being filial to parents and showing mercy to people. One of the highest values promoted in these stories is the display of good literary skills, and here too there is no clash between Buddhism and Confucianism. While Confucianism clearly lends itself more readily to maxims of good social behavior, it is interesting to note how Buddhism is presented less as a means towards enlightenment and more as a moral teaching. The moral quality of Buddhism is encountered in many Buddhist writings, which allow us to see how in practical terms Buddhism was widely used for its ethical teachings on how to live in the world and not just for taking leave from it.

In Kaibara Ekken (1630–1714) there is a more exclusively Confucian teaching on family values based on self-discipline, etiquette, mutual respect, "hidden virtue" (whereby acts of kindness need not be publicly recognized), and, most importantly, the joy of doing good. While Ekken's concern is clearly on the individual and family level rather than the political or ideological plane, his moral advice is given with a cosmic framework in which all things and beings of the universe are animated with a life force (*ch'i*) and therefore deserve respectful treatment. In speaking explicitly of the natural world and the moral responsibility to take life from it only as needed, Ekken developed an ecological ethic that demands individual care of the world. Each person is thus woven into the moral fabric that binds the individual with family, society, and the natural world.

Like the anecdotes about the maxims of good behavior, the Shingaku ("learning of the mind") teaching as interpreted by Nakazawa Dōni (1725–1803) is comfortably liberal in its conviction that no single tradition has a monopoly on truth. Since the true mind is universal, Confucianism, Shintō, and Buddhism all have wise teachings that uphold, among other things, the importance of a naturalness that does not interfere with nature. Buddhism, it has already been noted, embraces the world as much as it rejects it, and here we see how Confucianism has its own inward gaze on the true mind and naturalness. What this suggests is that both Buddhism and Confucianism have social and private orientations, and that it is misleading to characterize each just in terms of the individual or society.

So much of what has been written about Buddhism emphasizes the inward search for true self, the realization of emptiness, the attainment of ultimate enlightenment, and the outward journey to metaphysical heavens and hells beyond this life. It is true that Buddhism has a great obsession with such extra-social and metaphysical matters, but it is equally true that the teachings of karma and causality have very real lessons and consequences for ordinary people in all phases of their lives. Indeed, Buddhism should be understood for its strict sense of personal and social responsibility, as well as for its otherworldly interests.

The Buddhist insistence on personal accountability is unrelenting: no one but the individual is to be blamed for anything that goes wrong or is to be credited for what goes right. With good deeds and fortunate happenings, the buddhas and bodhisattvas may also share the credit, but the individual is seldom removed as a responsible agent for everything and anything that takes place. The heavy moral burden for all things that go wrong easily produces guilt and a deep sense of sin, and it is therefore not surprising that so many Buddhist rituals are designed for *metsuzai*, breaking the bonds and canceling the effects of bad karma. The moral burden is not limited to the happenings of this life alone, but is comprised of the cumulative total of karmic consequences of all previous lives. Illness, for example, can be attributed not only to any number of misdeeds in one's lifetime but to some moral failure from a past life now forgotten. Understood as the condemnation by others, shame is a powerful dynamic in Japanese society, but so is guilt, which is self-condemnation. The Buddhist teaching of karma is not as concerned about the shame resulting from what others think of us as it is about our own awareness of our failures and successes. There is no will of God or Providence to blame for what happens; the Buddhist finger can only be pointed at oneself.

The heaviest moral burden is borne by the Buddhist clergy, who dedicate themselves to nothing less than moral and spiritual perfection, and whose conduct must therefore be rigidly and specifically regimented. The clerical precepts define a monastic life of constant effort to combat the natural temptations that tarnish and even destroy the moral purity required for spiritual progress. Dedication to perfection requires total commitment, and seclusion from society and all of its temptations greatly enhances the possibility of achieving the goal. But even those who succeeded in living a pure life could not keep the world from barging into the quiet of their existences, and a serious practitioner, for instance, such as Myōe (1173–1232), known as the Pure Monk, constantly found himself embroiled in the affairs of his relatives and warring soldiers. The world is inescapable, even for those who escape from it, but if the persistence of its troubling presence was lamented as an obstacle to the pure life, the opposite was also held to be true: the virtues of a pure life can be cast onto the troubled world to pacify it. Just as Ekken saw the relationship between individual morality and the welfare of society and the natural world, and just as Nakazawa Dōni called for a balance between the inward cultivation of the pure mind and its outward manifestation in society, so too did the Zen master Eisai (1141–1215) explain the inescapable connection between a monk's moral purity and the condition of the world. It is the monk, but only the monk whose moral and spiritual attainments provide him with access to the truths of Buddhism, who can bring the power of the dharma and the deities to protect the nation. The welfare of society thus being at stake, Eisai argued that the ruler should support Buddhism, in particular Zen Buddhism. For their part in this mutual relationship, monks have a critical role to play in the upholding of society: they must maintain a strict monasticism, for the power of Zen is dependent on the purity of its monks, and any lapse in discipline damages the character of Zen and the health of the nation is put at risk. There is a paradox at work in the assertion that world rejection, which is essential for the monastic pursuit of purity, also protects the world and thereby affirms it. This assertion must be understood within the general framework of a morality that promises definite gains in return for self-denial. Eisai's call for monastic purity was also in response to the deterioration of discipline in the monasteries, a condition that pure monks in every age had occasion to decry.

In the mid-18th century, the Shingon monk Jiun (1718–1804), similarly concerned about the fallen state of clerical discipline, worked diligently to revive the monastic precepts, arguing that to follow those strict rules was to emulate the lifestyle of Śākyamuni himself; failure to do so spelled the death of Buddhism. As a young man, Jiun had received a good Confucian education, which emphasized morality as a matter of inner character, and he accordingly regarded the Buddhist precepts as prescriptions to be internalized into one's mind and body, and not just left as external rules. As a Buddhist monk, Jiun also advocated meditation and sutra study, but far from being merely rules of conduct, the precepts defined for him, no less than meditation and the scriptural teachings, attitudes and actions essential for becoming a buddha. Like Eisai, Jiun was convinced of the mutually beneficial relationship between monastic discipline and society, but his proposal called for taking the precepts out of the monastery and into the streets by placing them squarely on the shoulders of lay persons. Modified to suit the lifestyles of householders, the essence of the clerical precepts was applied to all: do not kill, steal, lie, and so forth. Even in our own time, Buddhist leaders, alarmed by teenage stabbings, school bullying, financial corruption, and all of the other human failings in modern Japanese society, call for the reapplication of the Buddhist rules for moral living.

Jiun was not the first to apply the precepts for the benefit of the world. Aware of the perennial problem of maintaining strict monastic discipline, Eison (1201–1290) vigorously reaffirmed the monastic code, but putting it into practice necessarily meant service to others. Renouncing the world meant working for it, and Eison provided relief for outcastes and prisoners, arranged public works projects like repairing bridges, counseled forbearance and forgiveness, and constantly taught that one must shift one's focus from self-interest to the welfare of others. His disciple Ninshō was even more active in his social work, which was extended to the sick, to orphans, and even to animals.

Though a monk of the Shingon Ritsu (Precepts) school, Eison drew widely from all forms of Buddhist teachings. In a similar fashion, Kokan Shiren (1278–1346), a Rinzai Zen monk, placed Zen within the matrix of other types of Japanese Buddhism. At the same time, Shiren had a very narrow view by which he regarded the bodhisattva Zen precepts to be superior to the Hīnayāna rules. One must, furthermore, believe in the efficacy of ordination, and by extension have faith in the Zen line of masters leading back to Śākyamuni himself. Yet this sectarian view contained a broad understanding that the significance of the precepts exceeds Zen itself since those rules were means for knowing the human heart and what distinguishes human beings from beasts. For those who fail to live up to its demands of being truly human, there is a remedy in the form of repentance. Since the final standard was that of being human, the precepts applied to lay persons as well as to monks and nuns. Breaking the precepts, after all, did not require a prior formal commitment to them, but did demand atonement. Anyone could break the rules, and everyone had recourse through repentance to the expiation of sin and guilt.

For monks and nuns, the moral requirement remained extraordinarily demanding. There were many exemplary monks and nuns who held true to the discipline, but there were also those who broke the rules. The enemy of moral perfection was not just out there in the world beyond the walls of the monastery but dwelt more seriously within the heart, mind, and body. Like Martin Luther, who so desperately felt the hypocrisy of a life governed by external rules that promised to but could not tame unruly passions, Shinran (1173–1262), the founder of the Jōdoshin (True Pure Land) school, declared that his attempt to live the monastic life was but a sham. Suffering from guilt of a failure resulting not from censure of anyone in his monastic community but from his own self-condemnation, he found his salvation in the grace of Amida Buddha rather than in the good works of personal effort. Having made the clerical code his personal standard by which he could judge his failings, he now abandoned it in favor of a new ethic that allowed meat eating and marriage, two of the more important infractions of the monastic rules. Criticized for excessive reliance on divine power at the expense of human action, Shinran defended his insights by insisting that while salvation was not dependent on human effort, morality was. While antinomianism and licentiousness would not make Amida deny salvation to sinners, such behavior was simply not acceptable for the moral life. Salvation and morality worked in different ways.

Other schools of Buddhism did not join in with the Jōdoshin sect in allowing meat eating and marriage, and in the early Edo period (1603–1867), the government enforced this clerical rule by state law. In the Meiji period (1868–1911), however, the government rescinded this law as part of its new emphasis on freedom of religion, and declared that Buddhist clerics were free to eat meat and marry without penalty. They were also free to continue their adherence to the traditional precepts, but, in time and despite some internal protests against liberalization, all of the Buddhist sectarian institutions changed their rules to allow monks—but not nuns—to eat meat and marry, effectively transforming them from monastics into ministers living a householder's life. The relationship between the monastery and the world was thus defined by an interesting, somewhat surprising, range of different proponents: the government removed itself from this aspect of monastic life; individual clergy protested the availability of voluntary laicization and demanded that the government maintain its regulatory intrusion into monastic life; and the sectarian institutions willingly allowed the clergy to embrace the world without breaking the precepts by getting rid of those rules that were offensive. In the context of actual practice, Buddhism in Japan, even as lived by priests, resolutely affirms the world and some of its best pleasures.

Buddhism, Shintō, and Confucianism, despite their many differences, share a common moral vision that takes the world seriously. The forms and specific prescriptions vary, but there is no major disagreement over the value of good human relationships, caring for the natural world, and finding religious meaning in terms of moral behavior. Even withdrawal from society produces benefits for it. This broad understanding of the interrelationship between religion and the world as well as the individual and society can also be seen in ritual practices dedicated to the land, gods, spirits, and self-realization.

Ritual Practices

As diverse as ethical practices, religious rituals cover an immense range of objectives, from benefits in this world to spiritual rewards in the next life. In all cases, however, rituals function generally as the means for establishing a relationship or making contact with normally unseen worlds, powers, gods, and spirits. These unseen worlds can become visible through ritual performance, can be described with a mythic imagination, or can be assumed to exist as places with familiar characteristics long accepted from the past. The objective of making the unseen world seen is an ambitious one, as is the hope of the rituals dedicated to creating the realization that one is a buddha or is already enlightened. The pursuit of this goal, which is also referred to by the term original enlightenment (*hongaku*), is so pervasive that it cuts across many Buddhist sectarian lines and crosses over into areas of Shintō and Shugendō practice as well.

The pursuit of such lofty goals is not likely to turn out successfully for all of those attempting to reach a state of utter perfection. Like the history of moral effort, the record of spiritual endeavor is filled with failure, and some practitioners, after years of effort, lost confidence in the power of certain rituals to produce insight and realization. Some therefore turned to different rituals, often reducing them to radically bare minimums. The founders of the new Buddhisms of the Kamakura period (1185–1333) were famous for their reductionist proposals limiting ritual to single acts: sitting in meditation for Dōgen (1200–1253), reciting the *nembutsu* for Hōnen (1133–1212), and chanting the title of the *Lotus Sutra* for Nichiren (1222–1282). Others, such as Shinran, gave them up altogether, preferring to relegate their salvation to the graces of divine powers instead of taking such weighty matters into their own helpless hands. Shinran's bare minimum, which was also a sufficient maximum, was faith, total trust in nothing other than the power of Amida to accomplish what neither moral acts nor ritual performances could achieve. While faith alone is an attitude or state of mind rather than a performance, it still is a means toward a spiritual goal, and as such can be thought of as a method. Jōdoshin philosophers would deny that faith is a method since they count faith itself as the receivable but unearned gift of Amida, but ordinary believers, feeling the need to be able to do something about their salvation, exert their faith in many ways, including the ritual of reciting the *nembutsu*: "All praise to Amida Buddha."

In stretching the definition of ritual beyond the limits of formal performance, we pass into the broader area of customs and cultural habits, the forms in which so much of Japanese religiosity is clothed. Contemporary surveys show that the vast majority of Japanese still visit family graves, and yet these same respondents at roughly the same percentage levels also say that they are not religious. The explanation of this seeming conundrum lies in the distinction made between formal expressions of religion—creeds, institutional memberships, and explicit beliefs—and cultural habit. Customs such as grave visitations or trips to shrines and temples are seldom placed in the formal and relatively new category of religion (*shūkyō*), the Japanese word for which was invented in the late nineteenth century. Yet customs bear the marks of ritual insofar as they are acts regulated, sometimes rigidly so, by clearly articulated prescriptions aimed at securing secular and spiritual blessings.

This is certainly the case with *Records of the Customs and Land of Izumo* (Izumo fudoki, 733), an early text regarded as one of the scriptures for the Izumo Taisha sect of Shintō. It does not describe a specific ritual but tells of the intimate relationship between the gods (*kami*), the land, and its inhabitants. Neither is an entirely separate mythic world described as the abode of the gods, but the ordinary world is explained as an arena of divine activity. The signs of the link between the land and the gods are the words used to name places, and in the prayers (*norito*) that were ritually offered to the gods, we see the use of words as a magical, potent medium linking people to the gods. As much as the gods, what is celebrated in *norito* is language itself, a verbal feast presented with sonorous richness, for it is primarily through a banquet of words that the gods can be induced to grant blessings, protection, and even the purification of sins. As it is with the Buddhist precepts, there is an element of repentance that depends on words, for it is in the *saying* of one's sins that their existence is recognized and laid open to expiation.

The Buddhist deities are also sources of blessings and sometimes curses. There is an entire genre of Buddhist literature that tells stories about the marvelous workings of the buddhas and bodhisattvas, and in *The Miraculous Tales of the Hasedera Kannon* we read about the miracles granted by Kannon, the bodhisattva of mercy. Here too the catalyst is prayer, supplication made to Kannon, who otherwise does not act. Certainly the extraordinary power of Kannon is lauded in these tales, but the underlying moral is the need for piety and its verbal expression, prayer. Morality is an important element in a nineteenth-century puppet play, also about Kannon, but the virtue of a blind man and his wife must be augmented by prayer and pilgrimage before Kannon restores sight to the blind man. Morality and magic take center stage in this puppet play about the Kannon at Tsubosaka Temple, which presents the old lesson of the Buddhist miracle tales in which good is rewarded and evil punished by divine powers.

The deities can also be petitioned for future blessings, especially when a new venture such as marriage is undertaken. The liturgical core of the wedding ceremony consists of sumptuous words inviting the bestowal of divine blessings on the couple. Though the modern Shintō wedding ritual dates back only to the beginning of the twentieth century, the ancient form of *norito* is still used to invoke nostalgic images of the venerable power of the *kami*. The ceremony is one of binding man and wife with each other along with the ancestors of the past and future progeny. The union is sealed with *sake*, rice wine sipped in an exchange of cups, and a pledge to extend the family from the past to an eternity of an ever increasing line of descendants.

The world of the gods is also the realm of the spirits of the dead, the existence of which is affirmed by all religious traditions in Japan. Along with morality and magic, the beliefs and practices associated with the spirits or souls of the departed form an enduring theme cutting across boundaries of time and sect. The *Man'yōshū*, the earliest of the poetry anthologies, presents details of *tama* (spirit) belief, and how words, again, in poetic form rather than prayer, are deployed to try to recall, bind, or pacify the spirits of the dead. While prayer is addressed to the gods, poetry speaks to people who, when they are gone, elicit strong feelings of love, longing, and loss. There is more to poetic function, however, than just the evocation of human sentiment and personal attachment; politics, too, is sometimes part of the poetry. The public elegy (*banka*) on the occasion of Prince

Takechi's temporary enshrinement was used to legitimate Emperor Temmu's violent assumption of power in the Jinshin War in 672 by rhetorically transforming the events surrounding it into what Gary Ebersole calls a "mythistory."[4]

That the votive document (*gammon*) by Kūkai (774–835) was dedicated to the deceased mother of a government official is an indication that politics may also have played an ancillary role in this ritual text. Kūkai wrote several votive documents for well-placed individuals and their families, and serving their ritual needs with new ceremonies featuring elaborate colors, smells, sounds, and resounding words aided his work in establishing the new form of Shingon Buddhism in Japan. The votive text presents an alternative to recalling or binding the spirit of a loved one and suggests a letting go, a release that is nevertheless comforting since the departed soul is to be received by the compassionate Buddha.

Life after death is not to be feared, ideally at least, especially when the spirit is placed in the care of a priest who has the sacerdotal knowledge for managing its fate through ritual. Even if something goes wrong in the afterlife, usually through ritual negligence on the part of surviving relatives, and the spirit turns out to be agitated and hungry rather than satisfied, the priest can perform a ritual to remedy the problem. The ritual for feeding the hungry ghosts (*segaki*) is one example of this kind of spiritual technology for resolving such crises, but it does require a trained specialist who knows how to form the hand gestures (*mudrā*) and recite the mantras in a greatly Japanized form of Sanskrit. In these mantras, we see again the magical power of words, the basic tool of the spiritual technician.

Related to the idea that words have power to manipulate matters of the spirit is the intriguing notion that one's final thoughts at the moment of death condition one's rebirth. Genshin's (942–1017) deathbed rituals prescribe the details for right consciousness at the critical moment of death, and while one's lifetime of actions and their karmic consequences cannot be totally ignored, negative karma can be offset by holding in mind images of Amida Buddha and chanting the *nembutsu,* "Namu Amida Butsu." Perhaps no other phrase has been uttered by so many people with the belief in the power of those words to guarantee rebirth in the pure land than the *nembutsu*. Mind and voice, thought and word work together toward the end of having Amida come to greet the dying person and provide escort to the pure land. Even women, whose nature and abilities for gaining salvation have been seriously questioned in Buddhism, can gain rebirth through *nembutsu* piety, as can warriors who, in taking human life, commit the deadliest sin of all. Priests belonging to the Jishū, the Time Sect founded by Ippen (1239–1289), typically borrowed ideas and practices from other forms of Buddhism, but basically promoted the *nembutsu* practice, especially among warriors and commoners. In *The Tale [of the Battle] of Ōtō*, which describes a war waged in 1400, the horrors of clashing armies shock the participants into a religious awakening centered on the *nembutsu*, the recitation of which is the simplest of rituals for dealing with the terrors of this world and for insuring peace in the next life. The battle scenes of chopped limbs, severed heads, and gushing blood make the realities of war comparable to the tortures of hell described in texts such as Genshin's *Ōjōyōshū* (The Essentials of Rebirth). The only difference is that they are inflicted by ordinary soldiers instead of demons and devils.

The taking of life assumes many forms, and in modern Japan abortions are carried out in significant numbers. Out of fear that the spirits of the aborted fetuses will curse their parents, or out of a deep sense of guilt, or out of a concern for the well-being of the fetus now in the spirit world, rites (*kuyō*) for a "child of the waters" (*mizuko*) have been performed in recent times. The abortion rituals also tell us much about the role that religious institutions play in promoting and even creating the need for these services, and temple literature brazenly promotes abortion rituals by playing on fear, guilt, and a concern for well-being. Herein lies a lesson in the realities of institutional religion, and while advertising is a powerful creator of need, or at least of felt needs, the promotion of services for the aborted fetuses would not have much effect if it did not resonate with preexisting beliefs about ritual and its capacity for handling the spirits of the dead.

Death carries an intimate association with enlightenment, and indeed the word *hotoke* is used to describe a corpse as well as a buddha. The state of nirvana is likened unto the quiescence of death, which is also the necessary precondition for rebirth in the pure land. But enlightenment is also a possibility in life, and the assertion that ordinary persons are already buddhas presents a paradox or contradiction that has invited many to resolve it. The idea is found in a constellation of other notions variously identified as nonduality, buddha nature, the womb matrix, original enlightenment, inherent enlightenment, enlightenment in this very body, the equality of passion with enlightenment, the identity of the ordinary world with nirvana, and any number of other related claims, including the Jōdoshin equivalent that rebirth takes place at the moment of faith or that everyone, saint and sinner alike, is already saved by Amida. The truth of these claims are not immediately apparent since human experience still seems to lie at a great distance from this ideal state that purports nevertheless to be immediately close by. If these claims are true and one is already a buddha, then the obvious question arises: why practice? The answer, equally obvious, is that one has to practice in order to realize the truth that obviates practice.

Suchness is another term for the identity of the imperfect with the perfect, and in the twelfth-century composition, *Contemplation of Suchness*, the paradoxical claim is put forth with startling simplicity. The text addresses lay persons primarily, and the level of clarity required for such an audience is achieved through a literalism that valorizes the world: even pigs and dogs are suchness, and to feed them is to make offerings to the buddhas. Pigs are buddhas, but in the light of ordinary perception, they falsely appear as smelly beasts. To see animals as enlightened beings requires new sight made possible by the contemplation of suchness, a ritual of realization.

In adopting yin-yang rituals, and especially the idea of inherent enlightenment from Shingon Esoteric Buddhism, the Shintō purification rite radically transformed the practice of ritual purity. According to the idea of inherent enlightenment, all beings are naturally endowed from birth with the qualities of enlightenment, which includes perfect purity, and the purification ritual, no longer needed to purge nonexistent impurity, was therefore placed in the service of realizing one's inherent enlightenment. The rituals of realization are more familiar to us in the context of Zen than in Shintō, and in Dōgen's treatment, the practice of *zazen* (seated meditation) itself becomes the actualization of ultimate truth, and the practitioner, just as he or she is, becomes the incarnation of perfect enlightenment. The Zen master Chidō (13th c.) adopted the less paradoxical view in which a distinction is made between ordinary reality, which is like a dream, and the ultimate reality of Buddhist insight, which results from being awakened from the dream. Aimed at lay persons, Chidō's work is an exhortation about how expansive the mind can be, how grand one's vision can be, if only people were to wake up from their dreams. While Chidō does not engage in the literalism of asserting pigs to be suchness, he does hold up a very ordinary experience, that of being awake rather than sleeping and dreaming, as the closest approximation of Buddhist enlightenment. It is a simile, but it evokes the language that valorizes the mundane. While he is critical of the Pure Land rejection of disciplined practice, Chidō does express a point that is often mistakenly credited only to Pure Land innovations, namely, that the power of faith can overcome the karmic effects of sin.

The idea that one is already a buddha invites everyone to be his or her own authority. Such an authority is assumed when a writer composes a sutra purporting to be a record of the Buddha's preaching. All of the Mahāyāna sutras were written long after Śākyamuni's time, but the fiction of authenticity is maintained in the distinction made between apocryphal and genuine scriptures. All Buddhist sutras begin with the standard phrase, "thus have I heard," which suggests that the writer was nothing other than a scribe dutifully recording the words of Śākyamuni, but the literary evidence in the texts themselves indicates that the sermons were composed by any number of mostly anonymous writers. A few sutras were clearly composed in Japan and could not have come from India by way of China and Korea, the route of so-called authentic sutras. Written in the early nineteenth century within the Shugendō tradition of mountain asceticism, the *Sutra on the Unlimited Life of the Threefold Body* argues that authority and meaning rest in one's own experience and not on some teaching transmitted through an institution. This is a convenient claim made by one who is passing off his experience as the preaching of Śākyamuni, and yet it cannot rest easy with the prospect that the truth it proposes is individually or personally derived, for that would reduce truth to opinion. There must be an external authority, but since it cannot be an institution in this case, it is located in the original buddha of no mind and no thought, the highest buddha. No mind and no thought are terms from the language of original enlightenment and its logic: the reason why we can claim authority in ourselves is because it is the authority of the original buddha. Hence, we can write our own sutras.

Writing a sutra in the name of Śākyamuni is easily seen as arrogant and presumptuous in the extreme, and therefore it is necessary to disguise such self-righteousness in the cloak of a scriptural diction that makes it sound as if it were merely recorded by a faithful disciple standing on Vulture Peak in the presence of the original master. Equally bold but less obvious is the interesting and complex act of interpreting a sutra whose apocryphal origins have been conveniently forgotten in favor of an attribution of authenticity. Interpretation allows for new insights to be derived from or invested in an existing sutra, and thus avoids the offense of writing a new one. This is the most common technique for developing new teachings in a tradition that prides itself on faithfully transmitting an original teaching without the distortions and heresies of innovation. Without interpretation, new schools cannot arise and take issue with received tradition.

In its criticism of traditional ritual practices, Pure Land Buddhism can be seen as a contrast to the other forms of Buddhism that place discipline and practice at their core. In another sense, however, the Pure Land conviction that salvation is not secured by the self-power of practice but only by reliance through faith on the other power of Amida leads to an immediate fulfillment that resonates with the rituals of realizing one is already a buddha. The rhetoric is different—being a buddha in this life versus being identified with Amida through the *nembutsu* in this life—but what is the difference between being a buddha and being Amida? The nonduality between the believer and Amida is the contention of the thirteenth-century work *Attaining the Settled Mind*; it claims that birth in the pure land has already been accomplished through the compassionate vow of Amida, and hence one can have a settled mind. To the question raised earlier as to why practice is necessary if one is already a buddha, the Pure Land answer, at least in this text, is that practices are not necessary as long as one trusts in Amida. The fifteenth-century collection of anecdotes in *Plain Words on the Pure Land Way* depicts monks who have thrown off concerns for status, fame, doctrinal learning, and intellectual calculation in favor of the simplicity of the *nembutsu*, the sole ritual that makes all other rituals unnecessary.

The letters of Shinran suggest that even true faith (*shinjin*) is a gift of Amida and not the result of human volition. There is nothing to do—no ritual, no practice, no contrivance. Faith puts an end to contrivance, and becomes the moment of birth into the pure land. Without removing evil, faith bypasses it and allows sinners (as well as saints) to be reborn in the pure land. This does not mean that people can justifiably commit evil, for compassion requires people to be good even though goodness is not a means to rebirth. Shinran, whose faith allowed him to ignore the clerical precepts and openly marry, occupied a position diametrically opposite to that of the traditional practitioners, but the line separating both can also be bent into a full circle such that his sense of immediate fulfillment meets the end point at which we find the rituals of realizing one is a buddha, perhaps Amida.

Institutional Practices

The rejection of ritual structure on the grounds of the immediacy of faith does not entail a repudiation of institutional structure. Indeed the Jōdoshin sect of True Pure Land Buddhism, which developed in the wake of Shinran's teachings, became one of the most formidable of institutions and could defend itself by force of arms when necessary. Religion and politics often clashed, but they also met on the common ground in which religious truth claims could be used to legitimize or enhance political institutions. The making of institutions requires founders, most of whom have been sanctified as great men, wizards, and even gods. Great efforts were also expended in defining the identity of sectarian institutions in terms of right practice or orthopraxis, and right thought or orthodoxy. In the arena of institutional life we see clearly what is appropriately called sectarianism, that is, the strict definition of exclusive zones of thought and practice. This does not controvert the repeated cases of syncretism across sectarian lines, but neither should such assimilative fluidity obscure the instances of rigid separation. Balancing the ideological tensions of sectarianism is the ordinary administration of buildings and furnishings, and the special social functions that some religious institutions play. Another lesson of the realities of organization is found in the gap between actual practices and stated ideals, and a view of these discrepancies is essential if we are to avoid the mistake of thinking that principles are always put into practice.

While we normally think that practice follows theory, there were times when actual practice preceded and then required the subsequent creation and support of principles. When one clan emerged in ancient Japan as more powerful than others, it could have ruled by brute force alone without concern for whether their rule was justified. The idea of legitimacy, however, made its appearance with some of the earliest writings in Japan, and the *Kojiki* (Record of Ancient Matters, 712) is a definitive text in establishing the principles that justified the practice of supremacy by the imperial clan. Departing from the Chinese principle that the ruler governed by divine right in the form of the mandate of heaven, which could be lost through excessive vice and claimed by another person of greater virtue, the imperial clan in Japan established the principle of divine birth as the basis of legitimate rulership. The *Kojiki* asserts that the imperial house descends from the deity Amaterasu, and the emperor rules by virtue of having been born divine.

Despite their divine origins, the imperial family functioned in a bureaucratic organization that was eminently human. The *Continued Chronicles of Japan* (Nihon shoki, 797) provides a glimpse into the everyday workings of the court, some of which sounds remarkably familiar: new bureaucratic rules devised to correct certain abuses, sanctioning a Crown Prince for his debauchery, and the difficulty of finding suitable princes of acceptable moral behavior. While the dominant values are identifiable as Confucian, it is also clear that there was an easy coexistence with and mutual use of Buddhism and (what we now call) Shintō. There was no need for a theory of syncretism since the assimilation of ideas and practices did not always follow deliberate design but was carried out for practical purposes. Though we can identify Shintō, Buddhist, and Confucian elements in the *Continued Chronicles of Japan*, it is clear that they melded into a single worldview, not three, in which spiritual forces, however they might be identified, were integrated parts of the temporal order.

This is not to say that there were no other circumstances in which religious traditions did appear differently and clash. The *Circumstances Leading to the Founding of the Monastery Complex of Gangōji* (Gangōji engi, 747) is an important document, not only for the founding of the temple but for the official introduction of Buddhism itself. The account is one of contention, strife, and even violence, as two political factions include in their opposing stances different religious understandings of the spiritual forces that affect worldly events. The deities are identified in opposition to each other, the one "Buddhist" and the other, for lack of a better term, "Shintō." Since the temporal world is directly affected by powerful unseen forces identified as deities, the violent struggle between the two factions was also a battle of the gods, and the Buddhist deities proved themselves to be the greater masters of war.

Emerging victorious, Prince Shōtoku (574–622), grateful for the support of the buddhas and bodhisattvas, became an influential supporter of Buddhism. The biographies of Prince Shōtoku are even more explicit about the relationship between Buddhism and power, and we read once again of how the war was won with the backing of the Buddhist deities. In his political uses of Buddhism, Prince Shōtoku is portrayed not just as a pragmatic warrior-politician petitioning the deities to be on his side, but also as a pious believer. Both stances go together, sincerity being an important element in the process of asking the buddhas to answer one's prayers for victory. Prince Shōtoku is reputed to have studied the philosophical teachings of Buddhism and to have gained an admirable mastery of them, but in the account of his struggles with his opponents, little is said about those teachings, although much is reported about the divine powers of the buddhas to help determine the course of history.

Spiritual beings can affect the outcome of wars and, in turn, those who lose their lives fighting a war can become special spiritual beings. The Yasukuni Shrine in modern Tokyo is a burial place for all those who died in service to the country, including the school children on Okinawa and the women telephone operators on Sakhalin who lost their lives in the Great Pacific War. Popular booklets and pamphlets written in an easy-to-understand style relate important lessons about how the war dead become spirits of the nation, a nation that is still symbolized by the emperor. All of Japan's wars, civil and foreign, were unfortunate but were fought for the sake of the nation and the emperor, contributing to the important mission, as a brochure puts it, of creating a marvelous Japan with the Emperor at its center. While this language evokes the diction of wartime Japan, the recently published pamphlets are good reminders of the continuing importance given in some quarters to the intimate connection between citizens, spirits, the nation, and the Emperor in modern Japan.

In turning from the imperial institution to those that are sectarian, we find, as we might expect, intimate connections between divinity and humanity, especially in the founders of sects. Shrouded in so much legend that it is difficult to discern the real man, En the Ascetic (late 7th c.) has become a paradigmatic holy man and wizard of supernatural powers revered widely even outside of the Shugendō sect of which he is the reputed founder. The account of him tells of the importance of mountains as places to acquire spiritual powers through strict discipline, but even this supernatural wizard is also described in very human and moral terms as being filial to his parents. Mountains are also the setting for the story about how Kūkai, the founder of the Shingon sect, established a monastery on Mt. Kōya and eventually died there. His death, however, was only a seeming one, for he remains alive, sitting in eternal meditation in his mausoleum. Even today thousands of pilgrims flock to Mt. Kōya to visit and pray to Kūkai, posthumously and popularly known as Kōbō Daishi, their living savior. The divinization of Kūkai was not the product of popular piety, but the construction by high-ranking monks developing the Shingon institution. They created the living savior, and wandering holy men dispatched from the monastery disseminated the story throughout the countryside.

The telling of tales is an important part of the process of instilling faith in the buddhas and bodhisattvas, as we have already seen with the tales and puppet play about Kannon, and it continued to be instrumental in the later development of Kōbō Daishi as living savior. While the story about Kōbō Daishi's eternal meditation was a creation by a monk at the top of the institution and was then disseminated to believers below, the stories about the encounters with Kōbō Daishi on the Shikoku pilgrimage were told by ordinary pilgrims making the journey. Stories were first collected from pilgrims in the seventeenth century by a monk who had ties with the Shingon headquarters. They tell of pilgrimage as a means of having direct encounters with the holy, and praise the virtue of doing the pilgrimage and offering alms to the pilgrims. Taken together, the stories of Kōbō Daishi's eternal meditation and the Shikoku pilgrimage show that in the making of belief through the telling of tales, stories can be told from the top down as well as the bottom up.

If, as scholars surmise, the *Personal Account of the Life of the Venerable Genkū* was written by Shinkū (1145–1228), then it is another example of a founder having been divinized by those at the top of the sect. Genkū, who is more popularly known as Hōnen, was the founder of the Pure Land sect (Jōdoshū), and Shinkū was one of his earliest disciples. The account transforms Hōnen into a divine savior, like Kūkai, and identifies him as a manifestation of the bodhisattva Seishi, who is often depicted along with Kannon as an attendant of Amida. Responding to criticisms that his master was a heretic for rejecting traditional practices in favor of the exclusive recitation of the *nembutsu*, Shinkū defends Hōnen as a scholar as well as a saint. History and myth depict Hōnen as both human and divine, and the text, like the *Kojiki*, is another example of "mythistory" designed to make something human more divine.

The Nichiren priest Nisshin (1407–1488) was not the founder of his sect, but he became a hero within his organization and the center of a personality cult. What is interesting about his story is that he is not portrayed as a supernatural or divine figure, but as a resolute man, a martyr at most, who withstood government censure and torture for the sake of his sect and belief in the *Lotus Sutra*. A similar case of intense faith can be seen in Teshima Ikurō (1910–1973), who had an intense Christian conversion experience in the midst of his own personal suffering. The founder of a small Christian organization, Kirisuto no Makuya (Tabernacle of Christ), Teshima emphasized individual faith and developed close relations with his followers, some of whom wrote testimonies about his extraordinary character, insight, and power. While his followers report cases of healing (in one instance by Teshima's wife) and revere him tremendously, they still do not regard him as anything other than a remarkable teacher whom they came to love and respect dearly. Personal commitment to each other as well as the gospel of Jesus Christ is the story told of a man remarkable for his humanity and faith.

Nisshin and Teshima were heroes to their causes because of their exclusive commitment to the truths they found respectively in the *Lotus Sutra* and the Bible. They were fundamentalists, unable to recognize other forms of truth. In contrast to this restrictive view, Mujū Ichien (1226–1312), ostensibly a Rinzai Zen priest, held that the Buddhist truth takes on various forms, and that no single way can be upheld over others. While Mujū also presents the idea of how Buddhism is compatible with the other religious traditions, it is important to note that the non-Buddhist teachings "softened people's hearts," as he states it, to make them more amenable to accepting Buddhism. Buddhism therefore enjoys a privileged position over the rest, and it is primarily within the Buddhist fold that pluralism and diversity are celebrated. The Buddha taught different teachings to suit different people, and in making such accommodations expressed his compassion. There is, in short, no single meaning to Buddhism, no orthodoxy.

It was not always the case that when institutions found themselves at odds with each other, the issues were free of concerns about the right articulation of truth. For Nisshin, the conflicts he experienced were directly related to his strict orthodoxy. The connection between conflicting orthodoxies and competing institutional (and personal) interests is not difficult to find even within single traditions. Intrasectarian tension, for example, is easily seen within the world of Zen, and again it is a story of the interrelationship between doctrinal understandings and institutional well-being. The competition between Shūhō Myōchō (National Teacher Daitō, 1282–1337) and the monk Musō Soseki (1275–1351) was not just a debate over the philosophical truth of Zen but about political correctness as well. The definition of doctrinal correctness or orthodoxy in this situation was a pressing issue even in a time of political stability; it is not just a change of rulers or the conduct of war that require religious support and justification. Cultural and even aesthetic realignments also affect the articulation of right religion, and a judgment of heterodoxy in one situation may be beneficial to the gaining of orthodoxy in another circumstance.

The influence of social pressures on the determination of truth can also be seen in the argument between the Inner and Outer Shrines at Ise, which waged their theological debate mindful of the economic consequences of their theoretical formulations. The Outer Shrine claimed that their deity, Toyouke, was equal to and identical with Amaterasu, the *kami* of the Inner Shrine. But the Inner Shrine priests rejected this formulation, saying that Amaterasu was superior. The theological arguments were in form about the *kami* but in function concerned donations from pilgrims who flocked to Ise, pilgrims who would, if Toyouke were inferior, bypass the Outer Shrine and go directly to the Inner Shrine and pray to the superior Amaterasu. The debate spilled into the streets as Outer Shrine priests set up barricades to block entry to the Inner Shrine. The issue was highly volatile at the institutional level, and difficult to resolve theologically. The great scholar Motoori Norinaga (1730–1801) addressed the matter with an aim toward resolving the conflict, but he seemed to have a split mind on the issue and managed not to provide any clear resolution.

Motoori referred to the controversy with the image of split bamboo, but the fracturing of relations between the Inner and Outer Shrines did not elicit cries of dismay about the loss of harmony within Shintō. When Buddhists denounced each other, they sometimes lamented the loss of the "single flavor of the dharma" or the breakup of the harmony of the sangha, the fault for which, of course, could be laid on their opponents. But little is said about the single flavor of Shintō: what, after all, is Shintō? A scholar of our own time, the late Kuroda Toshio (1926–1993) has been influential with his analysis of the nature and function of religion in Japanese history, and in a widely acclaimed essay on the subject, he criticizes the usual characterization of Shintō as an independent indigenous religion. Arguing that an autonomous Shintō is a modern construction, Kuroda sees that the beliefs and practices surrounding the *kami* are so integrated into Buddhist, Daoist, and secular affairs that they cannot be separated out to form an independent "Shintō."

The inextricable integration of Shintō beliefs and practices into the religious views of Buddhists has caused enormous problems for the True Pure Land (Jōdoshin) sect, which officially rejects all magical rituals aimed at acquiring this-worldly benefits such as health, wealth, safety, and happiness.[5] These rituals and beliefs are centered on the use of amulets, talismans, and other paraphernalia sold at most Shintō shrines and Buddhist temples. Concerned about field studies that show Jōdoshin members patronizing temples and shrines offering this-worldly benefits, Sasaki Shōten, a contemporary Jōdoshin priest and scholar, calls for a reconsideration of the official teaching banning such practices. Sasaki recognizes that this primitive magical mentality with Shintōism as its core, as he puts it, is an undeniable part of the Japanese religious view, including that of Buddhists, and it is useless to deny by doctrine what exists in fact. While sounding at times as if he is willing to accept those practices fully, Sasaki fundamentally cannot do so. His proposal is not to accept but to tolerate such folk practices so that people can be drawn in, or more importantly so that members do not have to be expelled. The final goal, however, is to transform such primitive practices into true Jōdoshin faith, which, even in Sasaki's version, cannot tolerate magic as true religion. His willingness to accept the primitive mentality in order to transform it is reminiscent of Mujū's attitude toward the non-Buddhist religions that function to soften people's hearts so that they can embrace the Buddhist dharma. Though they espouse pluralism and toleration, there is ultimately only a single truth defined according to their respective orientations.

Sasaki's argument takes us well into the area in which we see the discrepancies between official doctrine and actual practice. A good example of this can be seen in Sōtō Zen pamphlets written for temple members in which Zen as a religion for peace of mind and general well-being is emphasized to the exclusion of the practice of meditation. This is a striking position to be taken officially by an institution whose very name refers to the centrality of meditation. What is Zen, if not meditation? An overt clash between the original ideal and current practice is avoided simply by not mentioning the doctrines for which Zen is philosophically famous. The dilemma also arises in the matter of funerals. Sōtō Zen and Jōdoshin purists often point out that funeral rites and ancestor veneration are not Buddhist teachings, and yet we find in official Zen pamphlets positive, nostalgic affirmations of rites for commemorating the dead and memorializing the ancestors. This pamphlet Zen bears little resemblance to Dōgen Zen, though both are identified as Sōtō. It is quite significant that this sentimental Zen of general well-being is promoted by the sect itself without any mention of Dōgen's famous advocacy of seated meditation as the means to dropping off mind and body to reveal an originally existing buddha; a conflict between doctrine and practice is avoided by dropping off classical doctrine in favor of popular practice. Or, to put it in other terms, practice prescribes precept.

The priority of practice over doctrine is not limited to modern developments but is also seen in the writings of Keizan (1264–1325), who stands second in importance to Dōgen himself in the line of Sōtō Zen patriarchs in Japan. Keizan, displaying a pragmatism for what works rather than what is doctrinally prescribed, easily adopted ritual practices that Dōgen would not have condoned. The institutional development of Sōtō Zen would have been significantly retarded if Dōgen's successors had confined themselves to the limits of his demanding teachings and not adopted, for instance, mortuary rites and rituals for this-worldly benefits.[6] In his own writings Keizan is not as concerned with sitting in meditation as he is with rituals for warding off evil and inviting blessings, and with the more mundane matters of institutional administration. Women play an important role, as they do today, in the back room life of his temple, and Keizan has much to say about his grandmother, mother, and Sonin, the woman who donated the land for his temple Yōkōji.

Keizan built Yōkōji in a valley he named Tōkoku. Both names were chosen for their associations with Chinese Zen masters in whose lineage he was a dharma descendant. In his sermons, Keizan uses the language of original enlightenment to speak generically about every place being one's own self, one's radiant wisdom, the site of practice, and the practice of buddha activity; when he speaks specifically of Tōkoku Yōkōji, however—its buildings, its activities, its people, his relatives, and how he selected the site in a dream—it becomes apparent that the place is one of belonging, his home, the locus of his everyday spiritual life. Like the *Records of the Customs and Land of Izumo* (Izumo fudoki) and its naming of places in association with the actions of the *kami*, Keizan's *Records of Tōkoku* explains the naming of that place in association with his spiritual tradition and describes it as the venue of buddha activity as well as his everyday routine. Yōkōji is at once an ordinary and a special place.

Tōkeiji in Kamakura is a special place for women, specifically women who seek divorce from their husbands. The temple was founded as a convent in 1285 by Kakusan Shidō (1252–1305), widow of Hōjō Tokimune (1251–1284), the Kamakura military ruler who repelled the Mongol invasions in 1274 and 1281. Its name, Eastern Temple for Rejoicing (Tōkeiji), was an appropriate choice for a woman who seems to have enjoyed a happily married life. By the Tokugawa period, the temple had acquired other names: Enkiridera, Divorce Temple; and Kakekomidera, Temple into Which One Runs for Refuge. The popular verse known as *senryū* speaks poignantly about the unhappy experiences of women seeking refuge from their husbands. In a time when divorce was uncommon and difficult to obtain since it could only be granted by the husband, Tōkeiji was a very special place, but its unique function was possible because of the theoretically normal role any temple plays as a place for the renunciation of the householder's life. Monasticism had its secular use, and though it was not easy being a nun ("how difficult / breaking the relationship / with vegetarian food"), it was a temporary status to be endured until the husband could be convinced of sending a letter of divorce.

Monasticism and divorce are not usually associated in texts on Japanese religion, but the case of Tōkeiji illustrates how natural and practical an alliance it was. Dealing with the world by withdrawing from it was also practiced by Eison, whose monastic vows made it imperative that he work with outcastes and prisoners. On a more ambitious scale, Eisai argued that monasticism was necessary for the welfare and protection of the nation itself. There is a pattern of this association between monasticism and society, and to that degree we can state a generalization, a small one to be sure, but a generalization nevertheless: monasticism can perform social services. The more usual pattern is of monasticism performing services only for monastics; the monks who called for a continued ban against clerical marriage were not addressing the interests of society at large, though they tried to demonstrate that celibacy was not inimical to society. Herein lies another pattern: monasticism is self-serving. The patterns vary: monasticism is a hard rock, but it is used in shifting tides.

The traditions of Japan are filled with double-edged interrelationships that cut both ways. Religion, for instance, legitimates rulership, but the ruler, in turn, legitimates religion by legislating it. Sometimes the government intervenes in religious matters to the dismay of religious communities, and at other times the community complains that the government does not intervene enough. There are patterns of tolerant pluralism that stand in contrast with clear instances of sectarianism and censure, and then there is the kind of sectarian triumphalism that presents itself in the mask of pluralistic tolerance. Morality is a prevalent theme about reaping what we sow, but so is magic equally present with its promises of reaping even if we do not sow. Repeatedly we encounter the conundrum of being a buddha but having to become one nevertheless. This is attended by voices calling for strict practice in order to realize that there is no need to practice—voices that find counterpoints in those who said that there is no need to practice at all. At times the world is a defiled place worthy only of being left behind for the perfect pure land, and at other times it is the very abode of the gods where pigs are buddhas. Rules are external and need to be internalized, but internal realization makes external rules unnecessary. There are living spirits of the dead to be bound, recalled, pacified, or conversely let go; there are also dead masters whose spirits never leave but stay to bless and protect. Divinized humans and anthropomorphic gods grant miracles, induced from them through people performing rituals, reciting chants, uttering prayers, going on pilgrimage, being good, or just having faith. Myth is not to be confused with fact, but it can be blended with history to produce "mythistory," or with biography to create hagiography. For some, human institutions can never be sources of authority, especially when one is a buddha unto oneself, but institutions can also be the only source for defining what is true. Doctrine defines rituals and right conduct, but so can practice determine theory. There are also times when neither is the cause of the other, when one side, usually theory, is simply ignored. Shintō is a recognizable religion, but sometimes becomes invisible in its integration into Buddhist practice. Buddhism also has its own character, but it too can be hidden in a Shintō purification rite. Both Buddhism and Shintō can join together with Confucianism and other systems to form a single worldview, or they can clash to the point of violence. Buddhism is for peace, but also helps to win wars. Orthodoxies have definite consequences in society, and social conditions can help determine orthodoxies. The list of these double- or multiple-edged relationships can continue on and on.

All of the above are patterns that can be seen in repeated instances and therefore can be stated as generalizations, the making of which is essential to teaching and understanding; however, by showing that patterns have opposing counterparts, we see the limits of any generalization, and we see that counter-generalizations, equally valid, also need to be made. The resulting mosaic, seemingly on the verge of conceptual chaos, is what we are after, a kind of ordered disorder, a pattern of the uniformities and disarray that constitute the religions of Japan in practice.

Notes

1. Cited in Ryusaku Tsunoda et al., eds., *Sources of Japanese Tradition* (New York: Columbia University Press, 1961), p. 585.

2. See, for example, Ian Reader, *Religion in Contemporary Japan* (Honolulu: University of Hawaii Press, 1991).

3. See, for example, Stephen Vlastos, ed., *Mirror of Modernity: Invented Traditions of Modern Japan* (Berkeley: University of California Press, 1998); Robert H. Scharf, "The Zen of Japanese Nationalism," in *Curators of the Buddha*, ed. Donald S. Lopez, Jr. (Chicago: University of Chicago Press, 1995), pp. 107–160; Helen Hardacre, *Shintō and the State, 1868–1988* (Princeton: Princeton University Press, 1989); Neil McMullin, *Buddhism and the State in Sixteenth-Century Japan* (Princeton: Princeton University Press, 1984).

4. Gary L. Ebersole, *Ritual Poetry and the Politics of Death in Early Japan* (Princeton: Princeton University Press, 1989).

5. For a full treatment of the religion of this-worldly benefits in Japan, see Ian Reader and George J. Tanabe, Jr., *Practically Religious: Worldly Benefits and the Common Religion of Japan* (Honolulu: University of Hawaii Press, 1998).

6. For the institutional practices of Sōtō Zen, see William M. Bodiford, *Sōtō Zen in Medieval Japan* (Honolulu: University of Hawaii Press, 1993); and Bernard Faure, *The Rhetoric of Immediacy: A Cultural Critique of Ch'an/Zen Buddhism* (Princeton: Princeton University Press, 1991).